ANOTHER COUNTRY, ANOTHER LIFE

Other Books by J. Patrick Boyer

Raw Life: Cameos of 1890s Justice from a Magistrate's Bench Book (2012)

Solitary Courage: Mona Winberg and the Triumph over Disability (2010)

A Passion for Justice: How 'Vinegar Jim' McRuer Became Canada's Greatest Law Reformer. Rev. ed. (2008)

A Man & His Words (2003)

"Just Trust Us": The Erosion of Accountability in Canada (2003)

Leading in an Upside-Down World: New Canadian Perspectives on Leadership (contributing editor, 2003)

The Leadership Challenge: Effectiveness in the 21st Century (editor, 2002)

Accountability and Canadian Government (2000)

Boyer's Ontario Election Law (1996)

Hands-On Democracy: How You Can Take Part in Canada's Renewal (1993)

La démocratie pour tous: le citoyen — artisan du renouveau Canadien (1993)

Direct Democracy in Canada: The History and Future of Referendums (1992)

The People's Mandate: Referendums and a More Democratic Canada (1992)

Local Elections in Canada: The Law Governing Elections of Municipal Councils, School Boards and Other Local Authorities (1988)

Election Law in Canada: The Law and Procedure of Federal, Provincial and Territorial Elections. 2 vols. (1987)

Money and Message: The Law Governing Election Financing, Advertising, Broadcasting and Campaigning in Canada (1983)

Lawmaking by the People: Referendums and Plebiscites in Canada (1982)

Political Rights: The Legal Framework of Elections in Canada (1981)

ANOTHER COUNTRY, ANOTHER LIFE

Calumny, Love, and the Secrets of Isaac Jelfs

J. PATRICK BOYER

DUNDURN
TORONTO

Project Editor: Shannon Whibbs
Editor: Dominic Farrell
Design: Jesse Hooper
Printer: Webcom

Library and Archives Canada Cataloguing in Publication

Boyer, J. Patrick
　　Another country, another life : calumny, love, and the secrets of Isaac Jelfs / J. Patrick Boyer.

Includes bibliographical references and index.
Also issued in electronic format.
ISBN 978-1-4597-0840-2

　　1. Boyer, James. 2. Newspaper editors--Ontario--Muskoka (District municipality)--Biography. 3. Judges--Ontario--Muskoka(Districtmunicipality)--Biography. 4. Townclerks--Ontario--Bracebridge--Biography. 5. Frontier and pioneer life--Ontario--Muskoka (District municipality). 6. Muskoka (Ont. : District municipality)--Biography. 7. Law clerks--Great Britain--Biography. 8. Soldiers--Great Britain--Biography. I. Title.

FC3095.M88Z49 2013　　　　971.3'1603092　　　　C2012-907679-1

1　2　3　4　5　　　17　16　15　14　13

We acknowledge the support of the **Canada Council for the Arts** and the **Ontario Arts Council** for our publishing program. We also acknowledge the financial support of the **Government of Canada** through the **Canada Book Fund** and **Livres Canada Books**, and the **Government of Ontario** through the **Ontario Book Publishing Tax Credit** and the **Ontario Media Development Corporation**.

Care has been taken to trace the ownership of copyright material used in this book. The author and the publisher welcome any information enabling them to rectify any references or credits in subsequent editions.

J. Kirk Howard, President

Unless otherwise indicated, all photos, sketches, and images in this book are from the BOYER FAMILY ARCHIVES, BRACEBRIDGE.

Printed and bound in Canada.

VISIT US AT
Dundurn.com | Definingcanada.ca | @dundurnpress | Facebook.com/dundurnpress

Dundurn
3 Church Street, Suite 500
Toronto, Ontario, Canada
M5E 1M2

Gazelle Book Services Limited
White Cross Mills
High Town, Lancaster, England
L41 4XS

Dundurn
2250 Military Road
Tonawanda, NY
U.S.A. 14150

In tribute to

James Isaac & Hannah Boyer

whose fortitude and resolve
kept them resilient ...

whose love and secrets
are free at last

Our wills and fates do so contrary run
That our devices are overthrown,
Our thoughts are ours, their ends none of our own.
— WILLIAM SHAKESPEARE

Contents

1

Escape from New York

Was there no other way?

An anxious thirty-five-year-old lawyer from one of Broadway Avenue's biggest firms gazed at the scene around him.

Not even the cooler air of early autumn had been able to refresh New York's acrid skies or dilute the stench rising from the city's filthy streets, open sewers, and spewing smokestacks. The whole jammed-up place reeked like a fetid cauldron.

Even so, he still felt the city's tug. It was here he'd found chances to get ahead. He was enthralled by the exotic mixture of peoples, the pulsating rhythms of the place as ships arrived, buildings rose, and crowds jammed through streets chasing trade and entertainment. New York was a civilized jungle. Here he'd been able to turn dreams into realities.

He let out a slow heavy sigh, then turned and entered the station. He knew there was no other choice.

Boarding the train with him early that September morning in 1869 was a pregnant woman, their little girl, a curly-haired youth, and another woman in her early twenties. Other passengers would never have guessed that this family, dressed almost in Sunday best, was heading for Canada's wilderness to hack out a home from dense forest. Yet, such was their intent. Nor were they alone in this quixotic quest.

If New York had become a magnet drawing hopeful souls and ragged refugees from all corners of the world, Muskoka District was the newest, best refuge for anyone needing a further escape or yet another fresh start.

In the United States, the Republican Party had come to office in 1860 under President Abraham Lincoln with a pledge of free land for homesteaders willing to open the west, and Ontario's new government had implemented just the year before, in 1868, an identical policy. Some of those now flocking north were refugees from war, flood, fire, or famine. Others sought sanctuary from family tragedy, a crisis of love, a debt of money, or to escape the arm of the law.

Even as this New York family's early morning train steamed north toward Canada, "Captain" Pokorny, a furtive Polish immigrant whose rank was said to derive from prior service in the army of his homeland, was another of those unlikely pioneers seeking refuge in the remote northland. A trusted treasurer of Toronto's opera company, he'd fetched the Saturday night receipts from the theatre to count the haul, keep it safe through Sunday, then deposit the money Monday at the bank. Instead, he vanished, escaping to Muskoka's deepest bush in Franklin Township, an all but inaccessible section not yet surveyed, not even open for settlement. The edgy Pole found unpromising rocky land at the furthest end of Peninsula Lake for his out-of-the-way "farm," a place not to grow crops but escape the law. Pokorny would survive, as a squatter, aided by his wits and a suitcase crammed with cash.

Other desperate individuals heading to Muskoka were not eluding the law but forgetting tragedy. After Henry Bird trained as a milliner at his father's wool-weaving factories in England, he came to Canada, and before long was operating his own mill on the Conestoga River near Guelph, at least until the entire operation was flooded out by great rises in the river. The following year, severe flooding destroyed his rebuilt mill a second time. Then Bird's wife, Sarah, their three-year-old daughter, and six-month-old son were all killed in an accident. Devastated, Henry Bird abandoned both God and Guelph and headed to Muskoka. By the early 1870s, he would be operating a new mill at the Bracebridge waterfall.

Whether fleeing to Muskoka for reasons criminal or honourable, whether drawn by opportunism or just a sense of adventure, everyone migrating into the bush was on a quest for some kind of new life.

In time Muskoka would become accessible from all directions thanks to convenient transportation and contemporary communications; but in the 1860s the district was not even the end of the line, it was *beyond* the end. Loggers only reached Muskoka's southern edge by the late 1850s. Prospectors hadn't yet discovered Ontario's treasure chest of minerals in the northern districts beyond; until they did, no mining towns operated up there so there was no need for railways through Muskoka to haul resources south. By the mid-1860s, a couple of primitive colonization roads were being stubbornly pushed into Muskoka's unknown terrain, one from the east, another, the south. Only in the mid-1870s would a railway line get as far as Gravenhurst, but then not advance any farther north for another decade. When this family from New York headed to Muskoka in 1869, this frontier district was the remotest place on anybody's horizon.

New arrivals wanting anonymity for themselves asked few questions of others. They just hoped to cross over from one life to the next, a secular redemption, an unhallowed resurrection, entering a better world without having to die first.

—

Though people were propelled by urgent need to leave troubles behind, at the same time they found themselves pulled north by the bright prospect of becoming prosperous landowners. This alluring vision of being resurrected as self-sufficient individuals living on good farms of their own was even drawing people with no farming experience whatsoever, to land that was not yet settled, nor even cleared of its tangled forests.

These settlers hoped to cash in on a promise Ontario's government and its immigration agents were aggressively promoting through speeches, advertisements in American and British newspapers, and the booklet *Emigration to Canada: The Province of Ontario*, distributed widely in 1869 to publicize Muskoka's glowing agricultural prospects for new settlers. Whatever gloom haunted their pasts, these pioneers positively glowed as they imagined their hundred acres of "free" land. The Muskoka dream was grounded in the belief that having one's own farm was the foundation of society and personal self-sufficiency; it promised continuation of a centuries-old pastoral way of life, one not yet dislodged by heavy industry, the growth of factories, and the magnet of living in cities.

Few individuals heading north to Muskoka sought a transformation more complete, however, than this desperate Broadway lawyer. In New York he boarded the train as Isaac Jelfs. In Toronto he stepped off as James Boyer.

———

Not only was Jelfs abandoning his name. He was forfeiting a long-craved legal career with the politically influential, if increasingly embattled, Broadway Avenue firm of Brown, Hall & Vanderpoel. He was relinquishing his recording secretary's role with the Episcopalian Methodist Church in Brooklyn. He was abandoning the vice-presidency of the Brooklyn Britannia Benevolent Association, an office to which he'd been glowingly elected in May that year, being presented with a copy of Byron's poetical works and making, as the *Brooklyn Daily Eagle* reported, "one of his happy speeches on the occasion."

The real kicker was that he had closed the front door of the Jelfs's 18th Street family home in Brooklyn for the last time. Overnight, Isaac vanished from the life of his wife, Eliza, and their young daughter, Elizabeth.

The pregnant person on the train was not Isaac's wife in law, but had become a second wife in reality after she'd first captured his heart at a Britannia Benevolent Association dance one Saturday night several years before. The two-year-old girl on the train was their love child, Annie, whose birth the secretive lovers, Isaac Jelfs and Hannah Boyer, had contrived to leave unrecorded in New York's registries. Equally absent from official documents was any record of their marriage, since neither in New York nor later in Canada would they ever have a legal wedding.

Jelfs had become embroiled in a risky double life, his two families living only blocks apart in Brooklyn's Gowanus district. Beyond the snare of human complications inherent in such risky romance, his public role and professional reputation as a lawyer in breach of matrimonial laws escalated the danger. On top of that were his concerns about what might be going on at the law office. Some apparent practices at the fast-paced Brown, Hall & Vanderpoel firm made him fear a day of reckoning for corrupt practices might be in the offing. He'd already been swept up in something like that before, and paid a huge price despite never being a party to the wrong-doing.

The accumulating complications of his double life and the rising threat of what might happen at his embattled law firm, whose principal, Oakey Hall, was New York's mayor and an integral part of the Tammany Hall political machine running the city and bilking its coffers, combined to produce a bold plan: Isaac Jelfs would completely disappear from the life of one family and abandon his career in New York, then reinvent himself in a new role with the other family somewhere else.

Yet, for neither "James" nor Hannah Boyer would this be the first time they found themselves starting life over in a new country.

2

On the Path of the Law

Isaac Jelfs was born May 28, 1834 (a detail "James Boyer," with a much younger wife and also covering his tracks, would later obscure by giving 1836 as his year of birth), in Moreton-in-Marsh, an English farming centre in the northern Cotswolds west of Stratford.

Nestled along what centuries before had been a Roman roadway, Moreton-in-Marsh is aptly named, surrounded as it is by muck-rich acres. After 1227, when Moreton's market charter was first granted, the town's main event came every Tuesday, when the market hall and stone-cobbled thoroughfare filled with stalls of produce hauled by farmers from their fertile low-lying fields nearby.

When Isaac was a boy, a hundred-year-old tram railway ran the sixteen-mile distance between Stratford-upon-Avon and Moreton-in-Marsh, its pace gentle because the heavy freight cars were drawn by dray horses, its purpose chiefly to distribute coal that had first passed from the English coast on small sailing vessels up the Severn and Avon rivers to Stratford. On market days the railway's tram car, fitted with a special covered top, carried passengers from Stratford out to Moreton — maids, perhaps an actor or two, buyers from the inns and taverns, fun-seeking visitors to the theatre town who'd come for evening playhouse performances — to get the farmers' fresh produce straight from the fields that morning. A festive "market day" mood filled the Tuesday morning air and young Isaac Jelfs thrilled to it all, the dramatic highlight of his quiet week when he could enjoy action and observe strangers.

When Isaac Jelfs grew up in Moreton-in-Marsh, sheep moved unhurriedly through High Street's market square, except on Tuesdays, the day when farmers filled the place with market-day stalls and he enjoyed the excitement.
(Watercolour print: Sylvester Stannart)

Between market days, and between the two fair days in March and November each year when Cotswold games of woolsack races, shin-kicking, and the oddity of downhill cheese-rolling contests attracted lively sport and loud cheering, the town of a thousand inhabitants was serene. Sleeping cats sunned themselves in the middle of the streets, a curving array consisting of High Street where the Jelfs lived, Oxford and Church streets, Bourton and Stow lanes, Bakers Row and Back Ends, together with rear lanes and narrow burgage plots held on yearly rents. Most buildings in picturesque Moreton were warm-coloured limestone or white stucco, with thick, thatched roofs and large chimneys. The burning tang of coal smoke drifted over the town and pinched Isaac's nostrils. Each night he heard the town bell ring out from the sixteenth-century curfew tower just along the street at the corner of Oxford, a warning reminder to townsfolk of the risk of fire at night.

Isaac knew these houses and winding streets of Moreton-in-Marsh, all little changed when his great-grandson took this photograph in 1982.

Isaac Jelfs heard the bell from Moreton's curfew tower at right. He would still recognize these enduring buildings along his street, except for the puzzling television antennae and gas station, which appeared a century after he left the village.
(Copyright of the Francis Frith Collection)

Moreton was not only a market centre for farmers but a travellers' town, too, boasting several pubs, inns, hotels, teashops, and a coaching station. From one century to the next, despite advent of the linen production central to the Jelfs's way of life, or the shift from horse-drawn coaches to steam-engine trains when Isaac was in his teens, little else about Moreton-in-Marsh seemed to change. Lord Redesdale, for whom the market hall was named, was officially lord of the manor; however, though he occasionally held what was known as a court baron, mostly to appoint constables, effective local government here as elsewhere across England was principally in the hands of the county's magistrate, in whose office a heavy clock ticked away the hours even as time stood still.

―

The Jelfs household was headed by Isaac Senior, born in 1797 at the village of Bretforton. Isaac later relocated to Moreton-in-Marsh where, in 1824, he met and married Hannah Heath. The Jelfs family was set apart from others in that it prospered neither by farming nor through the hospitality trade, but to the extent Isaac Senior wove linens and Hannah made hats. "The only manufactory here is that for linen cloth," reported Pigot's 1844 *Gloucestershire Directory* on the economy of Moreton-in-Marsh. In spinning yarn for this cloth, Pigot's added, "some of the poorer classes are employed," without bothering to add that such workers were poor because they could earn only a pittance in this hard-bargain economy.

Reflecting his own steady rise in the business, Isaac Senior identified himself to the census-takers in 1841 as a weaver, a decade later as a linen manufacturer. His was the same initiative displayed by other enterprising Jelfs in the region, looking to see what people needed and then supplying it. Thirty miles north in Birmingham, Isaac's cousins likewise owned and operated small undertakings: John Jelfs was a shoemaker at 111 Holt Street; William Jelfs owned a bakery at 154 Unett Street; while James Jelfs was keeper of an eating house at 7 Lower Priory.

Ancestors of the Jelfs had migrated to England from continental Europe, most likely the Low Countries, in the late 1500s. There the name *Jelfs*, with various spellings, appears in records back into the thirteenth century. Although the family was Jewish, for several generations now the Jelfs had become adherents to the Church of England, the family and its descendants assimilating into English society, as such names as John, William, and James attest, although the girls still seemed to get more traditional Jewish surnames. In England, the Jelfs had morphed into Anglos in the manner of many other Jews, in order to get ahead in their new surroundings. The redoubtable British Prime Minister Benjamin Disraeli, whose clearly Jewish name never disguised his heritage, was a leading example of this phenomenon of social integration of which the earlier Jelfs were but a part.

From the 1600s onwards in England, Jelfs families had been concentrated northwest of Moreton in the Evesham and Badsey area, living in such Worcestershire villages as Honeybourne and Bretforton, down through generations. Many Jelfs marriages embraced other ethnic and national backgrounds. Over time memories faded until family heritage became fogged over with ignorance. Contacted in connection with the writing of this book, the Jelfs living in today's polyglot Britain, devoted to such diverse endeavours as pottery making, professional soccer, and politics, were as surprised as the delighted descendants of "James Boyer" living in twenty-first century Canada to discover their remote Jewish genes.

Back in the 1700s, a Jelfs family had lived at Moreton-in-Marsh, but then moved away. By the mid-1800s, the only Jelfs in town were Isaac, his wife Hannah, and their various children. The Jelfs's household shared High Street with many elegant eighteenth-century inns, houses, and the distinctive Victorian era Tudor-style Redesdale Market Hall.

Of the eight known children, three were boys, with Isaac the middle one. The first-born child was Samuel; nine years older than Isaac, he served as a fine example to the others for the independence which Isaac Senior and his wife Hannah required of their offspring. Sam had already moved out of the house when Isaac Junior was still quite young, to live with a retired couple named Lardiner. He became organist at Moreton's Anglican St. David parish church by age fifteen, married a Harriet from nearby Chipping Campden when twenty-two, then moved on to Dorset to work as a solicitor's general clerk, advancing in time, by then himself the father of seven children, to become clerk of the Poor Law Union.

Meanwhile Isaac's older sisters, Miriam and Sabrina, stayed at home, learning the skills of hat-making from their mother. Sabrina died from typhus at age seventeen. Other children died, too. Hannah gave birth to a boy in 1832, baptized Isaac to carry on his father's name, who perished within the year. Lest that be taken as a bad omen, the Jelfs tried out the same name on their next male infant who was baptized June 10, 1834 at St. David's as "Isaac Jelfs." Because this child lived, the name would be perpetuated — at least for thirty-five years until Isaac's disappearing act into Canada in 1869.

Just two weeks before Isaac was born, another child arrived under the family roof. Baptized George Jelfs on May 25, 1834 at the same local parish church, he was the child of Jane Jelfs, a single woman from Evesham who was secreted with her in-laws while she came to term in tandem with Hannah.

When Isaac was four, another child, named Rebecca, was born into the household. Although this little girl was found by the census-takers in 1841 living with her parents, that is the last trace of her, with no record of Rebecca Jelfs ever dying. Another girl, Mary Ann, born in 1840, died "suddenly from natural causes" at age eleven. Isaac was eleven by the time his younger brother, Thomas, arrived in 1845. Amidst this shifting galaxy of siblings, Elizabeth Heath, some thirteen years older than Isaac and more like a sister than an aunt, moved in to help Hannah with the children and household, thus freeing up her sister's time to increase production of straw bonnets. If the boy learned anything from all these comings and goings, it was that "family" was a very loose arrangement.

Young Isaac was bright and healthy, though somewhat shy. His boyhood adventures were innocent, limited by place. Filling the quiet interludes between market days, he sometimes hiked with other boys into the countryside, past water meadows and beech woods, across fast-flowing streams, through high turf alive with grasshoppers.

For a special adventure, the children walked a couple miles along the old Roman turnpike to the Four Shires Stone, nestled on a square yard of land whose exact centre formed the intersecting corner boundaries of Gloucestershire, Worcestershire, Oxfordshire, and Warwickshire. Taking turns to clamber up the nine foot high structure of Cotswold stone and perch atop the stone ball at the monument's apex, they would then gleefully proclaim magic to their chums: "Look at me! I'm sitting in four different counties at the same time!"

A few decades later, medieval scholar and author J.R.R. Tolkien would become as enthralled as Isaac and his chums by the Four Shires Stone, returning with excited inspiration from his discovery of it to a Moreton pub, The Bell Inn, to sip ale and write up notes about the "Three-Farthing Stone," the central place in the shire where three of the four farthings met, for his series of books about imaginary gnome-like creatures, the hobbits. The Bell Inn itself inspired, for Tolkien, the Middle Earth's famous pub named The Prancing Pony in *Lord of the Rings*, while the similarities between Moreton-in-Marsh and Tolkien's fictitious town of Bree are unmistakable.

—

Such delights aside, it was not as if Isaac or the other children around town had much free time.

His classroom education began at the local school when he was five. There he learned to read and write. Once his talents in penmanship emerged, Isaac was sent after school and Saturdays to earn small money as a copyist for Moreton solicitor Edwin Tilsley. This silent, solitary labour suited Isaac's temperament, but offered none of the body-strengthening work that fell to other Moreton boys with more robust tasks as farm hands and labourers' helpers.

Once he turned twelve, Isaac left school. He now worked full-time as an "attorney's writing clerk" in Tilsley's law office, joining another writing clerk, William Prosser, the nineteen-year-old brother of Edwin Tilsley's wife. Both youths spent their hours pinned at their writing desks under the supervising eyes of the firm's thirty-year-old managing clerk, Charles Wright. This arrangement continued for the next four years, with Isaac remaining in his parents' home to age sixteen.

During his formative years, Isaac's entire work experience thus entailed writing things out. It was not creative writing, but copying what he saw exactly and recording what he heard word-for-word. His skill resided in precise replication; his art embraced form as the essential handmaid to content. In this era there was no office equipment for typing documents. The first mechanical typewriter would only be invented in 1867, and even then, it would not enter practical office use until the turn of the twentieth century, which was about the time Isaac would finally be laying his pen down. To replicate multiple copies of documents, it was necessary to copy them by hand. Isaac Jelfs became a human replicating machine, one more scribe in history's long file of monastic monks and office clerks devoting their lifetimes to copying out text.

Had it not been for the Jelfs's well-founded belief that young men had to make their own way in the world, Isaac's clerical existence in the small English town of Moreton might have continued, unremarkably, for the rest of his life. But as soon as he turned seventeen, his parents made clear it was his turn to follow his brother Sam out of the family fold. They'd got him this far, still alive, and now it was up to him to take responsibility for his life. Possessing a transportable skill, Isaac climbed aboard the train to Stratford for a new venue, but still to do the only thing he knew — copying out documents in a law office.

Just where he lived in Stratford remains as unclear as whether he was engaged in the law offices of Umber & Snowden, or Hobbes, Slatter & Warwick, or Hunt, Oakes & Oliver. No census report mentions him in Stratford because he lived there between the recording intervals for such information, but his own published account of his life clearly states that this is where he lived and worked during these years, and a much later letter sent to him in Muskoka reinforces this fact. For whichever lawyers Isaac worked during the next three years, he no doubt applied himself diligently, as was his nature, acquiring through instruction and osmosis the dry learning solicitors apply to the affairs of others, simplifying the complex and complicating the simple.

In this era young men did not learn the practical work of lawyering by sitting in classrooms contemplating concepts, but by performing practical tasks under the watchful eye of older lawyers and seasoned law clerks — an apprenticeship system similar to any other trade. Isaac's clerkship entailed searching land titles at the registry office and assisting in the conveyancing of property. But in the main, his fine handwriting and artistic flare with straight-nib pens only meant more such work kept piling up on his high, slant-top copy desk. There the "quill driver" stood for hours shifting weight from foot to foot or perching on the front edge of his high stool, writing out authoritative contracts and attractive affidavits, filling in the blanks on pre-printed forms for deeds to property, and crafting wills according to the notes one or other of the solicitors provided him.

For the rest of his life, Isaac would earn his keep and make his mark by the pen: as law clerk, lawyer, calligrapher, newspaperman, clerk to municipal councils, artisan of illuminated addresses, and as the indispensable secretary for fraternal organizations, agricultural societies, and church congregations. His writing for newspapers and books, and his recording of minutes, would preserve for posterity a valuable historical record. His fine penmanship would also serve, for his quarter century as Muskoka's magistrate, to record the proceedings of all his trials. Had he not left behind that written account, this book's companion volume, *Raw Life: Cameos of 1890s Justice from a Magistrate's Bench Book*, which reproduces the cases he tried in that decade, would not exist.

—

After tedious hours in a Stratford law office, the faster pace of life outside beckoned the young man. Isaac enjoyed the famous theatre town's bustling atmosphere.

He sang in the church choir, something he would enjoy doing wherever he lived, beginning in Moreton where his brother played the organ, continuing in Stratford and later in Brooklyn, and through his decades in Muskoka singing in a Methodist choir. Handel's *Messiah* was one of his favourites — triumphal music that lifted him as he sang.

Isaac no doubt attended plays and enjoyed music concerts, given the penchant he displayed for theatre and performances at other times in his life. While in Stratford he learned to play several musical instruments, most notably what he dubbed "the challenging invention known as the clarinet."

William Shakespeare's influence, both in phrase and perspective, permeated Stratford and resonated profoundly with Isaac. His formative years in Moreton had included immersion in the works of Shakespeare, the rich literary gift he continued to savour throughout his life. He became well acquainted with the playwright's remarkable cast of universal characters, quoting their memorable lines at apt moments of conversation and alluding to their attributes in his writing. He stood in solemnity before the house where Shakespeare had been born, a wreck of a place but to him a shrine, thinking it a scandal that such heritage was being lost though disregard and decay. After he left the city, the birthplace would be restored in the 1850s and become a tourism mecca, as it still is today.

That Isaac was a reflective observer of others is clear from both his published writing and his few remaining letters. The way he described peoples' diverse characteristics reflects a perspective enriched by Shakespeare's own portrayal of people's pleasures, chronicles of robust adventures, and interpretations of human turmoil, all of it a study of the dilemmas confronting humans, whether regal personages or society's smallest players. The indelible imprint of his Stratford and Shakespeare-influenced years would endure throughout Isaac's life. In Muskoka it can still be seen in his preserved *Northern Advocate* and *Muskoka Herald* articles, which are sprinkled with Shakespearian phrases and embossed with the poetic flourishes much savoured in the Victorian age.

Isaac Jelfs liked to see William Shakespeare's house in Stratford-upon-Avon, and this is how the playwright's untouched birthplace appeared to him before its 1850s restoration. Isaac quoted apposite lines from Shakespeare all his life. (Copyright of the Francis Frith Collection)

To this point in his life, Isaac, who had been raised to be independent, seemed to display little rebelliousness or even much assertiveness. He was patient, kindly, observant, and somewhat shy. As a result, his life followed the arc set by circumstances of his birth and the plans of others. He relished life and its freedom but was willingly passive, content to take things as they came, a pleasurable but dangerous way to live in a world where others have more particular designs.

3

Calumny in Stratford

Isaac's law office work was running along just fine until a few months before he turned twenty. Although records shedding light on what happened next were lost in the 1930s, from what is known it seems a substantial sum of money went missing from an estate his Stratford law firm was administering. When this "came to light" with the other lawyers, it was alleged by one of them that Isaac was the culprit. He must have felt the blood drain from his face hearing such an allegation. There had to be some awful mistake. If there were problems in the estate, he protested, it was not the result of his wrongdoing, or any money that he had taken.

No doubt the lawyer who accused him would have stressed the delicacy of the situation, because if embezzlement or fraud became known, not only would the reputation of the firm be ruined, but Isaac would go to prison. The lawyers would endeavour to hide the loss and shield the problem until things blew over. The authorities would not be involved because the firm did not want charges laid, which would only bring the shortage of money into the open and make a bad situation worse.

There would, in short, be a cover-up.

Even if Jelfs repaid the money, as the culpable senior lawyer apparently insisted in his effort to frame the young law clerk, the law office could not have someone untrustworthy continue in its employ. Isaac was told that he had just to fade from the scene while they tried to prevent a scandal. Perhaps he could join the army, often a good solution when one needed to escape. The Dragoons, it was apparently suggested, might be a good prospect, because they were known to ask few questions of new recruits.

Humiliated and angry, Isaac continued to protest his innocence, saying he could not repay money he had not taken. Going away would only make him appear the guilty party he was wrongly accused of being. He would not be around to defend his name. Feeling as invidiously wounded by rank injustice as any of Shakespeare's pitiable victims, Isaac Jelfs, it seemed, had no choice.

Just as this stunning setback was taking place, romantic involvement, a reliable source for unwanted complications, created a second crisis for Isaac. He had taken up with Eliza Acocks, a dressmaker from nearby Bourton-on-the-Hill, three years his senior and a woman who doubtless saw in Isaac a worthy prospect for a secure future. Isaac and Eliza went up to Birmingham, a large enough centre where he could lose himself after the Stratford fiasco, find new work, and if real help were needed, perhaps look up one or other of his uncles in the city. The couple found modest living quarters on Pershore Street.

It was hard getting work as a law clerk, Isaac discovered, without references from his last employers. He had no one to turn to. Isaac was reluctant even to tell his mother about the bleak turn his life had taken, knowing the burden she was already shouldering in Moreton-in-Marsh. Hannah Jelfs's circumstances had been greatly reduced after Isaac Senior fell ill and left off weaving, earning money as a letter carrier until just the year before when his illness grew worse and he died. Why burden her further now with his inexplicable troubles? The same reluctance kept Isaac from appealing to any of his three uncles in Birmingham. He'd have to explain why he was in the city, and why he needed work. They would find his dismissal from the law office in Stratford suspicious. Could he be trusted?

Eliza's own father, Thomas Acocks, had already died back in 1848, and she no longer felt any discernible tug back to hometown Bourton. Young adults in this era did not even contemplate running home with their problems. Isaac and his companion set their faces to the storm, to brave life as best they could.

In the forlorn winter of 1854, on February 27, without a single member of their respective families present, Isaac Jelfs and Eliza Acocks were married in the drab parish church of St. Martin's in Birmingham. Besides the officiating minister, only two others were present, Thomas Brown and Ann Siddin, acquaintances from the Pershore Street rooming house, to serve as the required witnesses. Whether Eliza had been pregnant, or was thought to be, can only be conjecture. Official records contain no evidence that in the coming months, nor even during the next seven years for that matter, any children were born to Eliza Jelfs. Perhaps that was not too surprising, because her husband Isaac was not around to father any.

—

Whether it was his predicament in being made scapegoat for something terribly wrong in the Stratford law office, or his difficulty finding new work in a different city, or his desire to be independent and avoid having to make any appeal to his uncles, or the bleakness of the drab winter season in grimy Birmingham, or feelings of regret about the marriage, or the tempest of all these swirling factors combined, nineteen-year-old Isaac resolved his dilemma through a dramatic transformation.

The young man who'd entered a Stratford office as a law clerk stepped out of a Birmingham recruiting centre as a soldier in the Dragoons and was soon overseas fighting a war.

Isaac had enlisted in what, in two separate published accounts of his life, he would later call simply the "regular" Dragoon Guards. That term, obscuring his record of service with the Dragoons and their many distinctively named regiments, turns out to have been an intentionally vague reference to cover his tracks. As James Boyer, someone not wanting to be closely traced, he would further obfuscate his military service by loosely stating, without mentioning any dates, that he served with the Dragoons "for seven years." That was an impossibility, given that Isaac only enlisted in 1854 and by July 26, 1858 was in New York City filing notice of his intention to become an American citizen, based on already having been in the United States five years (itself an impossible stretch), in what by then had become yet another round in a series of disappearances and reconstitutions of himself.

No sooner had Isaac enlisted than the pace of history swiftly caught him up in its swirl. On March 28, 1854, just four weeks after his apparently rather loveless wedding in unfamiliar and unwelcoming Birmingham, Britain declared war on Russia, escalating the fighting that had first erupted some months earlier between Russia and the Turks in the Crimea area around the Black Sea. As Prussia, Austria, France, Britain and others were drawn into the conflict, the so-called Crimean War spread to a much wider theatre of hostile engagement, with naval blockades and battles taking place from the Pacific in the east to Scandinavian seaports in the north. The first engagement of British forces came in the Battle of Alma on September 24. That is why Isaac, and thousands more like him, were welcome recruits. Demand for enlistment would not abate until a quarter million British soldiers were serving in the increasingly unpopular Crimean campaign.

Begun over the pretext of which country should be "protector" of so-called Holy Lands, an antiquated concern fuelled by zealous religious differences that were underpinned by expansionist designs of rival imperial powers, Isaac found himself in a war that ushered in modernity: the first war to be photographed; the first with observers' reports sent from the front lines by electronic telegraph for publication in the next day's newspapers; the first involving strategic use of railways; advent of attentive battlefield nursing, led by social reformer, statistician, and pioneer of modern nursing Florence Nightingale when she and other women like her broke into the hardened ranks of indifferent male nurses; deployment in naval warfare of harbour mines, newly invented by arms merchant Alfred Nobel whose bloodied munitions revenues would later fund his exculpatory Nobel Peace Prize; and introduction of rapid-fire machine guns.

The Crimean War broke new ground, too, with abolition of the hoary British practice of selling commissions in the military, but only after scandals reached parliament about so many valiant men being led into slaughter by incompetent officers whose high rank had been purchased under England's class-system patronage. The suicidal "Charge of the

Light Brigade" — "Theirs not to reason why / Theirs but to do, and die" — expressed this treacherous stupidity.

Crimea also demonstrated how cavalry units, even in better-led armies, were all now riding into their battlefield twilight. In the face of modern, mechanized warfare and improved artillery fire, shouting mounted soldiers wielding sabres and lances were no match for the angry mouths of ranked cannon-fire deployed with cold calculation against them. Perhaps most sobering of all was the tragic evidence that inability to deal with hygiene was an even worse killer than those deadly guns. By the time the Crimean War ended in 1856, some 22,000 British soldiers had died, most fatalities resulting from disease. Isaac Jelfs acquired a visceral hatred of war.

Somehow, he survived. He'd avoided the slaughter as well as the creeping death of infectious disease by learning the fighting ways of the Dragoons and the practices of hygiene. In the quiet waiting that is a soldier's lot, he no doubt ruminated about the perverse fate that had brought him to this improbable place, and reflected on the inordinate

Although Isaac Jelfs's service in the Dragoons offered escape from predicaments in England, the horrors of the Crimean War — its deadly battles and unhygienic conditions — soon combined with Isaac's stretches of brooding reflection to propel him into another disappearance, this time to the New World.
(© Hulton-Deutsch Collection/Corbis)

influence others had exerted on the direction of his life. His prized penmanship was now used only to write infrequent letters from the front lines to his mother Hannah, his wife Eliza, and his brother Sam.

It seems that in one letter of reply, probably from Sam, who was connected to the legal world and had received inquiries about his brother during some sort of investigation, Isaac learned how he had indeed been blamed for the missing funds in Stratford. His sudden disappearance from the law office had been seen as confirming his dastardly embezzlement of funds from the client's estate. The cover-up had broken. The absent culprit, now untraceable, was easily blamed for money gone missing.

The quiescent approach urged upon Isaac by the senior lawyer had served someone else's interest, not his own, just as he feared would be the case. His "mysterious" departure taken as proof of guilt, Isaac now stood further condemned as someone who dared not even stay like a man to defend his honour. He realized a return to England was impossible.

Perhaps somewhere, far across an ocean, he could start anew.

———

After the Crimean War ended in 1856, it is unclear whether Isaac saw further service in India where Dragoon regiments were deployed to suppress an uprising, or in Ireland to check rebelliousness there; the regimental records contain no indication nor are there any other clues. The comprehensive, multi-regimental records system for detailing service in the Dragoons, in place for the previous hundred years, stopped just before 1853, only months before Isaac enlisted, replaced by an ever-accumulating mass of piecemeal records kept solely by regiments and almost impenetrable to anyone later searching for an enlisted man who never held rank nor received a military pension.

Whether Isaac made it back to England to see Eliza or his mother before crossing the Atlantic to the United States is uncertain, but most improbable. Those ties did not bind him very tightly. Even more, he feared his status as the scapegoat of Stratford would lead to his arrest, perhaps risking, despite his innocence, conviction and imprisonment. Who needed that?

That Isaac headed for the United States, rather than British colonies like Australia or Canada, may simply have been because dynamic America beckoned young men more than any other place in the world. Or it may have been that Isaac fled to a non-British country because he had deserted the army — his time with the Dragoons was short, given the date he applied for citizenship in the United States. As histories of the war record, many men slipped away from the army without benefit of a military discharge. There was no point fleeing a war to save your life, only to stand before a firing squad after a sentence of death at a court martial. Either way, he needed to cover his tracks and live in a jurisdiction where the British Crown's writ did not run. He certainly took measures to avoid detection, whether fearful that he might be charged with an alleged embezzlement from an estate in Stratford, or perhaps accused as an army deserter, or maybe even both.

Like many heading to the "New World," Isaac Jelfs did not look back. He sailed, almost certainly from a European rather than a British port. He travelled under an assumed name, easily done in an era before birth certificates, passports, and travel documents, when just having money enough to pay passage (or courage enough to be a stowaway, if lacking money) got a traveller aboard a sailing ship and into whatever country the ship reached. Isaac arrived in New York sometime prior to August 26, 1858, quite possibly a couple of years earlier, and walked down the gangplank into America a free man.

Back in England, meanwhile, another human drama was unfolding.

4

Hannah Boyer's Plight

Ely, in Cambridgeshire of East Anglia, was renowned for its cathedral, known locally as "the ship of the Fens" due to its prominent shape towering above the surrounding flat and watery landscape called fenlands. The second-largest cathedral in England, its towers pointed in silence to heaven and the better possibilities believers might one day experience there. By 1863 Joseph Boyer had reason to believe things would be better above than they were turning out here below.

Twenty-five years earlier, Joe, a good looking young man, was standing in summer sunshine one day along the road beside a field of ripening barley near Longthorpe when he spotted a stage "coming on the run with its horses, and a young girl running gust o' hell, well built, about sixteen, with her hair flying around her head. It was a coming thing for her to beat the stage into 'Thorpe. Just as she got up to me she stumbled and would 'ave fell only I caught her in my arms."

The wind moved upon those fields of barley and the sun gazed down, turning them gold. The pair walked the fields, stayed awhile, and Joe held her. Two years later, on March 2, 1840, she was still in his arms. They married that day in Longthorpe chapel of the Church of England, in Northhampton County's Peterborough parish.

Elizabeth White, Joseph's energy-packed bride, five years younger than he and still a minor when they wed, had come to England from Northern Ireland with her parents, two sisters, and four brothers. All her brothers were now in uniform, serving in either the navy or army.

Elizabeth's father, Tom White, a strong man standing six feet two inches tall and weighing two hundred pounds, was a labourer and brewer who each year made his rounds to "all the rich folks to brew their beer." Elizabeth's mother, Mary, a diminutive god-fearing woman and good housekeeper, lived on cookies and showered them on visitors. For her good living and bad diet she would be rewarded with 102 years on earth.

The Boyer couple, avid dancers with outgoing natures and a joyous sense of fun, shared a robust love. They began to populate their small house, "Woodstone Lodge," on the Huntington House estate. Their first-born arrived the final day of 1841. She was christened "Hannah," a name that would be rung for all possible changes over the years as friends and family variously called her Anna, Ann, Annie, Nan, Nancy, Nanie and even, on occasion, Hannah. In 1844 and 1846 Elizabeth successfully delivered two more children into the Boyer family, Mary Ann, and Thomas.

In 1848, after nearly a decade together in Longthorpe, Joseph and Elizabeth moved their children to Chettisham, about a mile from Ely, and lived in an old structure that had once been a monastery, its rooms

*From across their meadows, the Boyers could easily see Ely and its famous cathedral —
seen here in a photo from the late 1800s. Hannah led her brothers and sisters through an
abandoned tunnel from their home to a trap door by the cathedral altar.
(Copyright of the Francis Frith Collection)*

panelled with oak. Stone steps from the kitchen led down to a tunnel that came up a mile and a quarter away inside Ely Cathedral, right beside the alter. Hannah, an adventuresome girl, led the other Boyer children in exploring the tunnel's eerie length, lighting their way with dim flickering lights along the dank passageway which had been abandoned to spiders and rats for forty years and had caved in at places, making it tricky to navigate.

The year after moving to Chettisham, Joseph and Elizabeth added another daughter to their household, a second "Elizabeth" as she was given her mother's name, although the family would invariably call her just "Lizzy."

Then, in 1852, Elizabeth gave birth to twins. One was named Henry, at the request of Joe's brother Henry, a wealthy bachelor living near Peterborough who grandly pronounced that, if named for him, the boy "would never want for the rest of his life." The other twin, a girl, was christened Emma. Six months later, the village doctor diagnosed her cause of death as "water on the brain." Joe and Elizabeth still liked the name Emma, so tried it out again on their next daughter. Born in 1854, this one lived. Meanwhile, the surviving twin, Henry, mostly called by the familiar corruption of his name as "Harry" which his Peterborough uncle may not have fully appreciated, seemed to take on the energy of two.

Joseph Boyer's duties at Chettisham included paying out money and overseeing the work of the estate. As in Holland, England's watery fenlands depended on large dikes, with excess water behind them being continuously drained away by pumping. In the case of the Chettisham estate, four pumps carried water into the nearby river to flow away. Aided by the alert eyes of Hannah and Tom, who were daily learning about the cultivation and care of fine farm lands, Joe constantly watched that the water level didn't get too high and flood the crops. Each time a rainstorm came, whether day or night, he rode on horseback around the dikes to ensure the pumps were working, sometimes only seeing for sure in the stormy darkness when the scene became momentarily illuminated by bright flashes of lightning. All his life, in many ways, Joe Boyer was a responsible man on whom others depended.

His health, however, was deteriorating. Lacking any better diagnosis, the village doctor blamed it on "too much horseback riding" that had "ruined his insides." Doubting that, Joe went to London to see "a great doctor named Abernathy," who recommended his patient give up riding, prescribed some medicine, and implored him to take up smoking to improve his health.

Not long after, when the squire of the Chettisham estate died, the Boyers moved again, with pipe-smoking Joseph taking up similar work in a new setting. Hannah did not relocate with the family, as employment and a romantic attachment kept her in Chettisham. She liked being with her loving family, but wanted to be with her lover more.

Discovering what it meant to be on her own, Hannah Boyer began enjoying freedom. She was energetic, attractive, and, like her parents, an exceptional dancer. For the first time in her life, she felt a burden lift; her step was lighter, she did not need to explain where she was going, was no longer preoccupied looking after younger brothers and sisters. If those days of care and custody should ever return, however, they would come back with a vengeance because during the years of her absence, Hannah's parents continued giving her more siblings, two sisters and another brother: Lydia in 1858; Anne Alice in 1860; and finally, William White on September 23, 1863.

—

Never had Joseph Boyer been happier than that day in the golden summer of 1837 when sprightly, vivacious Elizabeth White fell into his arms and entered his life at the edge of those fields of barley.

Never was he more devastated than when she died in a darkened room that September of 1863, forty-one years of age, struggling to give birth to William. That day, the sun vanished from Joe's sky.

Elizabeth's funeral service required a long walk. Twelve pallbearers took turns with her coffin as the morose family procession wended numbly along three-quarters of a country mile to the Baptist churchyard in Haddenham.

Joe Boyer's despondency over Elizabeth's death made his poor health worse. Her vibrant Irish spirit no longer enlivened the familiar scene. Hannah, their first-born, now an attractive woman of twenty-one, rejoined the family to care for them all. Her heart was elsewhere; her duty, here. She struggled to look after the large brood, though she did have help with youngest child, infant William, who was being wet-nursed. Not Hannah nor wee William, but the seven other very lively children turned their expectant faces to their father with uncertainty. A complete change, a despondent Joe realized as the weeks dragged on, might be needed. He began to think of escaping this place with all its sad reminders, to somewhere completely new, to start over.

After several months he told Hannah, and then the other children, of his bold decision. The Boyers would make a fresh start. Joe called in his credits and sold most of what the family owned, except for essential cooking pots, some items of clothing, and a few keepsakes Hannah packed into a trunk along with family Bibles recording births, marriages, and deaths stretching back to the early 1700s. Using that money, he would buy passage for himself and the children to the New World.

Joe then travelled down to Southampton on the English Channel coast from where, on October 31, 1863, while still in port aboard the *Webster* and waiting to sail, he wrote instructions for his nine children who would follow in a second ship after he'd safely reached New York, got work, and prepared a new home for them.

My Dear Children

We expect the inspection this a.m. then we go to open sea. When you come bring some onions and potatoes, a bushel mixed in a sack, and all the bedding and blankets. You can get some sacks with good things to bring, anything. Do not have your best clothes on you for anything is good enough aboard ship. Bring your saucepans and brass pans with you. You cannot wear your crinolines; it is not convenient to go up and down the holds.

Dear children, my health is better than it has been for some weeks past. The vessel I am going in took about nine hundred passengers, and the one you will come by took seven hundred. I hope it will be the Lord's will we may all meet again soon, but if not then in that bright world above where parting is no more. Kind love to all friends. I am your loving father. You will want a water can large enough. I have spoke to the agent for berths for you.

J. Boyer
aboard the *Webster*

The children departed England two weeks later aboard the smaller ship *Orient*. The cramped vessel carried not seven hundred but nine hundred passengers, earning all the fares the ship's agent could extract. There was food and water enough for five weeks. Soon, the overcrowded *Orient* was blown six hundred miles off course by turbulent winds, ending up in frigid November seas — the peril of a winter crossing. The captain and crew eventually managed to sail her further south to catch warmer trade-winds for the rest of the voyage, but before the Atlantic had been crossed they were into their ninth week at sea.

Most on board had only a few hard ships' biscuits to eat and these had run out. Day by ocean-heaving day, starvation inched closer and dehydration was debilitating everyone, the thirsty passengers taunted by salt water stretching to the horizons but no more fresh water to drink. Even the desperate survival method of drinking one's own urine became harder with each cycle, becoming more concentrated in the absence of other consumed fluids to dilute its contaminated taste.

Passengers weakened, becoming listless and dazed. It is unknown how many died on the crossing, although the ship's official records suggest it was few. Different versions exist about how many people were even aboard the *Orient*. The shipping line officials had told Joseph Boyer, who'd purchased the children's tickets, she carried seven hundred passengers. His son Harry, who crossed the Atlantic aboard her, wrote in his diary of the voyage, which is the most direct first-hand report available, that there were nine hundred. Inexplicably, the ship's manifest for this voyage officially lists only 195 passengers arriving in New York, yet records only one death during the crossing, that of infant William Boyer.

It is not possible, nor necessary, to reconcile these differences. It was simply in the nature of that era's commerce that likely many more fare-paying passengers were crammed aboard the *Orient* than her official records disclose.

What is clear is that wee William Boyer, who came into the world at the cost of his mother's life, first lacked for milk, then even water, and finally perished, aged fifteen months, on December 16 at seven o'clock in the evening.

The beleaguered children, who had already lost their mother, their home, their friends, and their country, now watched as their baby brother was buried at sea that very night, a tiny cloth bundle sliding off a plank over the side of the ship, accompanied by a prayer to help his soul ascend and a lead weight to ensure his body reached bottom.

The eight who remained — Hannah, Mary Ann, Tom, Lizzy, Harry, Emma, Lydia, and little Anne Alice — continued to weaken. Most debilitated were the three youngest girls. Emma was seven; Lydia and Annie, both three. In their stupefied state, induced by starvation and more than sixty days on the hypnotically rolling sea, the Boyer children hung on to their only hope, reinforced by their dutiful sense of child's purpose and sister Hannah's urgings: they must survive this ordeal and reach New York because their anxious father would be there waiting for them.

———

When the *Orient* neared New York's harbour on January 12, 1864, as Harry's diary records, small tug boats came out to meet her with fresh bread and water. The three youngest sisters, so frail they could not walk, had to be carried off the ship to the Castle Garden immigration hall.

Around five o'clock in the afternoon, at the southern tip of Manhattan Island, the Boyer tribe was again on solid land, for the first time in over two months. In jostling crowds the bewildered children looked around for their father. Amid loud shouting and milling confusion of strangers, they asked for him.

Hannah, a distraught young woman in her early twenties stranded in this dismal and confusing setting, huddled her pathetically thin sisters and weakened brothers around her to keep the family from becoming separated. Tom and Harry ventured from the cluster to scout the precincts for their father, but kept returning to report they could not find him. Joseph Boyer was apparently lost. Or worse, he had abandoned them. All his life others had depended on reliable Joe, but never more than now.

The children remained after all the other disembarked *Orient* passengers had left or been escorted away. They watched anxiously as the crowds began to thin, and then disperse entirely. Joe Boyer was still nowhere to be seen. Clearly, their father was having trouble finding them.

That night they slept on the floor in the empty immigration hall. Rats ran over them in the dark. Harry, ten years old at the time, would later fill his diary with details. The next morning, when the hall stirred again to bustling passengers arriving and departing, they again waited anxiously for their father to fetch them. By nightfall the Boyer children again settled on the floor, hungry, cold, and very much alone. The rats returned, so far the only living things in New York to give them attention.

On the third day, a lawyer from the sailing company's office appeared. He informed the children that their father had died crossing on the *Webster*. Joseph Boyer had been buried at sea, the lawyer reported, off Newfoundland. The circumstances of their father's death were not made clear. None of his money, nor any of the papers in his possession, were turned over to them.

The forlorn children were now utterly on their own. The city authorities, accustomed to hardship cases, were notified about the destitute clutch of orphans. Hannah, along with Mary Ann at nineteen years and Tom at seventeen, were old enough to work. Boarding places were found for them while they searched for jobs. The five others were dispatched to orphanages which they could not leave until reaching age sixteen. Lydia, aged three, had been made an inmate of the city's District 9 Asylum for Orphans. From there she would be hired out to domestic service, even before reaching age ten, her child labour providing income for the asylum, although never enough, it seemed, for ever-hungry Lydia to get much food to eat.

After a month Hannah and Mary Ann, doing their utmost to keep the young family together, retrieved fourteen-year-old Lizzy from her orphanage by persuading the custodian she was really sixteen. The three youngest girls, Emma, Lydia, and Anne Alice, were scattered, and Hannah, to her unending despair, did not know where.

5

Crucible of War

Isaac, meanwhile, was discovering New York City.

Emblem of New World possibilities for those hoping to remake their lives, his boisterous new setting enthralled him. The massed jumble of individuals were busy competing in every conceivable pursuit around the congested port areas of lower Manhattan and Brooklyn, rushing along noisy thoroughfares, crowding office buildings with their commerce and stores with their trade.

He found a place to live in Brooklyn, on President Street. Rent was cheaper across the East River than in Manhattan. Isaac had no money.

Thousands who entered the United States through New York got dirty, low-paying factory jobs and menial helper's tasks, and then remained stuck in them because they could not speak English. America was a place of upward mobility, but only if you could communicate. A displaced deputy minister of finance from an East European country became a Brooklyn janitor, then continued the rest of his days pushing a broom and carrying garbage because the only languages he spoke were Slavic. A unilingual Polish blue-blood worked a foundry furnace in Manhattan, with no prospect for advancement. But any English-speaking immigrant could rise to manage, then boss, then even own a shop or factory — usually in short order. As an immigrant who spoke English, Isaac was fine.

Realizing his best chance to earn money would be using skills honed since boyhood, Isaac began making the rounds of the city's law firms.

On virtually his first call, he was hired as a clerk in the busy offices of Brown, Hall & Vanderpoel. Landing good work in the rapidly growing firm at 237 Broadway Avenue, one of New York's most bustling thorough-fares, landed him in the very heart of the city's action.

Before long he realized, from the variety of transactions swirling in and out of the firm's hectic offices, that lawyering in New York was utterly different from law practice as he'd known it in Moreton or Stratford. Isaac was soon starry-eyed, envisaging a legal career as his best possible future in competitive New York.

A sense of jubilation, rare for him, began to propel Isaac in his law office work. Some tasks were familiar, but many were new, such as the real estate deals and patent applications he helped with. New York was filled with manufacturing concerns, and almost daily some inventive person was coming up with a clever new way to speed a process, improve a product, or perform a function never before imagined. Isaac's intrigue with his patent practice grew not only because of the amazing designs, but because of his association with the fascinating people creating them.

The promise of the New World was, quite simply, that anything was possible, including advancing from mere law clerk to full-fledged lawyer. Because a person needed to be a citizen of the United States to practise law, during the summer of 1858 Isaac petitioned to become a naturalized American citizen. His petition was supported by J.R. Cumming, one of his firm's prominent attorneys, who attested not only that he had known Isaac Jelfs for five years and that the petitioner had resided in the country for at least that long, but also that "during that time he had behaved as a man of good moral character, attached to the principles of the Constitution of the United States, and well-disposed to the good order and happiness of the same." In this process Isaac also "renounced forever all allegiance to any foreign prince, potentate, state or sovereign whatever, and particularly to the Queen of the United Kingdom of Great Britain of whom I am a subject." Goodbye, Queen Victoria. Farewell, Britain!

While keen to embrace his future, he was not enthusiastic about reclaiming his past. Isaac hesitated to contact Eliza, whom he had not seen for years. He no longer felt close to her. Having renounced his queen, he felt like doing the same with his wife. It would be easy to let her think that, like so many others, he'd been killed in the war or gone missing in action and was officially presumed dead. That would make a clean, complete break from his brief association with her. Yet, after some time, propelled by a lingering sense of duty, Isaac took up his pen and wrote to let Eliza know where he'd landed. Yielding to her desperate pleas, he then sent her money for passage.

Isaac had relocated from one country to another under false identity and was intent to keep his tracks covered. He must have suggested Eliza likewise sail under an assumed name.

No passenger list on any ships to New York or any other American port of entry in the entire period between 1820 and 1870 record any Jelfs, with the sole exception of somebody named Henry Jelfs who arrived at New York's Battery Park facility in 1837, when Isaac was a three-year-old. In keeping with his clandestine plan, Eliza did not travel under her maiden name, Acocks, either. Passenger lists disclose only one family with this surname arriving in the United States from England, and those Acocks came some years later and settled in Wyoming.

Thus hidden from British tracing, Isaac, twenty-seven, and Eliza, thirty, took up life in the New World, together at last, really a married couple for the first time but in truth strangers to one another after their long seven-year separation. She had changed little, except to look older. Isaac, however, had been touched in his deepest being by the soldiering in Crimea, his desperate flight from Britain's jurisdiction, and his fulsome embrace of the American way. They had even less in common than before.

Eliza moved into her husband's Brooklyn home, now relocated to 15th Street near Fifth Avenue, with no thought they would ever again be parted. Their residence was in the Gowanus district of South Brooklyn, a neighbourhood of wooden frame houses inland from Governor's Island, not too far from the docks, its crowded streets sloping to the East River where a ferryboat crossed to Manhattan Island.

Isaac's trip on the jammed Brooklyn-New York steam ferry was a daily drill to get to the offices of Brown, Hall & Vanderpoel. He tried to insert himself into the waiting crowd early enough, because the adage "always room for one more" had become the governing principle for boarding this vessel, now far too small and infrequent for all needing to use her. Even as the ferry cast off, some late-running commuters hurled themselves from the dock into the cushion of crowded passengers, hoping for the best.

Like other New Yorkers worn down or injured using the city's inadequate transportation facilities, Isaac was fascinated by plans, frequently proposed, for construction of the much-needed Brooklyn Bridge to Manhattan, a bold engineering dream and in time, over the thirteen years it would take to complete, an even bolder financial scam. The massive bridge's construction would not begin however until after he'd left the city for the last time in 1869.

—

With his life now tugged in many contradictory directions, Isaac was a man in need of something familiar to cling to. Although an attendee of Anglican Sunday service in England, Isaac's detachment from Britain as a soldier, his renunciation of the queen as sovereign, and his pending status as an American citizen, all contributed to an emotional shift away from the Church of England. In the United States, he discovered, the Anglican Church was called the "Episcopalian Church," a change that allowed Americans to keep the denomination's essence while eradicating its English identity. However, he was not interested in such a superficial change. He was attracted to Methodism, finding its doctrines and practices a refreshing form of Christianity, more down-to-earth and Protestant than the Anglican Church, which was just Catholicism without the pope.

As a man in transition between these two denominations, Isaac was amazed to discover a church which embraced them both: *Methodist Episcopalian.* Just as great a miracle was that the Methodist Episcopalians had formed a congregation close to his Gowanus home. Isaac Jelfs stepped through the doors of Brooklyn's 18th Street Methodist Episcopalian Church, and joined up. Soon he advanced from sitting in the pews to singing in the choir. Ever the willing penman, he next was named recording secretary for church meetings.

Before long Eliza was pregnant. In May 1861 she gave birth to their son, Thomas, "Eliza Jelfs" being duly recorded as the infant's mother in the city's registry of births. Shortly after that, on June 1, 1861, and also under her name, Eliza Jelfs, she too filed a notice of intent to become an American citizen. They'd arrived under cover in the New World, but now the Jelfs were both on the public record and, it seemed, in America to stay.

———

Isaac and Eliza's reunion in the United States came just as the country itself was dividing.

The Civil War, which pitted northern against southern states, began that same spring, to continue with a bleak and mounting death toll until May 1865, when the Union Army defeated the secessionist southern states. In those four years, Americans would kill more of their fellow countrymen than would die in all the other wars Americans fought against foreigners, from the Revolutionary War in the 1700s through the world wars of the twentieth century, to Afghanistan in the twenty-first, combined.

Living in New York "during the whole of the conflict," as he wrote about it, Isaac resolved, having escaped the lists of Crimean War dead, not to again face death bearing arms for some cause not his own.

For Isaac, as for most people in the United States in the 1850s, when he'd arrived, the prospect seemed so remote as to be impossible that war could erupt inside the country, essentially over the issue of whether slavery, protected by the Constitution in states already having it, would be extended into new territories being added to the U.S.A. in the west.

After a series of compromises on the issue, an impasse led to most but not all "slave states" seceding from the United States and forming a separate Confederacy. The full-scale war, which escalated through a series of skirmishes and episodes that became emotionally and politically magnified in the tense situation, began in order "to preserve the Union," in other words, to defeat the Confederacy's army and bring the southern states back into a "reconstructed" United States, the "Union."

The election of Abraham Lincoln, candidate of the new Republican Party, as president, fascinated Isaac. Unable to vote because he was not yet a citizen, he nevertheless got caught up in the drama of the campaign and the early years of the Lincoln presidency. At the law firm, Oakey Hall, who'd allied himself with William Seward, the New York governor and senator who seemed a sure bet to become the next American president until he lost the nomination to dark-horse Lincoln, was writing articles in *The Continental Monthly*, which Isaac read, about Seward's diplomatic skills as U.S. Secretary of State.

The city newspapers, from the authoritative *New York Times* to Horace Greeley's outspoken *New York Tribune*, reported extensively on political developments, and Isaac, buying papers from newsboys hawking copies along Broadway Avenue, followed the unprecedented twists and turns with the intense focus of a new immigrant concerned about his chosen country and what its future would hold for him. His misgivings grew as each incident triggered in turn an even more astonishing development, until the country slipped into open warfare, focused on the Union and Confederate armies and navies but sweeping up everyone.

By July 1863 the protracted war — staggering the world by its excessive killing and maiming of soldiers whenever the armies engaged one another — led to battle at Gettysburg, in which over three days fighting 23,000 Union Army soldiers became casualties. The loss of men to casualties was made worse by the fact that the Union Army was already missing more than 100,000 soldiers, illegally absent. On top of that, the three-year term of enlistment for soldiers who'd joined up in 1861 was about to end. To replenish the ranks, conscription was introduced to force men into the Union Army.

Isaac felt sick. The terror, slaughter, and stench, the agony of the wounded and groaning of the dying, all flooded back from his Crimean nightmare. He knew a day of reckoning was at hand.

He stayed low. He avoided enlisting with the Union Army, despite repeated pressure from senior partner Aaron Vanderpoel's nephew, lawyer Benjamin W. Vanderpoel, who himself left the firm to take up the cause of battle with the 59th New York Volunteer Regiment.

In the midst of this push to enlist more Union soldiers, an event occurred that changed the Civil War and the history of the United States. President Lincoln issued his Emancipation Proclamation to end slavery. Overnight, the war changed from a fight to preserve the Union into a moral crusade to eradicate slavery, which is how some in the North had seen it from the outset, although many more assuredly had not. Many northerners despaired over the armed conflict being "turned into a nigger war," while a number of soldiers, proud to fight for the Union, no longer wanted to die fighting for black men. New York's huge and powerful population of Irish and German immigrants not only held racist attitudes toward blacks, but feared losing their desperately needed jobs once freed slaves headed north to work for a pittance.

In this tinderbox, as soon as conscription began, riots erupted. Angry New York workers laid siege to their own city, burning draft offices, ripping up railroad tracks, cutting down telegraph lines, and closing factories by intimidating other workers to join the insurrection.

Isaac "saw a great deal of what occurred during the draft riots, when the city was for nearly a week in the hands of the mob." The mob killed blacks on sight, drowning them in the rivers or beating them to death, and then hanging their bodies in trees. An orphanage for black children was burned to the ground, and windows were smashed out of buildings connected with Republicans or the federal government. Stores were looted, policemen killed, soldiers hunted down; more than a hundred people were killed, and some thousand wounded.

Along Second Avenue, Isaac witnessed the mob get badly whipped and some thirty rioters taken prisoner, once the tide turned after two Union Army regiments entered the city. Their muskets and howitzers outmatched the rebels' revolvers, clubs, and stones. Mounted soldiers and police now stood guard everywhere. Businesses placed private watchmen at their premises to keep guard, using special "dark lanterns" whose sliding panel could be closed to conceal the light and thus allow the sentinel to remain undetected in the dark until he needed to see a shadowy figure and demand, "Who goes there?"

Isaac became mesmerized by the raw power in the streets, appalled by the destruction and killing, and torn between his instincts for peaceful order and sympathy with those resisting the draft. He shuddered remembering his time in the Dragoons and how the deadly battlefields felt and smelled, but he soberly recognized that life in America was a two-way street: a man wanting to be a member of the New York bar could equally be a member of a New York regiment.

The urgency felt by men rising up against being conscripted into a war of unprecedented slaughters was countered by the government's determination to suppress the anarchy. Continuation of draft riots would send a strong message from the North's largest city across the Union, into the Confederacy, and overseas to vicariously interested foreign powers. Putting down the rioters would determine, for many reasons, whether the North could even win the war.

With order restored after a week of devastation and terror, the draft resumed. When deciding to apply for citizenship back in the summer of 1858, so he might one day practice law, Isaac never imagined he'd face military conscription. His petition, though still pending, placed him in a status subject to the draft.

Members of New York's law firms were not exempt. Isaac, in common with all men subject to conscription, received his draft number. Office boys, and lawyers on the brink of exceeding the draft age of forty-five years, were called up for military service. But conscription law contained a controversial provision enabling someone to pay a bounty for another man to fight in his place, causing critics to say made it a rich man's war whose battles would be fought by poor men. To use this escape hatch, Isaac began looking for anybody willing to be a soldier. Understandably, he was not alone. Across the North the raw new business of procuring "substitute" soldiers exploded; a marketplace that exchanged blood for money. Isaac was not rich, but resolved that whatever dollars he had or needed he would pay to a substitute, as authorized by the draft law.

Hundreds of others were about, too, hunting for men who would take money to assume their place as draftees. Only those not subject to the draft themselves were eligible as substitutes. That meant they either had to be aliens who had not yet applied for citizenship, or former soldiers who had already served their term of enlistment and were prepared for a further tour of duty.

Part of this soldier market was operated by the County Volunteer Committee, where men wanting out of the draft would deposit $270 for one-year and $335 for three-year substitutes, get their name on a list, then endure an anxious wait hoping the Committee could land a substitute for them, in which case they paid whatever balance was owing for the bounty. The "official" bounty price was no longer being paid, but amounts quite a bit higher, escalating because getting substitute soldiers was the hardest thing. Demand for them far exceeded supply.

Many prospective substitutes were intercepted long before they ever got to the County Volunteer Committee. Brokers and runners scoured the harbours and train stations, the taverns, and the known quarters where unemployed men hung out, picking up every person seeming to qualify. Substitutes in downtown Manhattan cost $800 and up, while along Broadway around 35th and 36th streets a man might still be bought for $650 or $700.

Castle Garden at the very foot of Manhattan, where immigrant ships landed, was in the hands of the city police, who themselves had entered the substitutes market as brokers, keeping everybody else out of Castle Gardens and grabbing for themselves men as they came off the boats. The New York Police also posted guards at the entrance of the Emigrant Building, where many brokers had been coming to procure men. They were now turned away so the police alone could drain this source, too.

On their own, few immigrants, not even one in a hundred, enlisted. Even men who were prepared to fight soon caught on to the game and held out for more money. Detectives were well placed to ferret out men, but then even they, too, began demanding more money for their part as middlemen in the grim business. Some, offered seven hundred dollars in hand so they could collect the three hundred dollar bounty for a substitute and pocket the difference, now were refusing even that, trying to bid the amount still higher. Isaac was growing desperate.

At the General Recruiting Depot at 39 Cherry Street, anyone being brought in for processing was escorted by the sharks, and the levels of complicity and duplicity were in evidence by the winks, whispers, jostling, and sly manoeuvres between the recruiting committee and brokers. Hovering around Cherry and Roosevelt streets was a shifting clutch of brokers, runners, and loafers. Down at Manhattan's southern tip in the Battery, predators were everywhere looking for greenhorns who'd come to New York hoping for work, pouncing to offer them three hundred dollars and a "job with prospects for advancement" which, once the duped boys had been signed up, they discovered was a "job" soldiering in the Union Army.

The Democratic schemers over at Tammany Hall, looking to diversify their services to the nation, had stopped receiving individual subscribers for substitutes. Instead, "the Ring," as Tammany's inner circle was known, had masterminded arrangements with the government to enlist men further south, a much larger scale operation, and were beginning to see success by getting plenty of substitutes and lots of money. It was a dirty business, but to Isaac, not as sordid as exploding into pieces when hit by battlefield artillery.

In such a cauldron of wartime speculation and corrupt dealings, it was little wonder that high-placed sons and wealthy families were able to orchestrate, for some undisclosed amount or benefit, an escape. Over at the law offices of Blatchford, Seward & Griswold, it showed that influence mattered. The firm's "Seward" had been New York's governor and was now none other than President Lincoln's secretary of war, and "Blatchford" one of New York's most prominent men, and Seward's partner when the two practised law in Auburn, N.Y., who'd organized the Union Defense Committee and staged a mass public meeting on the night of April 20, 1861 in Union Square for "all those desirous of preserving the Union," which a curious Isaac Jelfs and thousands more had attended. It was said to far surpass in size and enthusiasm any public gathering before in the country. In mid-September 1863, two partners at Blatchford, Seward & Griswold were suddenly removed from the draft, although the law firm's files, replete with other information about the war, recruitment, and substitute soldiers, are silent about the reasons for this special dispensation.

Isaac did not have such contacts as those, but he remained steadfastly resolved not to fight, and because Congress had passed a law permitting substitutes, pressed on. Eventually his unrelenting searches through the shadowy substitute market got the result he'd begun to despair of ever achieving, when he found an aggressive broker who took his money and did the paperwork at 39 Cherry Street.

Successful in keeping his blood from the flow saturating America's battlefields, Isaac focused on smaller personal fronts: advancing his legal career; expanding his family; and securing his American citizenship.

The war saw a falling off of much legal work for New York law offices, especially firms handling overseas matters from English and French interests who held back investing or doing business in a country in the midst of war. Wartime shortages and inflation meant that dollars, already hard to come by, had to be stretched further. Isaac managed to stay on at Brown, Hall & Vanderpoel but knew clerks in other law offices being let go after years of reliable service, and others whose desperate appeals for even the smallest pay increase had been refused.

Although less was happening in real estate than before war broke out, with depressed wartime property values, Isaac's patent work increased, spurred by new inventions and expanded manufacturing for everything from surgical devices in battlefield hospitals to naval equipment that enhanced deadliness in sea-battles with the Confederacy. The surge in war-related manufacturing brought opportunities for ingenious patentees, which resulted in new patent applications. Manufacturers yielded to the temptation to copy devices, which generated infringement actions. All this kept Isaac and other patent lawyers busy. Meanwhile, he was advancing his qualifications to become a full-fledged lawyer.

In October 1863, Eliza gave birth to their second child, whom they named Caroline. And a year later, on October 11, 1864, when his petition for citizenship was granted by an order of the New York County court of common pleas, Isaac Jelfs became an American, just in time to vote for the re-election of Abraham Lincoln as president several weeks later, on November 8.

He was confident of his future in the United States, if his past did not catch up with him, and if the long carnage of the increasingly fierce civil war, for which the Union Army would have over two million soldiers under arms, could end.

6

———

America's Promise

In his conveyancing work at Brown, Hall & Vanderpoel, Isaac had discovered the money-making potential of flipping properties. Taking the
sharp practice to be part of America's get-ahead society in which he was
now a participating citizen, he joined in.

Brown, Hall & Vanderpoel's close Tammany Hall connections kept
its lawyers busier than was the case for most New York firms languishing through the Civil War, which allowed Isaac to keep his job when
other clerks and young lawyers were losing theirs and ending up as soldiers in the Union Army. But more money was always needed, so he
was buying and selling houses whenever profit could be made in the
less than buoyant wartime real estate market. Isaac had already moved
from 27 President Street in March 1859 to 15th Street (near Fifth and
Sixth avenues) by the time Eliza moved in with him. In the spring of
1864, they went up to 18th Street (near Seventh Avenue), then a year
later moved down to 107 12th Street (near Third and Fourth avenues).
Their next move was to 166 9th Street, and three years after that, 259
18th Street.

Their homes in Gowanus district were all two-, three-, or four-
storey frame and brick rectangular boxes, with plain framed windows
and simple straight steps. These places the Jelfs lived, between moves,
were functional rather than elegant, row houses tightly abutting streets
running up from Gowanus Bay and the East River. Isaac's ambition to be
a player in the real estate game, however, was not the only thing driving

moves from one residence to another. Sometimes a change of venue was to escape unhappy associations.

New Year's Day 1865 got off to a sombre start for Eliza and Isaac when Caroline, their fifteen-month-old daughter, died from pneumonia. Isaac bought a plot for her remains in nearby Green-Wood Cemetery, a non-denominational burial ground with already a quarter-million bodies interred, and well on its way to becoming one of the biggest cemeteries in the United States. Now it had one more, very small, grave.

Soon after, more to escape the sadness hanging over their 18th Street house than to move up another notch, Isaac bought a house over on 12th Street, hoping to give Eliza a renewed start. Life's rawness, sadly, was not to be avoided by changing places. That same summer, on July 26, their infant son, William, just six months old, died from cholera in the new house.

The numb parents gazed once again as wind blew inland off the water, at a small coffin, for one more of their children. It was lowered by hand-held ropes into a fresh grave, near the bottom of a long sloping hill in Green-Wood Cemetery, where baby Willie's remains took their place beside his sister Caroline's grave.

These sad loses of life could not, in Isaac's mind, be separated from the relentless death march passing through his new country. Battles between the Union and Confederate armies resulted in deaths so staggering in number they were beyond comprehension. The ranks of incapacitated soldiers were just as legion, and the call had gone out for enlistment of another three hundred thousand men for the Union Army. Repeated shocks pummelled his sensibilities until it was hard not to be inured from feeling anything anymore. But no matter how bad things are, they can always get worse. On Friday, April 14, 1865, President Abraham Lincoln was assassinated in Washington. Isaac sobbed in despair.

A week later, he stood in stony vigil in New York, one among the millions of sombre Americans lining the route of the slain president's funeral procession which started out from Washington on April 19 and would end once his coffin had been transported one thousand, seven hundred miles, all the way home to Springfield, Illinois.

In the days ahead, when John Wilkes Booth, who had shot Abraham Lincoln, came to trial, Isaac followed the events closely. Lawyer and soldier Benjamin Vanderpoel, who had pressured him to enlist, and who knew Booth, was a witness in the trial of co-conspirators in the president's assassination.

—

The large drama of the war overshadowed the small enactments of individuals, but it did not obliterate them. While Isaac and Eliza adjusted to the death of their two small children, just a few blocks away Hannah Boyer was desperate for any job to earn money so she could survive. Seeking employment door to door, she finally found low-paying work in a New York millinery shop making and trimming hats.

With her intense resolve to reunite the Boyer family, Hannah got her sister Mary Ann, joined by their more reluctant brother Tom, to pool their earnings, move from the boarding house, and start housekeeping on Manhattan's 14th Street. From this base, she visited sister Lizzy in the orphanage, where she was forced to remain because of her young age. Hannah's devoted efforts to trace the three youngest girls, however, continued to draw only blank stares and unanswered letters.

Hannah's brother Harry had first been put to work as a cash boy in the large Arnold & Constable Dry Goods store on Bleeker Street but he "could not stand being closed up in a store," became weak, and then sick. So the New York bureau handling working-age orphans dispatched him next to the beneficial fresh air of a farming school at Westchester, New York.

The place, recorded Harry, "was kept up by the rich men of New York." It was really a working orphanage exploiting unpaid child labourers, "a large farm growing fruit for the New York market, shipping a garden truck into the city every day."

Harry did not attend classes at the Westchester "School for Boys," but instead became tutored in hard toil. He worked all day, every day, in the farm's extensive orchards, picking apples and pears, cutting grapes in the vineyards, and stooping for hours on end in the sweltering, prickly heat of a twenty acre strawberry field. The place was operated by Rev. Lewis Pease and his wife, Ann, whom Harry found "hard task masters." The boys "did all the work and only two men were employed" to supervise them and show new ones how to do the work. There were "from seventy-five boys to one hundred all the time."

"We got up at six and had our breakfast comprising of mush made from corn, a slice of bread, and coffee made from beans. At noon, some vegetables, a small piece of meat, skimmed milk, and water. For supper, bread, milk, sometimes butter. There were a lot of cows and we had to milk them night and morning. There was a large hennery. The eggs were shipped every day but we never got them unless we stole them. It was the same with all kinds of fruit."

Harry Boyer worked hard at this internment institution for a year. The boys not only did all the work in the fields picking fruit, collecting eggs from the hen house, milking cows and churning butter, but all the indoor chores too that were required to keep a facility for a hundred boys. "We had to do the house work, wash dishes, peel potatoes, make the beds, and wash the clothes." Harry was all alone. "I did not see any of my people for more than a year." He looked ahead, with no prospect for anything different.

One day Hannah arrived out of the blue, rescued Harry, and took her prized brother back to New York in triumph. She was determined against all odds, in an unspoken bond with her dead mother and lost father, to keep the Boyer family together. The place she took Harry was the house on 14th Street where she, Tom, and Mary Ann had started housekeeping in rented rooms. Now four of them had been reunited. Lizzy remained in the orphanage. The others were still out there, somewhere.

As she walked the streets of New York, Hannah would scan the faces of the young women in the crowds hoping to spot her missing sisters. It could be possible, couldn't it? On occasion, that crazy hope was mixed with dread, because the reality facing many girls was bleak. All around New York, flirting for business in any number of streets and side alleys, young women gave sexual action to men who offered a pittance, pitied them not, and were as likely to pound them as pay them after a tumble in a nearby shed or stairwell. Most neighbourhoods had become weary and quiescent about such scenes. Only the shrill blasts from a police whistle and the sound of running boots drawing closer broke up these hurried transactions.

Deeply worrisome for Hannah, always on alert for her sisters, would have been her discovery that several well-placed madams operated posh homes to which they enticed clean young girls. Acting as a mother protector, these women trained the girls in social graces and stylish dressing, but only to then offer them up for high fees to society men and senior officials of New York for "the virgin cure." Not knowing the whereabouts of her sisters, Hannah feared the worst.

Hannah herself was still working in millinery, using her talents to fashion the large-brimmed hats that women of means wore atop their high piles of hair. She kept her eye on what visitors to the shop liked most and what she saw attractive women wearing in public. She became adept in crafting high-priced superstructures with feather plumes, stuffed birds, dried flowers, painted wooden fruit, silk ribbons, and lace.

These monumental hats took an enormous amount of Hannah's time to make, an elaborate and painstaking effort but still not as extreme as other laborious works of the era, such as fashioning parlour art from carefully saved strands of a loved-one's hair, sewing passages of scripture in needle-point, or patiently assembling miniature wooden ships or notable public buildings to scale inside clear glass bottles.

Hannah was proud of what she made, and had fun modelling the grand hats in front of the mirror. Although part of her thought them silly, an indulgence for women with money, she herself wore one to church, and to public social gatherings she was beginning to attend. Not only were such showpiece hats the fashion of the day, but Hannah believed that wearing one placed her in a social set better than the one she in truth occupied. A woman could always dress up and hope.

She never needed to put on airs, or fancy hats, for her brother Harry. The two chums were so close as to have no secrets, and able to see each other beyond any surface blemishes or fancy head-gear. Having rescued

Harry and reunited him with her, Hannah was joyful in his resilient, good company.

Harry was clean, strong, and spoke good English. He soon got work as a cash boy in another New York dry goods store. From his perspective, Steward's was no better than Arnold & Constable's, but compared to the Westchester farm school it had many advantages: he could go home in the evening, was with his family, and no longer needed to fend off hunger by stealing food.

Harry "had to be at Steward's at 8 o'clock and if late would not be let into the store till noon. "If late twice," he wrote, "we were fined twenty-five cents, and we only got three dollars per week. Out of that small wage we could not afford being late much."

As a cash boy, his work was to take the cashbook and goods to the cashier and get the correct change. The price of the goods was marked in the cash book. Then he got the goods wrapped with paper and string and returned them, with correct change and a receipt, to the clerk who was still waiting with the customer. The cashier was on the second floor of Steward's, so Harry had to run up there, complete the procedures quickly, although he could be quite delayed by a line-up for the cashier, "then go back to the first floor, and on a busy day you sure got tired by the time six o'clock came." The place was often hectic. Harry was one of ten cash boys running, or standing at the ready, all the time.

Harry and his fellow workers were forbidden to sit down at any time during the ten-hour day. "Old Man Steward" ranged over his dry goods store like a hawk. "The floor workers were very strict as regards sitting down in working hours. If Old Man Steward saw you he would give you the sack."

The months passed. Mary Ann found work and separate lodgings for herself, and restless Tom struck out to be on his own. Hannah and Harry moved together into smaller and cheaper quarters, a house on 21st Street between Broadway and First avenues, where they boarded with the widowed owner of the place, a Mrs. Paine.

One night going home from Steward's, Harry was about to cross Washington Square when caught in a sudden thunderstorm. "The lightning seemed to run along the sidewalk and blinded me. I had my head down as

I ran and banged hard into an iron lamp post, knocking me down. I had a swollen pair of black eyes when I later got home. I was covered with blood."

Cleaned up and back at Steward's the next day, the "bad knock" to his head still made Harry dizzy. About to faint, he sat on the stairs. Old Man Steward spotted this breach of his rules and fired Harry on the spot.

After some days healing and looking around for a new job, Harry got work as an errand runner for a New York office, Mums & Company, which handled patent work. He liked this better because he was out and about, more independent, meeting interesting folk, and seeing sections of the New York City he'd never before dared visit.

As messenger boy for Mr. Mums, Harry "had to go all over the city and had strange places to go." He saw "all kinds of people, wood carvers who made the models for patents of all kinds of new inventions. Mums's firm got the patents passed by the Government for the inventors. The patent was published in the paper called *Scientific American*. The carvers were of German and English descent. They made large wages but most of them drank a lot and lived in the east side of the city, about the worst part. Low houses, dirty streets, and the stink from garbage and other things would knock you down. The children were undressed, and the mothers as well as the fathers drank whenever they had money to get liquor."

After scurrying around the rough Lower Eastside, venturing into dark tenements to fetch wooden models of patented devices hand-carved by alcoholic old sailors, Harry then scooted over to the United States Patent Office, where patent lawyers from New York's law firms also came and went, doing their part of the same business.

—

Constantly beset by worry about the younger children whom she considered her dependents, Hannah now also faced immediate concerns of her own. They arose from two of despair's most reliable agents: love and money.

In the spring of 1866, now a vivacious twenty-five-year-old, Hannah met and fell in love with a well-placed New Yorker named Will Smith. His first comment to her had been about the remarkable hat she was wearing. Their romantic attachment through the spring and into early summer thrived on Will's charms and Hannah's willingness to give herself to him. Then Hannah discovered her paramour was a married man, intent on remaining that way. In shock, she languished in wretched heartbreak and turmoil.

On August 24 her brother Tom wrote, with the uncomprehending glibness of those who observe someone else's love-wrecked life: "You are very silly about Smith. It is said in the Bible 'Love them that persecute you' but it does not say 'Make thyself miserable.'" Tom hoped his sister would "forget all about him, as far as possible." He asserted, with the smooth assurance of those who appoint themselves spokesmen for the Almighty, "God will reward you someday for what you have done for the little ones and for all of us." At least he was acknowledging, if tritely, Hannah's valiant efforts.

As for the money part, Hannah was flat broke. America's promise so far seemed just a taunt. Tom's pledge of eventual help from God provided no salvation from her immediate predicament. Any money Hannah did get she spent to support her sisters and brothers.

Custodian of her shattered and scattering family, she found her repeated letters to wealthy Uncle Henry in England, who'd grandly pledged that his namesake nephew "would never want for anything," went unanswered.

Hannah knew she would have to use her wits to survive.

7

New York Double Life

The "New World," by its very name, was an invitation to depart from the original trajectory of one's life.

Following Isaac's lead, Eliza Jelfs renounced her status as a British subject and became an American, too. Her application, supported by the affidavit of Henry Bookstaver, attested that she was "of good character." The prominent attorney at Isaac's law firm also swore, on August 2, 1866, that he had "known her five years."

Though Eliza and Isaac became citizens of their new country, they were having a harder time establishing their American family. It was not enough that their infant children Caroline and William lay buried in Brooklyn's expanding graveyard. On November 6, 1866, they again transported a tiny coffin to Green-Wood Cemetery, this time for five-year-old Thomas, dead from diphtheria.

For this forlorn, late fall scene, chiller winds blew off Gowanus Bay, crossing the hillocks and up the long cemetery slope where Isaac and Eliza shivered. They stood, not among the private plots of affluent Americans where marble sculptures and polished granite mausoleums marked final resting places, but in the cemetery's adjacent area for the general public who paid more modest fees for smaller burial plots. Here the cheaper white sandstone markers, engraved with their children's names, would gradually dissolve, like the remains of their three children whose places they marked.

Disease was a commonplace killer, for the Jelfs children and so many others, in crowded and unsanitary Brooklyn and New York. One person out of thirty-six was dying from poisonous living conditions in the mid-1860s, as New York's commercial avenues, paved with cobblestones, offered deep cracks where garbage collected and rotted. The city's many dirt streets, meanwhile, were filthy accumulations as decaying corpses of horses, dogs, cats, and rats merged into heaps of horse manure and garbage. Garbage boxes, seldom emptied, overflowed with offal, badly fouled old clothing, and vegetable waste. Stagnant water pooled in the carcasses of the dead animals and around clogged sewer drains.

In 1864 Isaac and other city dwellers read the sensational front page news of outraged William Thomas, sanitary inspector for the district, decrying the filthy streets that "generate pestiferous diseases." Thomas blamed the filled gutters and obstructed sewer culverts, noting "drainage is generally imperfect, the courtyards being below the level of the streets." Since then, no action had been taken. The city was being run by men whose focus was not on spending money to improve public health, but achieving greater efficiency diverting public funds into their own bank accounts.

Although poorly designed sewers had been installed throughout the city, most people in fact still used outdoor privies in the courtyards of their tenement buildings, close to the wells used for drinking water. These inadequate toilet facilities became a sinister hazard for communicable disease. Isaac and his fellow citizens hardly needed more reports telling them what they already knew, but the Citizen's Association Committee reported in 1865 that public toilets were "covered and surrounded with filth so as not to be approachable." Others were "merely trenches sunk one or two feet in the ground, the fluids of which in some instances were allowed to run into the courts, with stones and boards provided to keep peoples' feet out of the filth." Half the houses had no sewers connected to them at all.

There was little mystery about what was causing endemic conditions like tuberculosis and diarrhea, or the cholera scourges and outbreaks of diphtheria, which had now caused the death of three of their children.

The Jelfs household lapsed into bleak quietude. The absence of Caroline, William, and Thomas made it a forlorn place. Isaac and Eliza found themselves having less to say to each another, and seldom anything cheerful. An inarticulate hollowness crept into the core of their life together.

Hannah and Harry Boyer, scrimping to save money and hoping to find Brooklyn's streets less foul than those of Manhattan, moved across the East River, where rents were cheaper. This advantage, combined with Hannah promptly getting work at a Brooklyn millinery shop, improved their financial state. The new locale also helped Hannah deal with her broken heart, too. Sometimes a change of venue really can be a solution.

Though still preoccupied trying to keep her deceased parent's flock together, in a different setting and with better employment, she began to hit a happier stride. Hannah was by nature bright, resourceful, and quick to understand, and her resiliency made her adept at overcoming setbacks.

This talent was tested when a large water reservoir on a hill behind the house she and Harry occupied in Gowanus burst during a violent thunderstorm and flooded their basement "with water three feet deep," as Harry described it. Hannah and he "had to wade in up to our middle to get things out." The trunk from England, with its treasured Boyer family papers and Bibles, was among the flotsam the pair rescued and spent the coming days carefully drying out and cleaning.

Still, despite an inconvenience like that, or the lingering emotional wound from that dog, Will Smith, Hannah's life was improving. She was able to get out and tentatively sample Brooklyn social life by attending gatherings of the local Britannia Benevolent Association, another benefit of living in this new district. She was, despite living in the United States, still British. It had been her father's ill-fated plan, not her own desire to disengage from England, which had brought her here. By attending the Association's meetings and socials, Hannah could mingle with others of similar background, common understanding, and shared colloquial expressions. She could hear "news from over 'ome," sing along to familiar English songs, and happily enjoy a dance or two, a trait she'd inherited from her dance-ready parents.

Her brother Harry, too, was getting a better footing. Looking for work closer to home, he found it at Braun Bros. marble shop in Brooklyn. One of the owners, Frank Braun, took an interest in the energetic youth and taught him how to cut stone tabletops and polish marble. Harry liked this work, even though he cut his hands and rubbing the stones with sand grit wore skin off his fingers until they bled. His weekly wage was $1.50, just half what he'd earned as a cash boy at the dry goods store, but at least he was becoming a craftsman learning his own trade. He began to see a real future for himself.

———

One Saturday evening Hannah, looking radiant and wearing a new dress, her natural vivaciousness enhanced by paying close attention to fashion in the millinery shops that employed her, donned a bonnet with lots of ribbons and went to a Britannia Benevolent Association dance.

The musicians were playing popular music from England. A tall, slim man, handsome with high cheekbones, approached her, even though he seemed by nature shy. Employing flowery words of social grace, he introduced himself and asked Hannah if she would favour him with a turn about the floor. He'd noticed that she was new to the club and wanted to be sure she felt welcome. Pleased to find him a good dancer, she was even happier as they conversed, while embraced in step with the music, to learn he was a lawyer, an intelligent if somewhat diffident man, curious about life around him.

Her dance partner was just as delighted to discover that this appealing woman, a dozen years younger than himself, had not only the same first name as his mother, Hannah, but even shared her occupation as a bonnet maker. Their needy eyes glowed with a rare happiness.

Hannah Boyer and Isaac Jelfs shared more dances and animated conversation until the evening's social came to a close. Finally they parted, reluctant to separate.

———

Plucky Eliza Jelfs, still in their house on Brooklyn's 12th Street, gave birth on March 18, 1867, to daughter Annie Elizabeth, whose birth certificate recorded not only the girl's birth but also served to record her father's own progress: Isaac Jelfs, *lawyer*.

The annual legal directories trace his steady advance from copyist in 1860 to clerk in 1861 to notary public in 1865 to lawyer in 1866 when, to his immense pride and vindication, Isaac became a member of the New York State bar.

Still, he was a small-light attorney in a firmament of bright stars. Most published references to the firm kept Isaac and other minor lawyers at an inconspicuous level, though he was gradually rising; within a couple years, he began to earn more recognition, identified in New York newspapers as an attorney with Brown, Hall & Vanderpoel through the latter part of 1868 in connection with several civil suits. Like other lawyers at the firm, he was also active in outside organizations, such as his church and the Britannia Benevolent Association, partly out of personal interest and partly to attract new clients. That August, in addition to newspaper reports on cases from his law practice, Isaac was also being reported as one of the organizers of the annual picnic of Brooklyn's Britannia Benevolent Association.

Absent from the newspapers was any report that Isaac Jelfs, whose career in law and life in the community were on the ascendant by 1868, was leading a double life. By this date the romance he and Hannah Boyer shared had flared into intense love, and they already had a daughter.

—

The firm of Brown, Hall & Vanderpoel was now attracting greater attention from New York's newspapers because its colourful senior partner, Oakey Hall, was making large waves as district attorney prosecuting prominent people, connecting with a growing audience as a popular journalist and effective public speaker, and advancing his political career after switching in 1862 from the Republicans to the Tammany Democrats. If Isaac had not achieved his ambition to become a lawyer, and in particular a lawyer with Brown, Hall & Vanderpoel, he might never have left the United States for a new life in another country. But the very firm in which he achieved his dream of becoming a lawyer was beginning to give him nightmares.

Formed in the mid-1850s, Brown, Hall & Vanderpoel had quickly established a wide-ranging practice across criminal, civil, municipal, and bankruptcy matters. Its most luminous lawyers included principals

Augustus L. Brown, James R. Cumming, Abraham Oakey Hall, Aaron J. Vanderpoel, and Henry W. Bookstaver.

Brown, the first of the name partners, was a Harvard graduate who later became a distinguished judge. While at the firm he attracted less publicity than Vanderpoel or Hall and preferred it that way. When he did see himself reported in the *New York Times* in 1869, it was for having fallen short. The Gold Exchange Bank had been unable to meet its obligations and, amidst considerable controversy, Gus Brown was being replaced as receiver. On October 12, the *Times* reported that his replacement, a Mr. Jordan, "at once set to work to endeavour to extricate the bank from the difficulties which surround it, but the complications are so great that it will be a work of some time." The implication was that while the bank had its problems, so did Brown.

Aaron Vanderpoel, third of the name partners and for years an unwavering friend of Oakey Hall, was often reported in newspaper and court records for his high profile cases, especially many notorious murder trials.

But the true meteorite in this constellation was the man at its centre, in both firm name and fact, Abraham Oakey Hall. Rising from humble origins in New York where he'd been born in 1826, Hall graduated from university studying law and politics, practised at the bar in New Orleans around 1846, then returned to become a member of the New York bar in 1848. By age twenty-four, he'd become New York's assistant district attorney.

Failing to win reappointment, irrepressible Oakey resumed private practice by joining his university classmate and friend Aaron Vanderpoel to form Brown, Hall & Vanderpoel in 1854, soon making the firm, according to *Off-Hand Sketches of Prominent New Yorkers*, "the busiest, most profitable, and the most popular in New York, with Oakey Hall the most popular man of it, always *en scene* and in many ways engaging public attention." By 1868 the busy firm also had become a centre of great influence when the ever-ambitious Oakey was elected mayor of New York City. Editorials throbbed about his future potential to become governor, or even president of the United States.

No matter what public office Hall held, he always remained part of the firm, a partnership that would continue until 1875, to the financial benefit of all concerned. Isaac was fascinated by Hall, a man whom he observed in person at the firm, through the press, and at a number of public events he attended. Isaac enjoyed political meetings, especially if Oakey Hall was speaking. He was drawn by Hall's attractive energy, panache, stylish clothes, and powerful speaking style, which included large doses of humour and clever puns.

Yet something about elegant Oakey also made Isaac cautious. Like a number of citizens who stood back a little from politics, he was concerned that Hall was closely aligned with New York State Senator William Tweed, widely known as "Boss Tweed" for his commanding role at Tammany Hall, the power-wielding Democratic club which specialized in winning elections for its friends and then bilking the public with kick-backs from lucrative, highly inflated government contracts. The Tammany organization had become the epicentre of political patronage and electoral schemes plotted on whatever was feasible, rather than what was ethical or legal. New meanings for the term "spoils of office" were created at Tammany Hall, heated by coal in the cold winter and hot greed all year round. Delivering votes was Tammany Hall's form of currency, its use aggressively and shamelessly paving the way directly into the public treasury and access to real legal tender.

Flamboyant Oakey Hall, senior partner of the New York firm Brown, Hall & Vanderpoel where Isaac Jelfs rose from law clerk to attorney, was the New York district attorney, then mayor of New York, and a leading member of the powerful but corrupt Democrat Party political machine known as Tammany Hall. (Studio of Matthew Brady/ Library of Congress)

New York's electors voted Hall into office as the city's eighty-first mayor on December 1, 1868, by a landslide. Shortly after, the *New York Times* editorialized that, while it was the hope that Hall would be a reformer and the city "could be ridded of its corruption," that did not seem in the cards. He'd been made mayor "by the half-dozen men who constitute the Tammany Ring," explained the *Times*, and it was "perfectly understood between them and him" that he'd do nothing without first consulting his "friends," which "implied that The Ring administers the office of Mayor through Mr. Hall as their official representative and agent." In the spring of 1869, Tweed, using considerable political muscle and plenty of payoff money, got the state senators to enact a new charter for New York City. The revamped constitution established a board of audit, whose task was to review and approve expenditures. The board had only three members: Boss Tweed, Richard Connolly, who was New York County clerk and member of Tammany Hall's innermost circle, and Mayor Oakey Hall.

William Tweed, a large man in both personality and stature, with complete control over the city's 150-member Tammany Club, now loomed large in the institutionalized corruption of New York's government. Hall, in the mayor's office, named him commissioner of public works to further entrench him in structured graft. Along with other big-spending projects, Tweed resumed construction on the New York County courthouse, where building had been stopped during the Civil War, and where soon millions of dollars spent on the project exceeded many times its actual value. Now at the zenith of his power, Tweed shaped New York City business and tapped public coffers by skimming 15 to 35 percent from deliberately inflated contracts, a steady and substantial flow of cash for The Ring. Colluding contractors knew they would get no work unless they first saw public works commissioner Tweed and followed his instructions on the amount by which to pad their contract. When contractors submitted vouchers for work, they were approved by Tweed's loyal insiders, payments went through with nobody any wiser, and the overages were kicked back to The Ring.

Apart from his general reservations about corruption, which was being alleged in a growing number of newspaper stories he was reading,

Isaac was also becoming apprehensive about transactions he understood were being arranged at Brown, Hall & Vanderpoel when Oakey was around. His concern was fuelled by more than an insider's awareness of things the public and newspaper reporters did not know, however; it was instinctive alarm. He could never forget how in the Stratford law office he'd been made, as an expendable junior person, the scapegoat when the scheme of a powerful senior lawyer came unstuck. It was irrational to make such an improbable connection, of course. Yet, it was understandable that, already victim of a calumny that derailed his life before, Isaac anxiously wanted to protect himself.

To the outside world, in these early months of Hall's tenure at city hall, it still appeared that those who rode with Oakey and his friends would go far. Brown, Hall & Vanderpoel kept adding to its ever larger

Isaac Jelfs liked the excitement of New York's crowded streets, always full of people, wares, as well as the refuse of city life. Some order was introduced to the streets, however, during Isaac's time in the city. By the late 1860s, when he'd stroll north up Broadway Avenue from his law office, the garbage piles were less noticeable and the bustling midday crowds seemed almost orderly, as is evident from this photograph of his environs taken during the period. (Collection of the New-York Historical Society)

roster of attorneys and staff, needed to handle the additional work Oakey was putting through his firm. Although just a few years earlier it had moved up the street to larger premises at 271 Broadway, the firm again required more space, and so relocated to 291 Broadway. Isaac even got an office of his own in this move.

From his new vantage point, the well ensconced lawyer likely began to reason that, just maybe, he need not be so worried. Although some transactions at the firm caused Isaac surprise, part of him began to accept, as often happens for people in a large and dynamic organization, that he still had things to learn about the big leagues. After all, he earlier had learned to flip properties, once he saw how an entrepreneurial approach helped a person get ahead in the New World.

But as 1869 progressed, outcry about financial corruption mounted in the newspapers and from civic critics of The Ring, whose most public pivotal player was his firm's senior partner. Isaac's worries resurfaced.

———

At the same time, Isaac sensed with growing unease that his perilous private life could explode at any moment.

On December 9, 1867, nine months after his wife Eliza had given birth to their daughter Annie Elizabeth, Hannah Boyer delivered a girl, too. She and her "husband" Isaac named their daughter Annie Carolina Boyer, but did not register the birth.

It was one thing to keep Annie's birth secret: Hannah's sister Mary Ann had assisted with the delivery, and no doctor was on hand to certify the birth or register it in city records as required. It had been quite another thing to deal with Hannah being an unwed mother, facing her siblings.

In the early days, Isaac had been introduced to them as "James Isaac Guelph." By adding a new first name, "James," and fudging his surname as "Guelph," the couple sought to soften their predicament by keeping things unclear and his two lives separate. Once a baby was on its way and Hannah knew her sisters would see she was pregnant, they presented themselves to Hannah's siblings as a married couple, which caused consternation among her sisters, and resentment. The younger girls looked up to her as their leader, saw her like a mother, and loved her as a sister. Yet they had been excluded from the most important decision Hannah would ever make. Not only that, none of them had attended the wedding. This left the possibility that either Hannah had secretly eloped, for which they could see no reason, or that the marriage was a fiction. Either way, feelings among Hannah's sisters were raw. Things just didn't add up. Mary Ann seemed more understanding than Lizzy. Brother Harry, whose work as a runner for the patent office had taken him into the seediest parts of New York and whose many other experiences had long since made him worldly wise, didn't seem to mind. He was just happy his embattled sister, whom he cherished and lived with, had found happiness at last. Tom, too, seemed pleased; he was content to have an older male in the family again and liked the fact that Isaac was a lawyer and decided to become one, too. Least accepting of Hannah's situation was Lizzy, who as Harry prissily noted, "refused to call that Mr. Guelph by our name Boyer."

After the "marriage" Harry continued to live in the same Brooklyn home as Hannah and her new husband. Hannah had long been Harry's protector; now he in return had no difficulty putting the best face on her situation. "Hannah married James Isaac Guelph," he wrote in his diary, which would serve as a family record for several generations, but was a complicit gloss to obscure the fact that no wedding had taken place. His entry did not even try to square how James Isaac had taken his wife's name in an era when only the opposite was done.

Just how early Hannah came to learn Isaac's true identity as a married man is hard to determine. She'd met him through Brooklyn's British Benevolent Association where, as one of the organization's senior officers, he was unmistakably Isaac Jelfs. Despite her spontaneous romantic attachment to Isaac, Hannah must have felt some misgivings when she recalled her shattered love affair with Will Smith who'd also had a wife. Perhaps Hannah, desperate to overcome her plight and resolved to use her wits to survive, even saw a pattern in adult society and began to think this was the way the world really worked. The Victorian age was built on double standards, apparently even in America.

Their situation was indeed delicate. It involved Hannah's affair with a married man, his double life, and the fact that the couple had now started a second family. Isaac's success in becoming a lawyer added the most ironic complication. Whatever fictions they pretended for Hannah's siblings, Isaac's larger reality was that he was a lawyer with a prominent New York firm. Bigamy, which this arrangement resembled except for a second marriage certificate to readily prove it, was a criminal offence. If he were convicted, Isaac's days as a lawyer would be over. He knew Oakey Hall's firm was under close scrutiny from the public and prying news reporters, and while their focus was on municipal corruption, any transgressions showing that Hall's professional associates were a seedy lot could help taint the mayor from another angle. Isaac likely exaggerated his vulnerability, but his uncertainty led him to fear the worst.

With his double life and secret arrangements known in varying degrees to different people, it's hard to say who knew what, or who chose to believe what they suspected. In time their marital arrangement became accepted by most of Hannah's siblings, as they grew accustomed to it, although some frostiness remained, directed at Isaac far more than Hannah, on grounds of propriety, legality, and Christian beliefs.

It can never be known what suspicions Eliza had. What she did know was that her husband Isaac was increasingly away on legal work for the firm, sometimes even out of the country for days on end.

8

—

Canada Promises Another Life

Fate worked, as it routinely does, in unexpected ways.

If some of Isaac's absences were just excuses to free up time for his parallel life with the woman he loved, others were real sojourns out of town on legal business. Several times the firm sent Isaac to Montreal. One trip, early in September 1867, came just when Canada was in the throes of electing its first parliament, following creation of a new country of four colonial provinces.

Going up to Montreal gave Isaac the distance and time needed to review his circumstances with more clarity and dispassion than he could in New York. A part of him liked New York and the exciting life he'd been able to make there, becoming a lawyer and finding enriching love, for the first time in his life, with Hannah. But his first flush of enthusiasm for America's dynamic nature had faded, through the Civil War and the New York conscription riots and the killing of President Lincoln, and the more he saw of the country's daily reality. He now had serious reservations, reinforced by the hurt and anger over the conditions that claimed the life of his three children. Then there was his fear that corrupt acts linked to Oakey Hall threatened his career.

Living in the United States was making Isaac Jelfs nostalgic for British ways and values. His role with the Brooklyn Britannic Benevolent Association was an indication of that.

This seemed odd, given that he had seen filth in Birmingham, disease and the ugly underpinnings of war in the British army, and the sharp edge of corruption in his Stratford law office. Yet, fundamentally, it had not been dislike of England itself that forced Isaac to leave his country of birth. In America, despite taking a vow of allegiance when he became a U.S. citizen, Isaac continued to identify himself as an Englishman, clinging initially to a version of the Episcopalian church, and later finding an anchor in Brooklyn's Britannia Benevolent Association, where he could retain at least a portion of his identity as a son of England. His renunciation of Queen Victoria was, it seemed, becoming as forgotten as his marriage vow to Eliza Acocks.

Arriving in Montreal in such a frame of mind, it seems inevitable that the possibility of a different North American link with Britain would impress Isaac's consciousness. On his earlier trips, his personal circumstances and disposition had not made him so fully open to the reality of Canada. Now, especially with the blossoming of Confederation, the concept of a *British* North American nation stirred his ex-patriot's heart. He could embrace the best of *both* worlds.

Montreal appealed to Isaac not only as a bustling North American city, with an exotic, for him, French-speaking population and culture adding to its allure, but also because it offered comfortable familiarity of British ways and institutions. In New York he could stay connected through a British-oriented organization, but in Canada being "British" did not mean confining himself to an enclave with intermittent meetings. It was the daily norm, in a New World setting.

His legal business done, the intrigued New York lawyer stayed on in Montreal a few days longer to explore the city and test his new feelings.

The election for Canada's new Parliament was then in full tilt and quickly caught Isaac up in its excitement, especially Montreal's bitterly fought contest between D'Arcy McGee and Bernard Devlin. On the night of September 6, Isaac went to McGee's headquarters on St. James Street and listened in rapt awe as the eloquent Irish-born Canadian patriot, a "Father of Confederation" who had been one of the politicians instrumental in the creation of the new country, thrilled his audience with inspiring oratory and bright prospects for the fledgling nation. Fine speechmaking was something Isaac admired and sought to practise himself.

Darcy McGee's bold vision and uplifting 1867 speech in Montreal inspired visiting lawyer Isaac Jelfs to see Canada, with its British North America project, as an even better New World venue in which the ex-patriot Englishman could remake his life, yet again. The Irish-born Canadian patriot McGee, a Father of Confederation, would be assassinated the next year, before Isaac returned to Canada.
(William Notman/Library and Archives Canada/C-016749)

All of a sudden Isaac discovered that Canadian politics included more than platform eloquence. "The mob stormed McGee's headquarters in the Mechanics' Institute in Great St. James Street," he later wrote about the drama he was caught up in that night. In the darkness, the blind force of the impersonal crowd flared into a full-scale riot. The attempt to break into the building was repelled, but all windows on the first two floors were smashed and surrounding houses sacked. First bludgeons, then slingshots, and next revolvers escalated the violence. McGee's opponents, James added, "had to be dispersed by the cavalry acting under the orders of the civic authorities."

———

The next day, browsing in a Montreal bookstore, Isaac discovered a new work, published in Drummondville, Quebec, just three months earlier, entitled *The Lost One Found*. It told the overpowering true story of a "lost one," a young man named Norman MacKenzie, who found himself, against his intent, in military service, unhappy with his lot, and trying to escape.

The victim of "this strange series of events," seventeen-year-old MacKenzie, was a Canadian who had left Drummondville in August 1863, looking for work, only to soon be crimped into the Union Army as a result of a scam two opportunistic brothers were operating. American men called up for military service could pay a substitute soldier to fight in their place, and the Greenlaw brothers had made a business recruiting young Canadians in Quebec's Eastern Townships and America's northeastern states to serve as substitutes. The Greenlaws collected a two hundred dollar "bounty" from each wealthy man wishing to avoid enlistment, then delivered over to the Union Army the duped youths to whom they'd promised jobs.

"I had nothing particular to complain of with respect to my usage during my first soldiering experiences," explained Norman MacKenzie in the book Isaac could not put down, "but still I could not reconcile myself to this forced separation from home, and engagement in a service and in a cause with which I had no sympathy. My only thought night and day was directed towards the possibility of effecting an escape."

Isaac knew those feelings. He turned page after page of the book, riveted by this true account of the chaotic events involving conscription he'd experienced in the same Civil War. He was reading his own life into the story, thinking about his experience in the Crimean War, and then also how he'd managed to escape conscription into the Union Army where this young Canadian discovered himself trapped.

MacKenzie and two French Canadians, aged sixteen and seventeen, who also shared his plight as unwilling conscripts thanks to the Greenlaws, succeeded in escaping from camp on a dark moonless night. After several harrowing and hungry days, they were recaptured near Harper's Ferry and charged with desertion. MacKenzie was imprisoned in a dungeon and given only bread and water, then taken to Baltimore where he was imprisoned at Fort McHenry.

The fort's prison had been a horse stable, its stalls refashioned into bunks five tiers high, extending all around the structure. The room was one hundred feet long by forty wide, "and in it were confined between five hundred and six hundred human beings in a state of filth, vermin, and stench too dreadful to be described." The food was coarse and bad, the coffee "a disgusting mess" covered with "filthy-looking scum." The prisoners were "criminals of every class," a rough and violent crew. "They were accustomed to make 'fresh fish' pay on being admitted to the privilege of their society" by tossing them in the air. "One poor old man, after being thrown up, fell with his head upon a brick and was rendered insensible. He lay for two days in a precarious state, scarcely able to speak."

Young MacKenzie, the same age as Isaac when soldiering in the Crimean War, became worse off as the weeks passed. Meanwhile, his mysterious disappearance from Canada propelled MacKenzie's father to search for his lost son. A confident and seasoned man, he traced clues south into the United States, where he had many connections, including with President Lincoln going back to earlier years in Illinois. Eventually, the wily father's detective work brought him to his soldier son. But the Norman MacKenzie he found was now beyond any ability to recognize his rescuer.

"I was horrified by the spectacle he presented," said the older man later. "He wore no coat, hat, nor vest, his sole covering being a ragged and filthy shirt, and a pair of tattered trousers. His face, haggard and ghastly, was besmeared with dirt, and his bleary eyes were devoid of all expression. Want, disease, and ill-usage had rendered him utterly stupefied, and scarcely alive to what was passing around him."

The father's adroit use of political connections in Baltimore and Washington next placed in his hands Special Order No. 470 from the Adjutant-General's Office in the War Department, dated October 20, 1863, commanding young Norman MacKenzie's immediate release from prison and his discharge from the service of the United States Army. The two British subjects returned to freedom and safety in Canada.

Isaac was deeply moved. He'd had no father to rescue him from Crimea and his soldiering with the Dragoons, but had made his own escape. And earlier, at the Stratford law office, then again even in Birmingham, it had only been his own actions, such as they were, that helped him escape his predicaments. In a preface to *The Lost One Found*, noted Isaac, the narrator emphasized "the truth of the homely maxim" which holds that "Heaven helps those who are ready to help themselves."

That night in his hotel room, having read the tale to its astonishing climax, he dipped his pen-nib into black India ink and, on the frontispiece right above the words *The Lost One Found*, inscribed his name, *Isaac Jelfs*. The book, a timely inspiration, remained a treasured talisman he would keep all his life.

———

Back in the United States a few weeks later, Isaac found himself wrestling more urgently than ever with the dilemma he'd created for himself. A man who cherished his quiet universe of freedom, he was now desperate. But if he'd gotten himself into this fix, couldn't he also get himself out? *Heaven helps those who are ready to help themselves.*

His discovery in Canada of a *British* North America country suggested to Isaac the same artful blending of possibilities he'd discovered in the Episcopal Methodist Church. The church was not a compromise, but a reassuring linkage of Episcopalian and Methodist that, to him, extracted the best of each. Beyond the church, however, his life was no longer satisfying. His attempt to retain his British roots through part-time activity with Brooklyn's British Benevolent Association was, he now realized, more taunting and limiting than liberating.

Having experienced an alternative North American society with British institutions and ways, Isaac felt the tug of Canada. His diversionary role with the British Benevolent Association proved that while he might make oaths of allegiance to a non-British country, he could not really change his fundamental nature. By simply relocating north of the border, he could resume being British without having to return to Britain. Going back across the Atlantic was, in his mind, out of the question.

More pressing than even his rekindled fervour to dwell in a British milieu was Isaac's nerve-wracking effort to juggle his two families. His double life had to end. Its falseness was like acid eating at him inside. Having two wives did not square with his religion, nor with America's laws. By not actually marrying Hannah, he might technically avoid the criminal charge of bigamy, but he had certainly laid the two of them open, should it come to that, to a civil charge of "alienation of affections" from Eliza. He was, after all, presenting himself in some circles and with Hannah's family as her husband. If things became public, Eliza Jelfs would also have grounds to sue Hannah Boyer as the adulterous lover of her spouse — an easy case to prove now that Hannah had a child fathered by "James" who was simultaneously her husband "Isaac."

Such a prospect was not remote. In fact, it would have been on the mind of any practising New York lawyer like Isaac, because the adultery issue had been making news for several years. In 1864 New York's state legislature had codified the common law tort of alienation of affections, amidst vociferous public debate about "family values" and outcry over the need to shore up the faltering institution of marriage. Omitting to register the birth of Hannah's daughter only bought time. It had not offered a solution.

Isaac also remained worried about deals going through the law office, some perhaps central to the financial schemes of the corrupt Tammany gang. In all of these, Oakey Hall was front and centre. And even if no calamity befell the firm, Isaac had other considerations that bothered him, namely, professional recognition, trifling as that seems. Though well settled into his twelfth year in the firm Brown, Hall & Vanderpoel, Isaac saw that in New York he would remain a very small light in a dazzling galaxy of bigger stars. America had, it seems, made him more ambitious.

He again turned over in his mind other plights and perils. Unhealthy and diseased living conditions in New York and Brooklyn in these years after the Civil War appalled everyone, but in particular nostalgic Isaac, who began to measure this life against the rustic charms of Moreton-in-Marsh. Manhattan and Brooklyn were no longer fit places to live. Like other northern cities that had fully mobilized for heavy industry during the Civil War, smoke billowed over the landscape from a thick forest of factory smokestacks. The cities had swollen with ill-housed people. Manhattan Island, a mere slab of land in the Hudson River's estuary only two and a half miles across and nine miles long, was closing on a million residents as thousands more immigrants tumbled in, most on the island's lower half. Across in Brooklyn, the section around Gowanus Bay was just as crowded and foul.

Traffic along Broadway, which Isaac dodged coming from and going to his office, was a danger zone of stages, carriages, and carts, teamsters and pedestrians. People were injured or killed in the chaos. The horse-drawn streetcars Isaac rode were frigid as an icebox in winter, only to become infernos in summer, housing a stench of unwashed bodies, tobacco juice, and beery breath. Passengers, jammed like freight into spaces built for one-third their number, had their pockets picked and were harassed by insolent conductors.

The streets he walked were caked with animal wastes, filled with garbage piled as high as snow banks, and oozing with the overflow from clogged sewers. In the 1860s pigs came to reign in the cities, roaming the streets, including Broadway, rooting for food. The roadways served as pens for the dozens of nearby slaughterhouses in the cities, and the number of pigs climbed to the hundreds of thousands; in some northern cities, the pig population was almost equal in number to the human population. The pigs, unfed while awaiting slaughter, might have served a value eating garbage, since there was no municipal collection or other sanitation service, but such a role in waste disposal was quickly offset by their stinking semi-liquid excrement which flowed across the streets and walkways, creating a bed of slime.

Horses contributed generously to this scene. With a couple of million living in America's cities, New York itself was home to over a hundred thousand. A healthy horse would drop up to twenty-five pounds of manure daily, and as the steaming, stinking balls accumulated on the streets, so did millions of flies. The flies also swarmed in thick clouds around the livery stables and barns throughout the city. The stables' urine-saturated hay added to the universal stench of smoke and acrid vapours pouring from New York's hundreds of foundries, tanneries, refineries, bone mills, and machine shops. Work horses were underfed and harshly whipped, until they died and were left in the street to join the cadavers of other critters unable to survive urban conditions.

Beyond the city's built-up parts lay garbage-filled marshes, a suburb of sludge and stinking gases. When the outcry over dangerous conditions produced an inquiry by New York's Board of Health, it listed among the air's ingredients: sulphur, ammonia gases, offal rendering, bone boiling, manure heaps, putrid animal wastes, fish scrap, kerosene, acid fumes, phosphate fertilizer, and septic muck. Doctors identified how unending black smoke puffing from oil refineries made people sick and depressed, acid fumes irritated lungs and throats, and rank odours caused people to vomit. There was something to be said, perhaps, for small village life in an out-of-the-way corner of the world. Thinking of his past, Isaac was contemplating his future.

—

Seeing a way to resolve his dilemma and avoid the encircling unpleasantness, Isaac began to lay the groundwork for his most daring escape of all.

His first step came with purchase of a residence at 259 18th Street in the vicinity of Fifth Avenue. He paid three thousand dollars to Mrs. Frances Banks for it, a large amount for a substantial home. He then registered the title in Eliza Jelfs's name alone. If anything unexpected ever happen to him, he explained to his wife, she would have a home of her own. It was large enough that she and their daughter Annie could live securely while also renting quarters to provide income, should that be necessary, beyond whatever money Eliza might continue earning as a skilled dressmaker.

Next, fate intervened to direct Isaac's second step. Finding a flyer sent to the Britannia Benevolent Association, he rushed to show Hannah and Harry the incredible offer of free land in Canada. "He became entranced," Harry remembered, "with free grant lands."

The government in Ontario, one of the four provinces in the new Canadian Confederation, was seeking settlers for the lands it was opening for colonization in the province's northern districts of Muskoka, Parry Sound, and Nipissing. The promotional sheet gave details about the new Free Grant and Homestead Act, passed by the provincial legislature that February. Isaac summed it up: just cut down trees, clear some fields, build a cabin, live in it six months a year, and in five years the property would be yours. A homesteader could get a hundred acres, even two hundred.

Hannah was incredulous. "If the land is so good, why are they *giving* it away?"

Harry, however, became an enthusiastic ally for Isaac's plan, relishing the prospect of owning a tract of land as large as the one he'd worked with other orphans at Westchester.

The fact that Harry wanted to go helped to persuade Hannah. She had sought out the comforts of the British Benevolent Association in Brooklyn, and now she warmed to the idea of being back in a British country, as she'd heard Isaac describe Canada from his northern trips. Hannah had never become an American citizen, nor even considered it. She was only in the United States because her father had sought a fresh start and, duty-bound, she'd fallen in with his plan. So, leaving the country would not trouble her. In fact the prospect had one great appeal for Hannah, and it was not the lure of the land. Emigrating to Canada would mean she would have Isaac all to herself.

For both Hannah and Isaac, the anonymity possible with Muskoka's remoteness made migration north even more compelling.

Suddenly, something beyond their wildest imaginings seemed possible. They could escape their predicament just by going to Muskoka and performing the rewarding work of building their own home. Best of all, Hannah and Isaac could do this as an openly married couple.

—

The fact Isaac had fled to the United States without detection or detention by the British, and had since gone up to Canada and come back several times without repercussion, helped mollify somewhat his anxiety about the past catching up with him.

Although he had made prior trips to Montreal using his own name, Isaac saw that for this escape to work he would have to change his name. He would become a different person in another country, to close the door on any unfinished British business about the Stratford fiasco or his departure from the Dragoons, and to cover his tracks once he dropped out of the lives of Eliza and Annie. Isaac would henceforth present Hannah as his "wife." They would arrive in their new country a married couple, with one child and a second on the way. He hoped no official would ask to see a marriage certificate.

As Hannah prepared to take the bold step, her instinct to keep the Boyer family together was as irrepressible as ever. She wrote her brother Tom, now twenty-two and living in Massachusetts, inviting him to join them. Tom replied that he had no interest in heading north of the line. Inspired further by the example of his new "brother-in-law," Thomas Boyer was proceeding with his plan to become a lawyer himself. Looking to his future, he'd decided without difficulty that he'd rather practise law in Cambridge than clear land in Bracebridge.

His answer delivered the shock Hannah needed. At last she accepted that her family was scattering in all directions and she could relax somewhat her impulse to mother her younger brothers and sisters. The three youngest girls had disappeared, so far without a trace, and her unrelenting efforts to find them had been as frustrating as they were futile. Although the others were venturing further afield with careers and new relationships, the fact both Harry and Mary Ann would go with her to Canada delighted Hannah. Perhaps others would follow, sometime later.

Hannah had at last gained freedom to pursue her own wellbeing. Best of all, the fresh start could bring openness to the shadowy personal lives she and Isaac had been leading.

Meanwhile, over at the offices of Brown, Hall & Vanderpoel, Isaac set about completing work and transferring ongoing matters to other lawyers on various pretexts. He started withdrawing money from his bank account in amounts small enough not to raise eyebrows. With ink remover, he dabbed over the name "Isaac Jelfs" in the front of his book *The Lost One Found* until it disappeared, and with studied care removed other traces of his prior life.

Was there no other way? He knew the answer.

Isaac was anxious as he boarded the train early that September morning. With him was Hannah, their little girl Annie, seventeen-year-old curly-haired Harry Boyer, and an attractive woman in her early twenties, Mary Ann Boyer. Other passengers would not have guessed this family was heading for Canada's wilderness to hack out a home from dense forest, but such was their intent. They were making their big escape.

In the alchemy of a train ride, the thirty-five-year-old lawyer Isaac Jelfs became James Boyer.

———

The Boyer ensemble spent several days of delight exploring their new province's capital city, a developing centre of some fifty-five thousand inhabitants. The refreshing air of early September accentuated the exhilaration they felt in the pleasant, moderate-sized, British-like place, where the flag they saw fluttering atop masts was the Union Jack. For Hannah, these Toronto days were the closest thing to a honeymoon she'd ever have.

The Boyers' interest in music led them to a couple Toronto churches that Sunday, both morning and evening services, to hear the choirs. On Monday, while Mary Ann looked after Annie and Harry went exploring for stonecutting shops and other places of interest to him, Hannah compared the millinery shops to those of New York while Isaac lost himself visiting bookstores. His purchases included several novels, a book of poetry, and a copy of *Psalms and Paraphrases, with Accompanying Tunes for Use in the Presbyterian Church*, published by Blackett Robinson in Toronto the year before.

In this northern Utopia, the twin delights of sampling churches for music and stores for books transported Isaac, already afloat in a state of euphoria, into an even higher realm of bliss. He was with the woman he loved and their delightful daughter. Hannah's pregnant glow and her own great joy at the turn life was taking made her even more affectionate than ever towards "James." He reciprocated with feelings of pride and protectiveness. With the complications and tensions of New York and Brooklyn ebbing away, the relief they felt was palpable. Isaac tried to hide from Hannah his remorse about Eliza and his abandoned daughter, also named Annie, just like their own little girl.

Adept at getting himself into predicaments, he had freed himself by yet another escape. If he could pull it off, Isaac Jelfs would now improvise the role of a new man.

9

—

Homesteaders in a New Country

Keen to resume their journey to Muskoka and the future awaiting them, "the Boyers" arrived at the Toronto railway station early. After James and Harry heaved the family's heavy trunks onto the baggage car, they boarded the Northern Railway's 7 a.m. train for the north country.

As their trip progressed, James reflected on his strange journey, which had begun in England's long-settled towns, advanced through Crimea's well-worn villages around the Black Sea, continued to bustling New York, now well evolved from its Dutch colonial days, and then to Montreal, with its stone buildings huddled between the mighty St. Lawrence River and a hulking mountain, until he'd left behind the fresh little city of Toronto, a big town really, whose history as "muddy York" was so recent. He was now heading next to Bell Ewart, a tiny settlement not even close to two decades in existence. James imagined he was travelling back in time, reversing into an earlier, primitive age. In contrast to the ancient and settled areas he had known, everything in this unfolding northland was pristine.

Looking from the train, he studied the landscape as they moved through it. The cool, September morning air left fog patches hanging above the fields. A powerful modern machine carried them through mist into an unknown territory, its shape hard even to discern. Such a setting would be ideal for creating his new persona, he decided, so long as he and his time-travelling "family" made no slip-ups.

They arrived mid-morning in Bell Ewart at the south end of Lake Simcoe. For those going to Muskoka in 1869, this lakeside spur line was as far as the rails carried them. The Northern's main line continued northwest, passing through Allandale near the south edge of Barrie, then on to Collingwood. That fact alone reassured James that the Boyers' final destination would not be a readily visited place — certainly no busy thoroughfare — which reduced the risk of someone from a crowd of travellers taking him aside to whisper in his ear, "I know who you really are!"

The steam locomotive shuddered and passengers shook with its breaking stop. James picked up Annie and carried her in his arms as the four Boyer adults climbed down to the station's small platform by the lake.

Along with their trunks and other northbound passengers, they transferred to the *Emily May*. After a couple of "last call" warning blasts from her steam whistle punctured the calm morning air, the steamboat headed up Lake Simcoe, passed through the narrows at Orillia that Samuel de Champlain had once explored, and entered the green tinted waters of Lake Couchiching.

The Boyers felt alert to everything that was different and dramatic, from the new experience of the steamer's steady chugging throb — if you didn't count Brooklyn's ferry across the East River, this was their first ride on a steamboat — to the sunlight breaking through the majestic clouds over the lake, and the large flocks of ducks floating on its surface. The *Emily May* aimed for Washago Mills at the top of this lake.

Once she approached the little dock, Captain May ordered engines into hard reverse. The steamer's paddles changed direction and churned up eddies of frothing water. With a heavy bump, her side struck the dock. Passengers jostled to regain their footing, clinging to the rail and watching the spectacle. With hurried activity deckhands tossed mooring lines and quickly roped her secure, then pushed a gangplank between the vessel's side doorway and dock. That's as far as the *Emily May* could take them.

This time, it was Uncle Harry who carried Annie as they walked the gangplank ashore. The next leg of the journey was on John Harvie's Royal Mail stage from Washago north to a small settlement where a log bridge had been put across the Severn River. As they approached the place, perfunctorily named Severn Bridge, the Boyers were shocked to see the terrain transform abruptly. The gentle rolling hills they'd spotted from the train's windows north of Toronto, or reaching back from the shores of lakes Simcoe and Couchiching as they'd glimpsed from the *Emily May*, were replaced immediately north of the Severn by rough rocky ridges.

Crossing the bridge, they looked with awe up a mountainous rock face rising before them. Topped with pines and spruce trees, some scraggly oaks, and scattered clumps of sumacs, the massive outcropping of ancient rock had given the road-builders no choice but to divert course around its hulking base. James had been right about going back in time; they were encountering the oldest rock formation on earth.

Soon the Boyers learned the bruising way that such turns and twists, matched by steep climbs and sharp descents across a succession of rocky valleys, was the "Muskoka Road" experience. The jostled passengers hung onto the hard seats as the coach bumped and swerved toward Gravenhurst. As this winding, hilly, crude new colonization road penetrated the overwhelming silence of Muskoka's deep forests, Hannah fell silent. She gazed with intensity, stunned by the primordial wilderness crowding the very sides of their small coach along its narrow rutted track.

—

It was hard to remain sombre for long. An outgoing man riding in their stagecoach introduced himself as A.P. Cockburn.

Young but already something of a legend, exuberant Alexander Peter Cockburn was the member of Ontario's newly elected legislature for North Victoria, which included Muskoka District. He was also a lumber dealer, merchant, railway promoter, and the pioneer owner of a Lake Muskoka steamboat. Busy all the time, he was hardly quiet now.

Just three years before, Cockburn told the Boyers, he'd launched his first ship, the *Wenonah*, and been granted the government contract for mail deliveries during the navigation season. He explained that his boat carried passengers, freight, and livestock, as well as the mail, adding proudly that she made connections "with all stages, steamers, sailboats, and colonization roads." A natural salesman, he then boasted that the

Wenonah, because of these connections, formed "the only reliable and complete highway to the most important parts of Muskoka district."

After more conversation about public affairs, his interest in logging, the progress in building roads, and how Muskoka had a great future now that the Free Grant and Homestead Act he'd championed in the legislature was bringing in settlers, Cockburn returned to the subject of his steamboat, to emphasize that rates for passage were "reasonable." He had little difficulty clinching the sale of four adult passages. The jolted Boyers, already weary from their long day of new impressions and this rough coach ride, were readily persuaded that they'd find the last part of their trip from Gravenhurst to Bracebridge smoother, faster, and more scenic aboard his steamer *Wenonah* than by continuing over the treacherous Muskoka Road.

As the Boyers would come to appreciate, A.P. Cockburn was an adept salesman and promoter in all his endeavours. In politics he was "Reform," as the era's Liberals often called themselves, but he was also a "loose fish," as the Conservative Party's national leader John A. Macdonald described elected members who, rather than adhering to their party's line, swam wherever they wanted to advance their own or their constituents' best interests. Cockburn's knack for political swimming was enabling him to get timber concessions and mail contracts from governments, and would soon have the government constructing locks at Port Carling so his steamboats could overcome the five-foot drop on the Indian River and sail between Lake Muskoka and upper lakes Rosseau and Joseph.

Meanwhile, the man's continuous acquisition of valuable timber rights, repaid by Cockburn's votes in the legislature to support the fledgling government of John Sandfield Macdonald, drew strong attacks from Liberal leader George Brown in his *Globe* newspaper in Toronto. However his critics saw A.P. Cockburn down in the provincial capital, in Muskoka he was esteemed as a big local employer, developer of new opportunities, and rising star in the political firmament.

James Boyer and A.P. Cockburn hit it off well. The loquacious promoter and politician found an attentive and, at this stage in their relationship, unusually quiet, listener. Their views on the topics touched upon seemed similar, largely because James was passively agreeable to everything, not wanting to stand out by ruffling political feathers, least of all this man's.

Yet, early in the trip, James was suddenly taken aback when Cockburn, who'd quickly assumed the role of host and guide, informed him he would "not be allowed to pass Gibraltar unless he was a good British subject." Now apprehensive, the newcomer "soon discovered what this meant when the stage approached the Kah-she-she-bog-a-mog River," where at a turn in the road "what burst upon the view appeared at first sight as a massive fortification with guns mounted." There, at a large rock outcropping that to James's imagination resembled the vaulting rock promontory of Gibraltar, loomed a military checkpoint.

Then, as they drew alongside, James chuckled with relief to discover A.P.'s joke. What he'd seen was only "a perpendicular wall of rock with a flat top, upon the parapet of which had been mounted blackened logs with the ends projecting over the cliff, presenting what had appeared at a distance to be a tier of heavy guns." At the foot of the cliff stood the cottage and garden of an old soldier named James Cuthbert, who in time would own a real cannon, a small brass field-piece given to him by a Toronto gentleman, from which he thereafter fired salutes on public holidays or whenever a notable personage travelling into Muskoka passed his front door.

Muskoka's member of the Legislature, A.P. Cockburn, alarmed James Boyer by quipping that he'd not be allowed into the district unless he was "a good British subject," a fear compounded when the American first spotted an apparent fortress with six cannons (seen atop rock, upper right) by the first stagecoach stop.

For the rest of the tortuous fourteen-mile journey to Gravenhurst, the stagecoach groaned over poor roads, burdened by the weight of settlers' effects, including the Boyers' trunks. It was a heavy load for the team to pull up steep rocky terrain and across muddy, log-covered "corduroy" stretches of the colonization road. To lighten the horses' burden so that they could get to the top of steep inclines, male passengers were asked to climb out and walk up. Several times they had to put their shoulders to a wheel and lift the mired coach out of a hole or soft spot in the road. When the coach became stalled in one really deep rut, the men, including the honourable member of the legislature, had to give a herculean push. Twisting his ankle, James grimaced with pain.

From Gravenhurst, "Mr. and Mrs. James Boyer" and their affiliated family, with trunks accounted for, boarded Cockburn's *Wenonah*, for their second steamboat ride that day. They travelled out into Lake Muskoka, north up the lake to the mouth of the Muskoka River, then upstream along its winding six-mile course past a steep, sloping wall of rock and thickly wooded banks to the village wharf in Bracebridge.

A toot from the steamer's whistle signalled their trip had ended. Deck hands extended the gangplank onto the makeshift wharf. With

A steamboat enters the bay below Bracebridge falls as a rowboat crosses and two women look on. The primitive freight storage shed and original wharf stand in the centre; the empty area to the right had already been fully clear-cut by loggers. The Boyers arrived this way, but in the dark, not at first seeing the starkness of the scene any more than the artist who sketched this placid, bucolic rendition.

James leading the way but hobbling on his painful foot, the rest of the Boyers came ashore with trepidation, their way in the dark illuminated only by crew members holding tarry torches. They had reached the frontier of civilization.

—

Bracebridge in 1869 was a stark settlement, barely a decade old. It was a tiny scattering of shacks, tree stumps, and crude muddy pathways, isolated, primitive, and much further from New York than all the miles the Boyers had journeyed to get here. James cherished the remoteness.

They had quit a bustling, overcrowded, foul city and travelled to a pristine wilderness, whose thick silence was punctuated only by bird songs, the hollow swishing of a light breeze in tall pines, and the steady, comforting roar of waterfalls. Muskoka's pure air had special buoyancy, its dampness releasing pungent earthy muskiness of fresh woods and mossy rock, an aromatic mixture swilling with heady evergreen scents. It was even fresher when the wind brought air carried across the district's rocky plateaux, clean forests, and crystalline lakes.

Until they could get settled, the Boyers took rooms in a small tavern on the south side of the falls. Still struggling to get used to his new name, James was hesitant in describing to others just who he was or even what he did for a living. Signing the guest register at The Royal, he simply wrote "gentleman" in the column for occupation. For his new persona, he would try casting himself as someone a cut above the ordinary, without disclosing that he was a lawyer, since such a fact could make him easier to trace. Their days in Toronto had allowed his unshaven stubble to form the early beginnings of the beard James hoped would disguise his appearance and increase the odds against him being found out.

The rustic inn, built of logs and newly enlarged by a two-storey frame addition, had been dubbed "The Royal Hotel" by its proud proprietor, Hiram McDonald. Looking over the place and taking in its dirt floor, James considered that "a pretentious name." This frontier propensity to use grandiose names was, he would discover, by no means confined to McDonald's small hotel. Bracebridge's humble barbershop enjoyed an elevated status as "His Majesty's Old Reliable Shaving Saloon." One modest general store was called the "House of Commerce," another "The District Exchange." Who was "James Boyer," anyway, to quibble about names?

Only a year before the Boyers arrived, the provincial government had designated Bracebridge, geographically at the district's centre, judicial and administrative capital of Muskoka. A "government square" had been planned for the settlement's central Dominion Street, a dirt track, also named above its status, to honour the new Dominion of Canada. Here the Crown lands office and land registry office would be established, then a jail built and, in a few more years, municipal buildings erected.

The boy who'd grown up in the settled English town of Moreton-in-Marsh near the abutting corners of four counties now found himself starting life over in a raw frontier Canadian community emerging near the four corner points of Monck, Macaulay, Muskoka, and Draper townships. Settlement around the falls would spread into the nearby parts of these townships as the influx of newcomers claimed free land in each of them. The best lots were going fast.

James and Harry, pooling tips from helpful locals, caught a good dose of land fever and right away began scouting for property, exploring the rugged bush outward from the settlement. Hiram McDonald, their hotelier at The Royal, appeared well informed about local prospects. He directed them to good potential land to the east, along the "road" between the Second and Third Concessions in Macaulay Township. Still bothered by his twisted ankle, James found it painful to make these excursions, but stoically refused to mention it, not wanting to attract attention.

Years later, he would quip that during his novice weeks in Muskoka, he "could be considered as a 'tender-foot' indeed."

10

——

First Muskoka Winter

If timing is everything, seasons matter.

Drawing on the experience of the province's first big waves of settlers in the 1820s, several books and guides published in Ontario warned prospective homesteaders that autumn was no time to start.

That warning resulted from what had transpired in milder southern Ontario. Further north in Muskoka, winters were even more severe. So the Boyers listened as seasoned settler Hiram McDonald took them aside and explained that, since it was already September, it would be impossible to claim a lot, then clear enough land, build a cabin, and outfit it, before winter set in.

What he said was true, of course. But it also turned out that McDonald had a vested interest in the Boyers' well-being. Keeping hotel was part of his life, but so was developing land and dealing in property. As an early settler, he'd acquired "squatter's rights" to Lot 7 in Concession 3 of Macaulay Township, merely by occupying the land, putting up a building, and living there. Now, having convinced the Boyers of their dilemma with the calendar, he presented a solution by offering to sell them his Macaulay shanty.

James and Hannah talked it over with the others. They would either have to pay the wily McDonald for rooms in his Bracebridge hotel all winter, or bite the bullet and come up with the one-time fee to buy McDonald's Macaulay Township dwelling. They had budgeted for neither. But Hannah, anxious about coming to term with her pregnancy, wanted to be in a private place with her sister Mary Ann, rather than in a crude hotel with a mostly male clientele. Supporting his sister, Harry offered the practical thought that because the land they would claim would no doubt be even further out from Bracebridge, McDonald's place, although it was already deep in the township, would likely be closer and prove convenient for clearing trees during the winter. Mary Ann did not think either prospect appealing so suggested they all just head back to Brooklyn and return next spring — an idea the others knew was more than impracticable. For his part James knew he would be at greater ease further from the settlement, hidden deeper in the Canadian bush, away from any emissary who might arrive from New York or Brooklyn.

Their decision having been made by the logic of circumstances, James bought the hotel keeper's cleared property with its existing cabin, paying McDonald somewhat more than three hundred dollars for it. After completing the deal, Hiram then added that, by spring, James would need to pay another hundred dollars to the Crown to get to the squatter's rights assigned to him at the land registry office, should he ever want to sell the place after the Boyers' own cabin was ready and they'd moved into it. James was chagrined. He was learning more about Ontario land law. Each of his unexpected lessons was further reducing his limited cash. He was shocked to see how quickly it was being spent.

Tranquil and sparse Bracebridge as it appeared in early days, where winter greeted the Boyers only weeks after their arrival from bustling and crowded New York late in 1869.

Relocating from McDonald's hotel to McDonald's squatter's shanty, the Boyers hauled their trunks yet again. Hannah's coveted trunk from England contained family letters and Bibles inscribed with records of family births, marriages, and deaths, which had now survived an Atlantic crossing and a flood in her Brooklyn basement; she'd also kept some souvenir stationery from the New York and Brooklyn millinery shops. A second trunk was jammed mostly with James's things: law texts from New York; the new books bought in Toronto; some works by Shakespeare; his prized copy of *The Lost One Found*; and his clarinet, nicely given added weight by Harry's stonecutting tools. A third one held clothes, with some dishes, pots, and a frying pan at the bottom.

The next day back in the village at the House of Commerce general store, James bought axes for himself and Harry, a rifle and box of cartridges, rope, matches, and coal-oil for the lamp that he found in the cabin. Hannah purchased cups, flour, beans, some apples, baking soda, salt, tea, salted pork, and a few other staples for a household of four adults and a child.

———

The Boyers' cabin was only interim accommodation to get them through the first Muskoka winter. James still had to locate his own "free land." During the next four weeks, autumn chilled the air; nature ripened foliage into warm orange, crimson red, and bright yellow colours; and then the leaves fell to the ground. With the deciduous trees bare, the lines of vision became clearer, which helped the two Boyer men as they continued to scout the terrain for a potential farm.

A dozen years earlier, when provincial land surveyor John Ryan had subdivided Macaulay Township's 41,902 acres into lots, he estimated more than half were "fit for cultivation." That meant the rest of the township's land, almost half, was unsuitable for farming, which is why James and Harry found themselves exploring a lot of uneven rocky ground before coming across a run of land that seemed flat enough. They took its covering of large trees as a sign that arable soil lay beneath the tangled forest floor, believing they could create good fields once they cleared away the dense bush.

The chosen land was seven lots further east along the same concession line from the cabin they'd bought. Just as Harry had anticipated, it would be convenient to reach from McDonald's old shanty during winter, when they could begin clearing trees. On October 16 James went to the Crown lands office on Dominion Street in Bracebridge, confirmed that the lot was still available, and got his "ticket" for it by filing claim to Lot 14 in Concession 2 of Macaulay, a rectangle comprising ninety-nine acres. The missing acre had been lost where surveyor Ryan's concession line dodged south to get around a rock ridge and swamp, a tactic not unlike the one builders of the Muskoka colonization road resorted to as well.

A month later, James helped Harry file his own claim for property abutting Lot 14 to the south. On the surveyor's plan of survey, Harry's rectangular piece showed as a separate lot in Concession 1, but for nature and to the Boyers the two properties were a single continuous stretch of land. Overlooked in filing Harry's claim was the fact he was not yet eighteen, the minimum age to qualify. The government land agents were on duty, however, to see that able-bodied and willing settlers were taking up Muskoka's land. Any legal impediment on Harry's part, especially one that would be remedied by mere passage of a few more months, did not matter in the spirit of this frontier society, if everybody just looked the other way or didn't ask questions.

Hannah, too, wanted a lot in Macaulay. Why not? Under Ontario law married women had been able to own property since 1859, a right extended into the Free Grant and Homestead Act in 1868. No one in the Crown lands office at Bracebridge asked to see her marriage certificate.

The land she claimed in late 1869 would be for the future. For now, the energetic twenty-seven-year-old, well into her pregnancy, confronted more immediate realities. Far away were the fine millinery shops of New York and Brooklyn with their fashionable indulgences of ribbon-trimmed bonnets. Gone were the dance halls and live bands playing music she enjoyed. Hannah, preoccupied with the crude conditions to be overcome or adapted to, focused on how she and her family were to survive in the bush.

Despite the challenge Hannah never felt so confident. She was now with the man she loved. Her cherished brother Harry was at hand. Mary Ann was a companion and helpmate, even if she longed to return to Brooklyn and voiced her feelings a bit too often. Special pleasures greeted Hannah as she watched little Annie making discoveries. She anticipated soon giving birth to the family's first Canadian, but that thought also brought a chill. Looking at the dark cabin interior, she remembered her mother's tragic end in childbirth.

Winter arrived early, astonishing the settlers when they rose and ventured out of the chilly cabin, dazzled by a blanket of glistening snow in early morning sunlight. Seeing dark tree branches outlined in white lace, the landscape enthralled the Boyers like some heavenly fantasy.

As winter advanced the dark nights grew longer, the snow deeper, the temperatures colder. In McDonald's old cabin at the edge of the forest, the Boyer family hunkered down as best they could to await the even harsher conditions they'd been told would be coming. Harry'd picked up a tip from a neighbour and strung a rope to the rudimentary outdoor privy, to guide the way through darkness and blizzards. He and James chinked holes and gaps in the log walls to keep the draughty dwelling warmer. Once more snow fell they pushed it up the lower parts of the cabin as extra insulation against the icy wind's penetrating blasts.

They had little food but Hannah managed to have something, perhaps salted pork, some boiled dried beans, biscuits or a type of flatbread, and hot tea, on the table at mealtime. Their next meal, and the one after it, would be much the same. During the daylight hours, when weather permitted, James and Harry went hunting for game, bringing back a partridge or rabbit, sometimes a deer.

After cleaning the animal or bird for Mary Ann to cook, they'd head up the concession line to cut trees on Lot 14. As they spoke together during rest pauses, Harry and James talked over past events and laughed with amazement once they'd figured out they had encountered each other before in New York at the patent office, before Isaac had met Harry's sister and become James Boyer.

Together in the small cabin during the long evenings, James read books by coal-oil lamplight, while the others chatted about things they'd done, or had to do next, taking turns to add firewood to the small box stove. Sometimes James heard them recalling the suffering aboard the *Orient*, or remembering the hardships of New York, or wondering how much worse the Muskoka winter might still get. He'd put down his book and take up his clarinet, making music to the accompaniment of howling winds outdoors. Harry would join in, and hit the high notes with his clear tenor voice. Mary Ann wrapped her blanket tighter around her shoulders and hummed along. It was James's way, when he could not do it by reading, of insinuating something else into the moment. Music crowded out the past and put the bitter cold at a distance. The future they could face a day at a time.

Month after frigid month, the four Boyer adults and wee Annie weathered physical demands and emotional testing, in common with Muskoka's other huddled and exiled city-dwellers from England, Europe, and the United States, all of them fighting off frostbite and starvation, despair and illness. The snow, Harry recorded, "was six feet deep."

———

The new year arrived with much joy, thanks to the appearance of a healthy baby. In the small draughty cabin, with Mary Ann's help, Hannah gave birth on January 3 to her second daughter. The girl was named Mary Ellen White Boyer, to perpetuate Hannah's mother's maiden name, "White," and perhaps even, as a little humour of the kind Hannah and James enjoyed, to honour Muskoka's snowy landscape that greeted her arrival. As she grew the little girl would be called "Nellie," and then "Nel," all her life.

Through the rest of that long winter and into spring of 1870, Harry recorded, he and James trekked to the first of the lots the Boyers had claimed and "cut down trees to build a log cabin and then clear the land for crops." As the two men continued to wield their axes, spring's warming breezes dispatched the snow, and the countryside came to life with buds pushing out and sprouts up. In this season of new growth, a sturdy cabin began rising in the clearing.

Knowing what the Free Grant and Homestead Act required, and getting a lot of advice around the Bracebridge settlement, they built the dwelling just sixteen feet wide and twenty feet long, the minimum dimensions to get their grant. Most Muskoka homesteaders took the legal minimum as their maximum, at least when building their initial structure.

It was "a well-built cabin with logs shaped, especially the corners, so they fitted together well," wrote James and Hannah's son George, years later, after he visited the family homestead, by then abandoned. James and Harry had not only been advised by neighbours to "keep it small," but also got tips in construction. The logs for its walls "were about sixteen inches in diameter, the corners squared and framed, with wooden pins to hold them together. The four inner walls were mostly squared up and the cracks filled with moss and clay."

Pioneers favoured a smaller building because it was easier to roof. Simplest was a flat roof of logs covered with earth, common for many Muskoka homesteads, but that created a dank interior more resembling a root cellar than a fit human dwelling. Several buildings James and Harry studied in the village had slopping roofs, with shingles made by splitting thin flat lengths off a short section of log, which worked well. Hannah favoured shingles because they would add a civilized look to an otherwise crude abode, but cutting and nailing them required tools and materials the Boyers did not have.

James, remembering the thatched roofs "as they had aplenty in England," tried to use the coarse "beaver grass" close at hand to finish their roof, but after an initial attempt did not press on with the technique. When the rain dripped through, he realized the method was not as easy as it appeared and required the talent of skilled thatchers. The Boyers then turned to roofing their place with easy-to-handle poles, "dozens of them laid side by side, the gaps filled with pine gum, clay, and moss," as George saw. It looked more primitive, but the cabin was drier inside. The floor was dirt. Whenever they could get boards, they laid them to plank over the ground. Later, more boards were used to line the interior walls.

———

If Muskoka's homesteaders had romantic back-to-the-land notions about the virtue of "roughing it in the bush," such sentiments did not last beyond their first year in the district.

Frigid winter had forced the Boyers to huddle in their cramped cabin with a little girl and newborn baby. Surviving winter, they believed they had come through the worst ordeal. But the family, arriving in September, had not yet experienced Muskoka's warm, damp spring and hot, early summer. "Black flies and mosquitoes swarmed everywhere," recorded Harry. The Boyers found these seasons, said uncomplaining Harry, "strenuous."

Hunger, and the ache to overcome it, was constant. The little stores in Bracebridge had limited supplies which occasionally dwindled to nothing. "We sometimes had to go many miles for supplies of food, the nearest place Gravenhurst, twelve miles away, but often to Orillia or Barrie, from thirty to fifty miles away," Harry recorded. "On these trips we sometimes had to carry a bag of flour on our backs, holding other supplies under arm. These trips would take a couple of days. The nights were spent in the wild woods." James made these trips, too, to "back" the flour, in a fifty-pound sack from Washago, "through the bush, and over so-called roads of the worst description, which if somewhat fatiguing, was guaranteed to be a certain cure for the worst cases of indigestion."

After spring drove them to distraction with its bug infestations, summer brought a new species of setbacks for the Boyers as they sought to plant and raise crops amidst stumps, roots, boulders, hungry animals, and pecking birds. They decided, for the first season, to plant seeds in their cleared land at McDonald's old farm, and then try to establish little planted patches and garden rows on James's first lot as soon as they cleared it enough.

Face to face with unbroken bush, settlers struggling to make their farms in the forest amidst rocky outcroppings could be overwhelmed. For most this was their first experience of forestry and farming. Between a homesteader and his "free" land stood years of back-breaking labour. As soft hands hardened and backs grew stronger, the race was on. By law the ancient wilderness had to be transformed into an agricultural operation in five years to qualify for the grant. Recent arrivals in the district, learning from the example of pioneer neighbours, cleared their selected lots in small sections rather than all at once, first cutting away the underbrush, then felling the many trees. The work never ended.

Often the odds were insurmountable. In Muskoka's Morrison Township, non-swimmer William Johnston, exhausted after a day chopping trees, drowned in the Severn River trying to catch fish for his hungry family. As he sank to the bottom, Johnson also went down in history. He was the first settler to die in Muskoka. His courageous widow, with two young boys to care for, then pressed on alone, managing by valiant spirit, with tears of determination in her eyes, to clear about nine more acres on the Johnston's lot, until she herself weakened, sickened, and died.

The common denominator for all Muskoka homesteaders, whatever the quality of their land, was the raw struggle to survive against isolation, shortage of food, accidents and illnesses with no doctor at hand, predatory animals, freezing winters, and black fly and mosquito-infested summers.

For many who'd come north with the dream of having their own farm, adjusting to this harsh existence was the main thing, the only thing. James and Hannah, like many settlers who had burned their bridges, or sold their assets, or escaped a personal hell, had gambled everything on a fresh start. They had to make a success of homesteading, or at least find some tolerable way of surviving.

There was no going back.

11

Opening the Frontier

With no possible retreat, the only direction was forward.

In early spring James, determined to prevail whatever the odds, walked into Bracebridge and at the land office paid the Crown a hundred dollars for Hiram MacDonald's squatter's rights. Because married settlers who met the criteria could acquire a second lot, he registered another claim as well, in Macaulay's Second Concession, for Lot 20. Land officials seldom resisted homesteaders wanting a second lot, because provincial policy was to get the large district opened up, and they also knew many hundred acre lots contained only a fraction of that acreage in farmable land.

All the while James and Harry pushed themselves hard to clear their land. They wanted their farms since this was the new life they'd envisaged and knew that only work would make it reality. An even greater imperative was their need to plant in the spring because with next to no money they had to grow food to survive. On top of that, they were driven by the homesteader obligations they had to meet if they were even to qualify for their land grant. The setting was peaceful; their sense, one of urgency.

Working his Macaulay land was also changing James's perception of himself. Struggling to fashion his new persona, he'd entered Bracebridge describing himself as a "gentleman." Now he described himself, in his March 1870 title document, as a "yeoman." A year later, when asked his vocation by a census taker, his answer was plain and direct: "farmer." James had changed his name, nationality, grown a beard, and evolved from gentleman to farmer. In place of his law office on Manhattan's bustling Broadway Avenue and the creature comforts a ferryboat ride away at his home in Brooklyn, he now avoided stumps and mud puddles while treading the crude roadway between Bracebridge's modest collection of buildings and his primitive log cabin in Macaulay.

The Boyers had even more to come to terms with than the shock of difference, in this land that now possessed them. James sensed a mystery about Muskoka, through the unseen presence of its Natives. Clearing their land and digging a vegetable garden, he and Harry found a couple of arrowheads. When he heard about a place near Bracebridge entirely clear of trees, stumps, and boulders, James's curiosity drove him to look until he located it. He paced out the area to measure some thirty-seven acres. Strolling around the tranquil clearing, he developed a primordial affinity for its isolated, eerie space. In its silence he felt somehow an intruder. Yet he was drawn back whenever he wanted to withdraw and reflect on things. At such times, had he been in a city, he might have slipped into a cavernous cathedral. Now, in the frontier, he was instead drawn to this roofless cathedral. Each time, whatever else he was pondering, James puzzled anew about the clearing's significance.

———

There were newer clearings in Muskoka, too, but of a very different order.

Loggers had begun moving like irregular armies through Muskoka's deep pine forests. For ten thousand years, since the time of the last ice age, these woods smoothly carpeted the Canadian Shield's rugged rocks and ravines. Now, in short order, the rough underlay was again revealed as the woodsmen cut down the biggest and the best of the trees.

In the 1870s they felled the giant white pines by axe. The concept of a cross-cut saw was known, but improvements in blade design and construction were still needed before saws could be used with success. When that day arrived in Muskoka, pairs of men would use the saw blade, one at each end, cutting high enough so they needn't bend, which was easier on their backs. That practice would leave thick, solid, pitch-filled stumps three or four feet high that lasted for decades, some still visible in sections of Muskoka today.

Until cross-saws became common, however, settlers like the Boyers and their neighbours faced even harder work. Their hands became calloused and leathery wielding their axes to bring down thousands of evergreens and hardwoods, working to fulfill their bargain for free grant land by clearing the acres they'd claimed. The homesteaders and the loggers both were making hundreds of clearings across Muskoka's forested landscape. Their reasons were different, the results the same.

Muskoka was becoming a maze of felled trees. The place was piled with logs, littered in slash, and dotted by brush piles. Logs awaited winter roads when teams of horses could pull them to rivers, to float to sawmills downstream at falls where the water's plunging power had been harnessed to spin the circular saw blade. Everywhere on these clear-cut lands, thin soils began eroding and newly exposed rock blinked at the sunlight for the first time in millennia.

In Macaulay Township James and Harry made a well-matched team, contributing their share of logs. Now aged forty and eighteen, they were healthy, men of growing strength and even greater determination, steadily creating stumps around the expanding Boyer homestead. Once felled, each tree had to be limbed, leaving one log and a hundred bulky branches that littered the ground. After they'd used the first several hundred logs to build the cabin, a barn, a shed, and an outhouse, other logs from clearing the land became surplus.

At first these thousands of extra logs did nothing to increase income. In fact, it was the opposite. The Boyers and every other Muskoka settler grew incensed to discover they had to pay stumpage fees to the government for the trees they were cutting down. Most had little or no money. This extra charge was a new hardship not mentioned in the free grant publicity pamphlets. It was harsh and unfair, an example of mindless provincial policy.

Once the Georgian Bay Lumber Company and other lumber concerns began operation, settlers got some financial relief because they had a market for all the logs they were producing, getting paid one dollar per thousand feet for logs dumped on the river. For homesteaders lucky to be close to a logging road or near a river, this income would help cover the government's royalty. But pioneers with lots deeper in the bush, unable to get their logs to a mill, now felt even more resentful because of their double disadvantage.

The more the Boyers discussed the stumpage fee issue with neighbours, the greater everybody's ire and sense of injustice grew. The Free Grant and Homestead Act made clear that all pine trees on a settler's property, as well as all minerals below ground, still belonged to the Crown. As a result, the provincial government's foresters and agents came through the woods counting all stumps to calculate the royalty fees owed to the provincial government. They did not distinguish pine timber taken by lumber contractors from trees brought down by homesteaders. To the government's representatives, implementing government policy, a stump was a stump was a stump. So the fees were extracted from the settlers, too. The land might be free, but not what was on it.

Resolved to get a better policy, the struggling homesteaders, bitter over this unexpected financial imposition, erupted in a major "timber dues protest." James Boyer was among those making the argument, including to A.P. Cockburn, Muskoka's member in the legislature and a lumberman, that they were not logging companies levelling virgin stands of white pine, pocketing money, and leaving a clear-cut wasteland. They were pioneer settlers working hard to clear the bush for farms, something that the same provincial government demanding stumpage fees obliged them to do to qualify for the "free" land. The government was being, they said, both hypocritical and exploitative.

The standoff was only resolved when the Ontario legislature passed an amendment to the Free Grant and Homestead Act that implemented a stumpage fee compromise. The new policy clarified that while all pine trees would continue to be reserved as property of the Crown, the dues payable on cutting them would no longer apply to any pine trees a settler felled in clearing his land and which he used for a dwelling, fencing, or fuel.

As a result of the exemption for trees used as fuel, hundreds of Muskoka homesteaders began burning their logs. The "fuel" loophole saw uncounted thousands of high-quality logs burned just to clear land. In a staggering waste of exceptional wood, again the consequence of provincial policy, log burning became standard for those opening the Muskoka frontier. Large burns proved a quick way to get rid of everything else. In addition to splendid logs, the slash, brush, chips, and deadwood on the forest floor would be incinerated, too. Homesteaders embraced the practice because they were anxious to begin farming.

—

Once spring turned to summer, drying out the last patches of dampness from melting snow shaded under piled logs, James fetched Robert Dollar, a neighbour who'd told him to seek him out when ready to burn the brushwood jumble off his "fields." When they returned, Dollar confirmed by looking at the clear sky and noting the steady breeze that, yes, it was "a good day for a burn."

For several weeks, James and Harry had been building piles of wood the way they'd been instructed by another seasoned homesteader, neighbour William Barron, whose previously cleared farm had natural springs that supplied pure drinking water to Bracebridge.

Preparing the site as directed proved heavy work. The tree trunks had been piled up, something like loosely building a log cabin, to create hollow squares. Then they'd thrown inside all the nearby easy-burning softwood slash, mostly pine, hemlock, and cedar. Other boughs and winter-dried branches from hardwoods, such as maple and oak, they piled on top of these squares, like roofs. At this stage the clearing resembled a primitive village, in the twilight.

Next they began arranging more of the brush into windrows between the square log structures. For this they used their supply of tree tops, lighter boughs, and underbrush, which seemed limitless after all their winter's axe work. They found a place for everything. William Barron had emphasized mixing the evergreen and hardwood so the burn would catch in the dry needles and then take hold in the solid wood. The piles also had to be loose enough, and set cross-wise, so the wind could fan the flames. At last all was ready. The clearing's ramshackle of waste, transformed into a systematic pattern of rows and piles, awaited only the right weather and a flame.

Muskoka's settlers had learned the art of a "burn," which was not like a campfire for cooking but a blast furnace with intense heat that took on a combustion force of its own, a firestorm. Creating one took real know-how. Hannah brought out a pail with the fiery embers she'd readied, on Dollar's instruction, into which Robert himself, James, and Harry each inserted long shards of pine kindling until their tips burst into flame. Each man then headed toward different sections of the clearing to ignite the small clumps of birch bark and pine branches set throughout the rows and under the logs structures.

At first all there was to watch were lazy curls of smoke clouding the scene. But after ten or perhaps twenty minutes, the drama escalated. Dozens of fires — or maybe a couple of hundred, it was hard to tell as dense smoke clouds filled the "clearing" — now crackled and hissed. They all backed away from the heat and sparks, watching flames dance upwards, higher and higher. Time passed, but Dollar and other veteran homesteaders who'd since come over to watch, impassive and waiting, said nothing. They hoped to enjoy the spectacle, but wanted to be sure the fire did not get out of control. Sections of Muskoka had been heavily burned over by rampaging forest fires. More than an hour passed, everyone's gaze fixed on the big timbers burning. Stumps close to the conflagration began to smoke, and then sprout flames of their own. It was a strange sensation to be mesmerized by something so dangerous and close. Hannah had backed all the way to the cabin, whose walls were scorching. Mary Ann took Annie and Nannie further away, back down the concession road.

In one sudden flash, the Boyers startled in alarm and their neighbours' solemn faces burst into huge smiles. A forceful explosion swooshed upward with a roaring blast. Its updraft turned the entire clearing into a single, noisy inferno. They had a "burn."

Flames raced high into the sky, burning embers and black chunks of wood ascending with them, as if shot out of a cannon. For hours the noise and heat roared from the opening in the forest. At dusk the biggest charred logs were still smoldering. Now a giant step closer to having a field to plant, the Boyers could not stop trembling from nervous excitement.

In Brooklyn they had never imagined a scene like this as part of "farming" in Muskoka.

—

Southern Ontario's flat lands, once stripped of the overgrowth of their trees, presented a clear run to farmers' ploughs and fertile soil for their seed. That pioneer experience led advocates for colonizing the empty northland to believe Muskoka's forested frontier would be just as yielding, despite surveyors' reports and cautions to the contrary.

The Boyers found to their chagrin, like most settlers on the Canadian Shield, that clearing the trees was not the final hurdle before growing crops. Next came the stones.

Cramped farm fields, first cleared of forest, and then freed of stumps, next began to sprout rocks. The boulders were worked to the surface by ploughing in spring and fall, and by winter's frost. The Boyers spent a lot of farming time harvesting, not vegetables, but stones. They were using their horse to pull, not a wagon loaded with hay to sell in town at a livery stable, but a stone-boat loaded with rocks to the edge of their field.

Field stone was a handy building material to pile up for barriers at the perimeter of fields, for the walls of root cellars and wells, and to construct barn foundations. But most settlers, including those in Macaulay, discovered a surfeit of such material. More rocks just kept appearing. Some farmers quipped, if asked what crops they had, "I'm growing stones!"

Often there were so many large stones that the effort to haul them off the field was too great, so weary Harry just made additional mounds throughout the Boyer fields, a series of rock pile islands. On some farms, after several years, these piles resembled taunting grave markers, monuments in the burial ground of a homesteader's earlier aspirations.

12

Moneyless in Muskoka

If the land was hard, the Boyers themselves were hard-up

Like other destitute settlers, the moneyless family realized that farming would not be enough to rely on for survival. In addition to living off their land, hunting game, and working Muskoka's barter economy, James and Harry adopted the well-known pattern of impoverished farmers everywhere, seeking other jobs to supplement whatever they could eke from the earth.

Some homesteaders with trades found intermittent work as the settlements began to grow, but Harry Boyer found no demand for polished stonework or his stone cutter's skills around pioneer Bracebridge. His chisels and polishing tools remained idle, stored in the barn. As an alternative Harry offered his strong back wherever someone needed manual labour.

Harry was seeking more than money or barter, however. He was struggling to find a footing for himself. If James was busy working out just who he was in Canada, his brother-in-law was unclear about his own identity and purpose, too. Harry had been easily persuaded to come to Muskoka. He was adventuresome and the idea of owning his own farm tantalized his youthful mind. Up to this point, his presence and willing strong arms had been invaluable for his sister's plan to escape with James from the United States and settle in the Canadian bush.

Yet now, facing the reality of Muskoka homesteading, Harry figured any time he would spend planting, tending, and harvesting crops would be just a fraction of the time he'd have to spend clearing more land, burning more brush, and removing more stones. He was losing interest. All he saw ahead, like his older brother Tom had envisaged, was a hard road to end up as nothing more than a back-bush moneyless farmer trying to trade some eggs for a pair of socks. Harry knew now his Muskoka farm would never compare to the productive operation in Westchester with its good soil and ideal growing conditions. He began to say, looking for something better to do with his life, "I've farmed enough for one lifetime."

By the time he and James finished building the Boyers' initial homestead cabin and outbuildings, exposed some fields by all their tree felling and dramatic burn, and got a reasonable amount of soil worked and planted with seeds, he decided to postpone doing anything more with his own Macaulay lot. Instead, he hired himself out working for other settlers, building their log cabins and clearing their land through the rest of that summer, and into the autumn of 1870.

As a second Muskoka winter loomed, neither Harry nor Mary Ann wanted to spend it in a small cabin again with Hannah, James, and two children. Mary Ann returned, with great relief, to Brooklyn. Harry, although having now made many log cabins, had not yet put up one for himself. Even though he seemed to be giving up on homesteading, he did not want to return to the United States. So, following other Muskoka men needing winter work, he signed on at a logging camp deep in the bush.

—

In camp, working hard for long hours and separated from the enjoyable company of Hannah and the rest of the family, Harry thought about the bleak times at the Westchester farm in New York, which in retrospect he now described, when telling others about it, as "slavery."

In the logging camp, he and the other men put in ten hours or more a day, in exchange for ten dollars a month plus their board. Rising at five o'clock in the morning when it "was still dark as midnight," the men sat down to a breakfast which, like all their other meals, "chiefly consisted of fat salt pork, molasses, bread or slapjacks, and green tea." Then it was off to work.

In the evening back in camp, the men made their own amusements. Harry enjoyed some respite and the men "often had hilarious times, as some would play mouth organs or an old fiddle while others would dance the sailor's hornpipe or Irish jig." Harry was popular as a step-dancer and a singer, possessing a fine tenor voice that could move people deeply. At times, cards or wrestling matches provided the evening's pass-time. Another popular game involved blind-folding two players, giving each a sock with a potato in the toe for weapons, then letting the "sock him" contest proceed "amidst an uproar of laughter and shouting from the onlookers." Other times, things got uglier, "the men growing rough when too much whiskey was in circulation" so that "numerous fights ensued" — Harry's way of describing a camp brawl, which could lead to revenge fights in the woods the next day.

Each camp had a store of supplies where such items as tobacco, socks, and warm clothing could be bought. Payment for whatever Harry acquired was deducted from his monthly wages. "When the camp broke up in the spring, very little money was left to take home."

With winter over, and his limited earnings in hand, Harry next signed on with a work crew putting through the first telegraph line to Rosseau from Parry Sound in the northwest corner of Muskoka. "It was a terrible task," he recorded, "as swamp and logs had to be overcome and blackflies made life miserable." His handkerchiefs were bloody, his "neck and face like a piece of raw beef steak" from the blackflies. He survived that, however, and once the telegraph line was in, Harry again worked between Rosseau and Parry Sound, this time with crews building several of the main roads.

While working in this part of Muskoka, Harry boarded with an Irish couple, the McCans, at the community of Rosseau. Mrs. McCan washed out his bloody handkerchiefs, and in repayment he'd go to the local tavern to coax her hard-drinking husband home, especially when he remained on a binge for several days. One time, when the "wild Irishman beat a man up so badly in a drunken fight the police were coming to arrest him," Harry did not coax him home but helped him escape. Harry "drove him all night out of the reach of the law." The road superintendent saw the pair pass in the wagon and told the police, but when questioned by the authorities, Harry "refused to say for what destination his friend was bound when he took the boat at Parry Sound." For "this act of kindness in helping Mr. McCan escape, I lost my job."

From Rosseau the eighteen-year-old adventurer, still needing to earn money, went by boat to Port Carling and got his first Muskoka work somewhat related to stone cutting. Harry found a hive of activity buzzing around the tiny community's disorganized cluster of workers' shanties, and sought out the contractor. The fact he'd worked with stone, though on a different scale, was recommendation enough for the site boss to put him to work dynamiting a channel through the solid rock to bypass Baisong Rapids. The locks between lakes Muskoka and Rosseau represented a major advance in the district's development, a project extracted from the government by A.P. Cockburn to allow his steamboats to ply between central Muskoka's upper and lower lakes, something young Harry could never have dreamed he'd be doing when he first studied the fulsome character A.P. Cockburn on their bumpy coach ride to Gravenhurst and heard about his steamboat.

That summer Harry met some Chippewas of the Ojibwa tribe who had come up from Lake Couchiching to stay at the place he was working, his first direct encounter with Native people. He was amazed, almost disbelieving, to learn a Native village called Obagawanung had earlier been in this spot along the Indian River. It consisted of some twenty log huts, with cleared land for garden plots growing potatoes, corn, and other vegetables. The inhabitants had dogs, and many birch bark canoes.

By the time Harry came upon the scene, Obejewanung had been replaced by Port Carling. The inhabitants had been cleared from their village and relocated north to much poorer Parry Island in Georgian Bay, under protest and with heart-breaking appeals to the governor general, Lord Monck, that went unanswered. Only a small reserve on part of the riverbank remained, to which some of the impoverished Chippewas now returned in summer. When Harry met them, they were troubled to see the changes being made as he and the others blasted rock and further transformed the setting.

While working on the lock and canal that summer, earning the best pay he had so far, attentive and ever-helpful Harry "looked after Mrs. McCan, making many a long trip on her behalf during the couple of years the old man was away, before he came back and took his punishment." He kept seeing her for months. The lively Irishwoman enjoyed Harry's singing, washed his clothes, and appreciated his handsome company as a definite trade-up from her absent husband, who was often drunk when around anyway. When he did come back, he was soon gone again, to serve his jail time. Harry continued to visit his companionable friend.

—

James, too, took steps to bring in money, but his path was less colourful than Harry's.

Broadening out was easy enough. Muskoka's fledgling settlements had more roles to go around than actors to fill them. James made a natural progression for someone who only months earlier had been making his livelihood in a Manhattan law office. Seasoned at doing property deals in New York and Brooklyn, and having already learned some features of Ontario land law from his own experiences, he now took a lawyer's detailed interest in the Free Grant and Homestead Act. Knowing the statute's provisions better than others gave him an advantage as "counsellor at law," another description he began using for himself, edging back into the role he'd seemingly left behind on Broadway Avenue.

Demand for his services grew, because more settlers arriving every week sought to register claims for free grants, or to buy or sell properties in Muskoka's land boom flurry. Earning money as a "land conveyancer," James was soon spending more time in the government offices on Dominion Street than on his fields in Macaulay Township. He drafted agreements of purchase and sale, checked titles, prepared deeds and other documents, and registering transfers of ownership, leaving a legacy of numerous real estate documents in the Bracebridge Registry Office bearing his name as witness to transactions, including on documents he had drawn up in his distinctive penmanship.

From all this work, he collected welcome fees. In the process, important adjustments were being made to his work-in-progress, the "James Boyer" persona.

Although he seemed to be practising law in all but name, James knew he could not hang out his shingle as a full-fledged lawyer without first becoming a member of Ontario's self-governing body for the legal profession, the Law Society of Upper Canada. To join would require evidence of his credentials as a lawyer and his qualifications to practise. That would lead directly to New York, where he had been a member of the state bar and actively practising in Manhattan, but under a different name, with a different wife and family, and as an American citizen. James found himself stranded in the gap between his new and former lives. He had no choice but to formally pay the price, although decades later he would admit in his own published accounts of this period that he'd been "doing conveyancing and other legal work."

At the always-busy Crown lands office, hub of real estate transactions and registrations, men pose outside for a mid-1880s photo. Camera-shy James Boyer was likely inside, registering deeds and checking titles.

A second opportunity to earn money came when James learned of a vacancy in one of Macaulay Township's remote schools. Few settlers were interested in teaching, especially away from the action, but that was a bonus as far as James was concerned, still uneasy about being found out.

Even fewer settlers were able to teach. The dire shortage of qualified instructors had already been demonstrated in Bracebridge. The village's first teacher, a weathered wreck named Foster, had learned whatever he knew during long sea-faring years in the Royal Navy. The sailor found teaching barefoot urchins so thirst-inducing that he frequently was forced to slip away from the one-room frame schoolhouse (atop the Queen's Hill on the town's main street, about where Bracebridge Public Library stands today), to the tavern next door to slake his immediate need. Often Foster only dimly remembered to return to his charges after school hours, when his pupils had already self-dismissed. One day the boy pupils even rolled Foster, dead drunk, down the Queen's Hill from the school as part of their improvised athletics curriculum.

In such a talent pool James, who had never taught a day in his life, stood out as exceptionally qualified. He was contracted to teach in Macaulay School No. 5, some seven miles from Bracebridge, on the Second and Third Concessions. Enrolment for all his grades totalled thirty pupils. For the next two years, in addition to working with land by farming it himself and conveyancing it for others, James also, as he himself put it, "conducted educational instruction among the children of the district."

A pragmatic teacher, he soon began to supplement the official curriculum. Being a trained veteran from the Crimean War, he "taught the young idea how to shoot." In James's account of these years, published in 1905 by the *Muskoka Herald*, he would again use that odd "young idea" phrase, which he'd come across in the books of Charles Dickens and Herman Melville. However described, his extra-curricular teaching of marksmanship and rifle operation provided a valuable lesson for youngsters living in Muskoka's wilds. He gave instruction to the girls as well as the boys. Hunting game was helping James keep his own family fed. He knew this was an important part of homesteading life, and believed well-rounded junior Muskokans should be able to shoot a rifle as well as read and write.

Other survival skills depended on fortitude, and luck. Returning once from Toronto in the first week of November, James boarded the stage at Washago, just as it was getting dark. There were about six passengers on board, including a young lady who had been to Orillia to purchase a new hat. "All went well till about four miles from Gravenhurst," he wrote, "except that the rain fell in torrents, there was a very high wind, and it was as dark as a stack of black cats — but that was not thought much of in travelling in Muskoka at that period." Then, just as the stage had descended a steep hill and began onto a crossway over a swamp, "the horses went too near the edge of the logs. Over went the stage, horses, mail bags, and passengers into the soft mud of the swamp." James had been sitting out on the front seat with John Harvie, the driver, but after the vehicle went over, found himself "lying on my back with a mail bag on my breast." The horses, in trying to regain their feet, "distributed the mud, impartially and plentifully," over the passengers, the vehicle, and everything within range.

"It was no small undertaking to detach the horses, get them on their feet, and lift the vehicle onto the crossway as there was no lantern. You could not even strike a match because of the high wind, and the rain still descended in torrents." By about one o'clock Sunday morning the stage reached the steamboat wharf, "and the *Wenonah* received on board half a dozen of the most disreputable looking passengers that ever boarded a steamboat in Muskoka, but not one of whom had received the slightest injury."

——

Besides earning much needed money as a land conveyancer and teacher, James discovered that this incessant activity kept his mind engaged, too busy and weary to think much about the past crises in his life or the fate of his wife Eliza or their daughter Annie. Though he had left them behind, he would never forget them. His transformation in Canada might be far-reaching, but could never be complete.

13

—

Northern Advocates

It was not only the frontier's roads and survey lines that made twists and turns, but also James's career as he continued to look for additional ways to earn money.

It turned out that his work conveyancing properties at the land registry office, and his duties as recording steward at the Methodist Church, which he and Hannah joined shortly after arriving in Bracebridge, had been creating a local reputation for him as a man who prepared documents well and gave attentive care to details.

There were other dimensions to how people saw him, as well. Many found him reserved and deferential, yet forthcoming with practical suggestions if asked. He was known to be a hardworking homesteader, which meant he was familiar with conditions faced by Macaulay Township folks; and a dependable teacher in one of the local schools, which showed he could assume responsibility for others beyond his immediate family. The funny thing, to some, was how he left the odd impression of being both furtive and dignified at the same time. Others just thought it reticence, and judged this aspect to be another of James Boyer's assets.

Now that Macaulay was a stand-alone township, with population large enough to withdraw from the "united townships" arrangement with Draper and the others, the time had come to set up its own municipal government. On January 1, 1871, a council was elected in Macaulay's inaugural elections. Meeting on January 16, the new township council discussed James Boyer's qualities, considered him the ideal person to serve them as township clerk, and offered the job. James did not hesitate for a minute to accept the part-time position.

The clerkship could be combined with his other tasks, and would provide a modest but dependable trickle of additional cash. Even more important, occupying a neutral office with a role in government was an ideal next step for James as he sought to establish himself in Canada. It was, for Hannah, a pleasing sign that her husband was rising in the esteem of others.

For the next six months, everything went well. James and the councillors developed a harmonious relationship. As for the township itself, settlers continued to arrive and push along the crude roadways on Macaulay's concession lines which subdivided the township into a neat grid, or at least such approximate rectangles as surveyors and road-builders could manage when crossing lakes, circumventing swamps, and skirting rock outcroppings. Macaulay's new homesteaders were clearing bush and erecting cabins everywhere. Settlements such as Fraserburg and Stoneleigh, and part of Falkenburg at Macaulay's west boundary with Monck, now dotted the township map. The largest settlement was Bracebridge. With all the activity, Macaulay's council had important duties to perform. The township clerk liked the work and felt he was really hitting his stride.

Then, just when James believed he had his activities nicely balanced, into his life blew a human dynamo named Thomas McMurray.

McMurray wanted him to become editor of his newspaper.

—

No ordinary person could have started a newspaper in Ontario's northern districts in this era. Only someone with Thomas McMurray's unique combination of advocacy, entrepreneurship, and irrepressible energy was a ready match for Muskoka's daunting pioneer conditions. A big man with a full face, smooth forehead, and long black beard, McMurray stood out from others, a man possessed by a grand mission.

Born in Scotland in 1831, he'd sailed to America and Australia as a young man, then settled in Ireland, married, and begun a family. But the Irish were aching from famine and disease, distraught by drink, and crowded into filthy cities. Despairing of this decadent scene, resolute McMurray, now thirty and having seen an alternative, departed Ireland with his wife and children in May 1861, sailing from Londonderry straight back into the promise of the New World.

When he reached Toronto, he rented a house where he deposited his dependants, and then pressed on north, alone. At McCabe's Landing (Gravenhurst), he rented a flat-bottom boat, rowed it up Lake Muskoka, then further up the Muskoka River to North Falls (Bracebridge) — clearly a man on a quest.

Upon landing, the outgoing Thomas McMurray was greeted by the hospitable James Cooper in as exuberant an exchange as Muskoka had yet seen. The district's newest immigrant spent that night at Cooper's camp near the thundering waterfalls, feeling the fresh energy of the place surge not only past him, but within him as well. Bright the next morning, McMurray pressed his craft into the newly surveyed township of Draper by rowing up the nearby south branch of the Muskoka River. Part way he encountered a barrier in the form of most scenic waterfalls.

McMurray was overwhelmed by the grandeur of the canyon's rock walls facing him as he gazed up. He became mesmerized watching the

A real pioneer, Thomas McMurray was an idealist, visionary, and entrepreneur who became a political leader in central Muskoka, promoted the district's free land to immigrants, started the north country's first newspaper, and hired James Boyer as its editor.
(Engraved sketch by Damoreau. Boyer Family Archives)

high, narrow funnels of white water plunging into the abyss, dancing wildly on the rocks, dispersing spray into dozens of colourful rainbows. He felt small in the thundering roar. He grew intoxicated inhaling, until he could fill his lungs no more, the heady scent of fresh pines, churning water, and musky wet rocks. He beheld in awe the black water with its crystal bubbles swirling past his boat, the green vest of pines dressing the cliffs above, and the summer sky with billowy soft clouds in the sunshine heavens above. Thomas McMurray said a prayer.

Ashore, he clamoured up the rugged steep rocks and, after a while, tracked down the road crew James Cooper told him he'd find in this vicinity. The men were extending a colonization road into Muskoka, under the charge of contractor Richard Hanna.

McMurray and Hanna met most happily. In the isolated wilderness, the bush-whacked contractor got a lift to his spirits from the energetic interloper who looked him square in the eyes when he talked. In turn, the would-be homesteader was delighted to come across someone knowledgeable about the very area in which he hoped to locate his new farm.

The latter had no difficulty persuading the former to take a break. While guiding the prospective settler, the road builder began catching up on news from the outside. They picked their way east along the unfinished Peterson Road to examine some good land Hanna had scouted near the next set of falls upstream. About two miles along, shortly before the Peterson Road swung south for a couple concessions, the promising land came into view along the river's banks.

McMurray selected what would later measure out some four hundred acres, when his claim and his subsequent purchase of adjacent lots were taken together. This property along the riverbank and inland was good farmland on which he would prosper for the next eight years, a fact that reinforced McMurray's favourable impression about Muskoka's agricultural possibilities as a whole.

During their conversation, McMurray learned how Hanna was building the western extension of the Peterson Road into Muskoka because the government hoped this colonization track would stimulate the district's settlement and its economic development. It was part of a network of some two dozen such roads being scratched through the unsettled interior of the province, this one to connect with the colonization road being pushed further into the bush from the south, a section of which McMurray had already travelled crossing the Severn River to reach McCabe's Landing. That "Muskoka Road," it was envisaged, would reach the Muskoka River in this central part of the district, connecting with the "Peterson Road" here at Muskoka Falls, the most majestic and scenic place in all Muskoka. Hanna said with great enthusiasm that it was thus the ideal town-site for a major municipality.

McMurray was beside himself. He had landed dead center in a new society even before it had begun.

The prospect of this virgin territory being opened up to newcomers keen on making a fresh start in their stale lives struck Thomas McMurray with the force of a religious revelation. A new social order for a truly better life could arise here, should arise here, *must* arise here. He now saw that this "New Jerusalem" would not be just for the McMurray family alone on this farmland in Draper Township, as he'd first vaguely imagined when escaping the cesspool of human decadence in Ireland, but for hundreds, nay thousands, of others wanting freedom from societies in decline. He could, by God's mysterious working, fulfill his true destiny as a leader, a champion, indeed a Prophet, of what was to come.

Seized by this shimmering idea, Thomas McMurray became infused with zealousness, like Canada's temperance preachers crusading to eliminate debilitating alcohol and establish a better world, or like Mormon leader Brigham Young leading a wagon train of true believers through rugged 1840s wilderness to create their own New World in Utah. McMurray would espouse settlement of Muskoka as a haven for those wishing the new life, a heaven on earth.

—

Before this glorious new chapter in human progress could be written, with homesteaders converging over the Peterson Road and up the Muskoka Road to be reborn in Muskoka, McMurray first had to install himself in the district.

The man's persuasive charm and ready dollars proved enough encouragement for Richard Hanna and his work crew to leave off road-building for a spell and redirect their energies to clearing ten of McMurray's newly claimed acres. Into the bargain went the building of a house.

A month later McMurray returned with his wide-eyed family, now retrieved from Toronto. Wife and children could not wait to see the wilderness paradise he'd been endlessly praising. During his absence Hanna's men had cleared the acreage and erected the house, but no roof was yet on it. So the exhilarated McMurray family enjoyed their first Muskoka nights in the best of both worlds, sleeping indoors but under the stars.

Focused on his new mission, McMurray organized Draper Township's few other scattered settlers to sign an 1863 petition requesting that while surveyors were in Muskoka laying out the new roads, they also survey a townsite and lay out lots. He took the petition to Lindsay's James W. Dunsford, who represented Victoria County and Muskoka District in the legislature. In turn, the government was prompt to order the townsite plan for "Muskokaville," because creating communities dovetailed with its program of filling the territory with people. McMurray's initiative to lay groundwork for a new town signalled to his neighbours that this man, barely off his ship from across the Atlantic, was a born leader landed in their very midst. When the "United Townships of Draper, Macaulay, Stephenson, and Ryde" were organized in 1868, they elected him their first reeve, top political office for the four townships.

Charismatic and entrepreneurial McMurray was an ardent, unrelenting advocate for land settlement because it was key to creating his New Jerusalem, a refuge for the families he'd seen in Ireland and elsewhere who needed to start afresh and build better lives, and with it, a better society. It would be more than a refuge, but a citadel of light and honourable living. He pondered what it would take to get things moving.

After the northern districts had first been opened for settlement, arrival of settlers was sporadic and light. McMurray and his family had themselves been among the earliest trickling into the empty north. Settlement was still so sparse that several townships — here it had taken four — had to combine for local government just to get enough people to do anything. More, he knew, must be done to bring people to Muskoka.

McMurray spread his urgent vision to others. One was road-builder Richard Hanna, who'd played a big role for Muskoka getting McMurray's evangelistic mission launched in the first place. Once his road contract was completed, Hanna returned with his wife, Christina, excited to become a homesteader and a founding father of Muskokaville, too, having already seen the place's great future potential.

Hanna applied for a post office and became first postmaster at "Muskoka Falls," its improved name. At McMurray's side, Hanna would have continued to advance local expansion and become a major pillar for the rising community. But when the Civil War broke out in the United States, although many did everything they could to avoid the carnage, Richard Hanna could not wait to enlist. He went south, leaving Christina with their sons William, James, Richard, Peter, and Joseph Francis, and their daughter Rachel. They never saw him again. Richard Hanna died fighting as a volunteer in the Union Army.

Meanwhile, McMurray was reading letters in the Toronto newspapers from some settlers complaining about bleak farming conditions in Haliburton County to the east of Muskoka. Such whiners angered him. He felt their plaintive messages discouraged others from coming to Muskoka. He, after all, was doing so well on his Draper acreage that he had even bought more land. Still believing his vision for this northland would be fulfilled, McMurray was doing whatever he could as reeve to spur settlement, urging the provincial government to speed land settlement by stronger incentives.

Finally, when the Free Grant and Homestead Act became law in 1868, McMurray joyously believed the future of his vision was secure. Ontario's new government had included the incentive of free land for any qualifying homesteader. Empty Muskoka, Parry Sound, and Nipissing districts were each just biding their time until receiving countless thousands more settlers who, like him, could leave the diseased, drink-ridden, and impoverished Old World and make a fresh start with dignity as homesteaders on their own land.

In fact, settlers who began arriving the very next year, though hoping to make a fresh start, were not just coming from the Old World. Some would be leaving behind the "New World," too, coming from places like Brooklyn.

—

At the same time the Boyers were anxious to get to Muskoka, McMurray was becoming restless to leave.

After eight years on his Draper farm, McMurray had taken stock. In his grand vision, the key to settlement, the opportunity for social redemption and a better life, the promise that could make Muskoka the New Jerusalem, was *free land*. But because no land rush yet corresponded with the vision he'd had, he now became convinced something was still missing. Even though Ontario's legislature had voted to support the government's contentious plan to open Muskoka using "free grant" settlement, McMurray now saw that what the development program lacked was an effective communications plan.

Yes, some newspaper advertisements, posters, and pamphlets were circulating in New York, London, and other major cities in the northern United States and Britain. Yes, Canada's immigration agents, and spokesmen for the railways as well, were in these and other cities delivering recruitment speeches. But a really successful approach, McMurray reasoned, required an authoritative publication that could continuously inspire new recruits to the northland by informing them, from practical experience, about the advantageous new life awaiting them in the free grant districts.

McMurray's ideas meshed with the Ontario government's aggressive program to fill the province's undeveloped northern lands with homesteaders, itself part of the larger project being undertaken by John A. Macdonald's national government to push surveyors, settlers, and a railway into the "empty" Prairies. The strategy in both cases was to staunch America's expansionist desire in the post-Civil War period, by sheer physical presence of Canadian settlers, in the open and beckoning stretch from northern Ontario to the Rocky Mountains. The Yanks were keen to annex this northern territory, many Americans now gripped by their bellicose belief that it was the "manifest destiny" of the United States to occupy the entire North America continent. More than he could realize from his vantage point in Draper Township, Thomas McMurray was about to become an important player in this Canadian defense policy, as would James Boyer, although he, too, didn't yet know it.

All of McMurray's enthusiastic plans might have come to naught had he not reluctantly accepted the truth that his own community of Muskoka Falls was moribund. Nearby Bracebridge, though far less scenic, had become the magnet for growth and economic development in the region. It was, after all, the first place he'd landed when rowing upriver, before retracing his route a bit and proceeding up the Muskoka River's south branch. Since then, others, and Cockburn's all-important steamboats, had likewise been drawn to Bracebridge, head of navigation on the river's more accessible north branch. McMurray could also see that Bracebridge was likely to prosper, while his more idyllic Muskoka Falls settlement languished, because Bracebridge Falls, although smaller than South Falls, nevertheless channelled a vast amount of water power, far more than was needed for its pioneer mills, but with the crucial difference that Bracebridge's cataracts were more readily harnessed due to the more open terrain around them.

These factors made McMurray reconsider how, in the beginning, the conjunction of the Peterson and Muskoka roads pointed to Muskokaville as the community of the future. That had been before advent of the steamboats. The more he studied the overall free grant region's geography and transportation, the more he appreciated the village of Parry Sound as a pivotal mid-point for all three districts. Just as Gravenhurst and Bracebridge were pulling ahead as well-situated transshipment centres, Parry Sound, already the most settled of the northern communities, appeared to have the greatest potential of all. Its harbour on Georgian Bay connected Parry Sound to the Great Lakes by ship, while inland, the village was linked to the interior country by wagon and coach along the new colonization roads to Rosseau and Falkenburg, and from Falkenburg both south to Bracebridge and Gravenhurst, and north to Utterson, Hoodstown, Huntsville, and beyond.

Thomas McMurray decided to relocate, determined to be at the centre of the mainland settlement action.

—

In August 1869, just before the Boyers arrived in Bracebridge, Draper's pioneer settler auctioned off everything at his farm and sold the property to the Trethewey family, who took over his good acreage and gave their name to the adjacent falls. McMurray took the proceeds of sale and moved his family to Parry Sound.

Relocating was only part of the plan. Upon arrival he immediately set up the equipment for publication of what would become the first newspaper in Ontario's northern districts. By ship it had been possible to transport a heavy printing press and the requisite cases of metal type to the village. With a publishing day of Tuesday, the first issue appeared quickly, on September 14, 1869.

The weekly's masthead showed his intended reach and ambitious purpose: *The Northern Advocate and General Advertiser for the Free Grant Districts of Parry Sound, Muskoka, & Nipissing.* With no other newspaper in the north, why not stake claim to it all? Thomas McMurray was nothing if not ambitious. And his vision really did encompass the entire region open to settlers.

Of course nobody called the paper by its full name, just the *Northern Advocate* — not only a clear indication of the publication's mission, but the very definition of the publisher himself.

As the only newspaper for Ontario's northland, the *Advocate* soon carried advertisements from all three districts, as well as businesses in Orillia, Collingwood, and Toronto serving the north. A four-page broadsheet, about a third of its space was used for ads, the rest given over to news and features. After just a few months, the Parry Sound publisher proclaimed his labours "successful," noting that, "A great many copies go to England, Ireland, and Scotland for the information of intending immigrants, and through its advocacy many have been induced to settle in our midst."

However, McMurray was again focused on location. He'd discovered that for both Muskoka and Parry Sound districts, the inland lakes and rivers region formed a separate universe from the Georgian Bay shoreline. Despite the two zones' proximity inside a common political boundary, their culture, economy, and natural features were different. The map he'd studied when deciding to move to Parry Sound had not lied. It had just been silent about social, cultural, and economic dynamics. McMurray, ever decisive in his actions, moved his family back again to Bracebridge because, as he now explained, "Bracebridge was more central" to the larger region.

Thus, in the summer of 1870, when the *Northern Advocate*'s printing press arrived in Bracebridge after being hauled with difficulty over the rough colonization road from Parry Sound, Muskoka's capital became the new home of the only newspaper north of the Severn River. McMurray not only relocated his sheet from one district to another, but made other changes as well. Publication day was shifted from Tuesday to Friday. The masthead was set in more authoritative typeface. David Courtney, a skilled printer whose craft was indispensable in producing a new issue of the paper each week, was hired.

And James Boyer, homesteader, conveyancer, family man, municipal clerk, and ardent reader, was enticed by Thomas McMurray to assume "editorial supervision of the paper."

—

The publisher and editor had met several times before, including at a major banquet at the Dominion House hotel in Bracebridge the previous September. On that occasion Ontario's premier, John Sandfield Macdonald, and other leaders from the district and province gathered to toast their apparent success in "opening up Muskoka."

McMurray's speech that night included a proposal to the premier that Muskoka become a provisional county, a higher status in municipal government hierarchy than its "district" designation. That suggestion was just one example of the many ways the man exuded confidence about Muskoka's future, and promoted plans to advance it.

That September night's celebration gave James a glimpse of something grander he could be a part of, too. It could somehow even justify everything that had caused him to restart his life in Muskoka with a different name and new identity.

14

An Editor's Life

Becoming editor of Ontario's first northern newspaper, an astonishing advance for James, came at a price.

McMurray, with Boyer's full knowledge and secret pride, had printed in his first Bracebridge issue that the newspaper was "under the editorial supervision of Mr. James Boyer, our present Village Clerk." That created problems.

Despite the small community's need for people to double up roles and James's belief that he could handle the work of both jobs, the neutrality required of a municipal clerk did not mesh with the possibility that, as an editor, he might have to take stances critical of local government. As well, the work of clerk and editor would demand Boyer's time and attention on different tasks with different people in separate premises simultaneously. Even more, it appeared the *Northern Advocate* was somehow controlled by, or authorized by, or officially connected to, the village of Bracebridge. The councillors bridled at the implication.

As well, calling Boyer "Village Clerk," when in fact he was clerk of the township, was to the council an example of McMurray's puffery. He, of course, wanted to impress distant readers about Muskoka's state of development, and thought an image of "village life" evoked a more pleasing and familiar scene for potential immigrants than "township life." Even though Bracebridge had other businesses such as hotels and barber shops, bars and general stores, all vaunting their status with overstated names, Macaulay councillors didn't like the way McMurray exaggerated.

Perhaps even Boyer, too, for all they knew, was guilty of trying to make things look better than they were.

Even if McMurray's tendency as a promoter to overstate things did not perturb the Macaulay councillors all that much, because civic pride and local boosterism was a currency most of them traded in, too, the real truth was that McMurray's friendship with Liberals, including A.P. Cockburn, did. Most members of council were Conservatives. The community throbbed with continuous, heated discussion of politics, and partisan differences were as intense as denominational separation in religion. They did not want their clerk, Boyer, in the employ of McMurray, who was, although important as a newspaper publisher, still just another municipal politician like them, and worse, a Grit. James had been appointed clerk because he'd remained pleasantly neutral in a highly divided community.

Macaulay's councillors said Boyer could not have it both ways. There could be no such animal as a "political" clerk. James, feeling quite embarrassed, acknowledged the incompatibilities. He resigned as clerk of Macaulay Township, to throw his lot in, at higher pay, with Thomas McMurray.

In August 1870 his promising career in municipal administration had come to an end, just eight months after it began.

Having forfeited one great avenue along which to remake his Canadian life, as municipal clerk for Muskoka's most dynamic township, James would now fully embrace the other, his new job as the *Advocate*'s editor. For a man adept at changing roles, it would not be hard.

The closer he got to know and work with McMurray, one of the most visionary and enterprising of all Muskoka promoters, the more James found a man who shared much with Muskoka's other entrepreneurial evangelist, A.P. Cockburn. Both of them, and James as well, held views that lined up with Liberal positions. But each man was also an independent sort who, even more than a party, believed in Muskoka. James increasingly viewed the district's future from McMurray's and

Cockburn's higher plateau. He was not a player the way they were, with money and business connections, but he could embrace his publisher's bolder view of the free grant territories, and did. It was, almost, like converting to a new religion.

Annoyed that Macaulay's council had stripped his new editor of the pivotal clerk's office, which initially made McMurray see Boyer as his best person to edit and supervise his newspaper, he still believed him right for the role. He was, after all, a homesteader himself, doing practical things to convert the dream of successful agricultural settlement into reality. He had been clearing and farming his own acres, conveyancing titles to new homesteaders at the land registry office, and promoting good farming practices through the Agricultural Society he'd helped form. He also could write, and had a certain literary flare. If McMurray wanted to give readers of his newspaper information and advice "from practical experience" about settlement in the free grant districts, Boyer was his man.

James was even better suited than McMurray understood for the *Northern Advocate*'s mission of drawing settlers from Britain and the United States. From his days of prominence in the Brooklyn Britannia Benevolent Association, a past connection he did not disclose to anyone in Muskoka, he knew the mind of ex-patriot Brits living in the U.S., as well as the impulses that drove Americans themselves. In that very setting where the *Northern Advocate* was now trying to make an appeal for immigrants, he'd learned about Muskoka's free land in the first place. He knew perfectly how fear and self-interest could motivate others to come to Canada and claim some of Muskoka for themselves. He knew free grant lands, in short, from both ends.

James, like an acolyte being inducted, listened as McMurray explained his three missions for their paper. One was to serve the local community by publishing news, commercial information, and entertaining stories in which the readers could see themselves reflected, giving them a feeling of belonging to a real place, drawing together the scattered people across the north's free grant districts with a cohesive sense of the whole. Another reason for the *Northern Advocate*'s existence was the overarching program of populating Muskoka, and its sister districts to the north, with worthy immigrants from the British Isles and the United States desirous of a better life, by artful praise and astute promotion of the *free* land to be had. "This," James heard McMurray say with emphasis, "is the *Advocate*'s main business." Finally, the newspaper would espouse good living through moral uplift, which mostly centred on McMurray's campaign for temperance in the use of alcohol, which, to James, increasingly seemed like a crusade for outright prohibition.

James sometimes rode into town to the Advocate building, some four miles from the Macaulay homestead, leaving his horse at Samuel Armstrong's livery stable, but he usually walked the distance so the steed could remain for farm work, or for Hannah to use to come into the village if need be. Some people thought the *Northern Advocate* was located on Manitoba Street, the village's "downtown" commercial thoroughfare, because the most prominent sign to be seen, high on the south side of the Orange Hall, proclaimed NORTHERN ADVOCATE. That was, however, just advertising space McMurray had paid for. The Advocate offices and print shop, where James headed, were housed in a large frame building up on Dominion Street, part of the "public square" section of the village where the land registry, the jail, other government buildings, and hotels clustered. The building stood on high ground, at Dominion's southwest corner with Quebec Street. The newspaper's premises did not exactly lack for prominent signage, either. In addition to advertising NORTHERN ADVOCATE in capital letters full-width across the front, and again down the building's side, a further sign at the front declared: THOMAS MCMURRAY, PROPRIETOR & PUBLISHER.

Soon James had fallen into the weekly rhythms of producing a newspaper, getting the ads in so David Courtney could set them in display

At the corner of Dominion and Quebec streets in Bracebridge, the prominent Northern Advocate building became a hub where James Boyer edited the weekly newspaper and, across the street at the registry office, continued to conveyance land.

type, harvesting information from the city papers and his countryside contacts, writing reports on meetings held and announcements about events forthcoming. As Monday turned to Tuesday, then blurred into Wednesday, intensity built to get everything done. A publication date of Thursday meant that by late in the day Wednesday David had to be able to start printing the second run of that week's edition.

James and the *Advocate*'s indispensable printer worked closely together. David Courtney set the type by hand, using a type-setter's "stick," which he'd adjust to the width of the newspaper's columns, then fill row-by-row with letters picked, one at a time, from a wooden type-case. Each piece of type had its own compartment in the case. The foundry-cast type included each of the twenty-six letters of the alphabet, the same twenty-six in capitals, all numerals from zero to nine, punctuation such as periods, commas, and quotation marks, and spacing. For commonly used letters such as "e" there were more of the small pieces of type than for rarer used ones such as "z." When James handed David some copy, he'd prop the news report above the type case and begin to assemble the letters into words, the words into sentences, the sentences into paragraphs. His fingers flew. His eyes moved back and forth from the copy to the type-case to the stick. He knew by rote where to fetch a "w" or find an "a." The process was the same if the copy was for an advertisement, but a different case of type with larger letters, and much more spacing, was used.

Once the story or ad or public notice had been set in type, David carefully slid the assembled letters into a "form" on a large, flat stone counter where the pages were being made up. The so-called form was a rectangular metal frame, a little larger than the size of a newspaper page. When all the stories and ads for that page in the next edition of the newspaper were complete, he'd lock everything tightly in place using narrow wooden blocks and metal wedges along the top and side of the frame. Then he'd carefully turn it up on its side, and lift the heavy assembly over onto the *Advocate*'s flatbed press, lowering it with great care to avoid a disastrous "spill" of all the contents, thousands of individual pieces of type. One more page was then ready.

When two pages were on the press, which would be the second and third pages of the *Advocate*'s four-page broadsheet, David would leave off typesetting to start printing the first run of the papers. About a thousand copies were printed each week, one at a time. The metal type was rolled by hand with printer's ink, then a single sheet was laid across the two inked pages, then a flat press the size of both pages was lowered by hand to force the paper onto the type. David then released the press by raising it up again, removed the printed sheet, and set it aside for the ink to dry, taking care not to let it smudge or smear. He then repeated the process, another 999 times. James often helped with this printing process, lifting the printed sheet away to start drying while David rolled on ink for the next impression. After a time, when there was no place left to leave the sheets to dry, James gathered the driest, handling them lightly, to make room for more.

When a thousand or more had been printed, the job was half done. The *Advocate's* front and back pages, kept for the latest news, were finished on Wednesday, with James hurriedly writing the report of a court case that morning or a barn fire at noon, which David set into type and got into space kept open in the waiting front page for such fresh news. If there were no last minute items, David had a poem, or a bit of national or international news cribbed from the city papers, ready to insert instead.

Then the printing resumed, now on the blank sides of the sheets already printed. Once dried and folded, another copy of the four-page weekly was ready for readers, out on Dominion Street, in the United States, or across the seas in Great Britain. Mailing out the papers was another of the publishing tasks to which James turned his hand.

The *Northern Advocate* began to promote the need for libraries. James ran a weekly "Poetry" feature. Below that, under the heading "Literature," he serialized a novel from week to week, inspired by the way a London newspaper ran Charles Dickens's stories in installments. It was a handy expedient to fill space when there was little news or a shortage of advertisers, and an extra way to make readers want to buy the following week's edition to see what happened next. It also helped get each week's paper ready in the final rush. David Courtney set more of the novel into type in the quiet times of the week, after he'd finished other chores like washing the last edition's type with kerosene and redistributing each piece back into its respective compartment in the type cases. On Wednesday, as a final step, he'd use as little or as much of the novel as needed to fill any remaining space at press time. Books had many roles such as filler for dramatic news that never broke.

Moral uplift embraced a wider gamut than merely ridding society of demon rum's evil scourge. "Moral maxims" began dotting the paper's columns, many addressed to young girls: *"If you want to marry, do not court or attract the attention of gentlemen. A little wholesome indifference will be more likely to accomplish the object."*

A later week's tip for the blossoming female: *"Consider that it is better to be a woman than a wife. Do not degrade your sex by making your whole existence turn on the pivot of matrimony."*

When it came to alcohol, Boyer simply deferred to McMurray, who was keen to write whatever the *Advocate* published on that topic himself, anyway. As for other areas of emphasis in the paper on "proper conduct and ethical living," James, as a churchman, could not help but embrace the general concept as McMurray espoused it, yet he seemed more circumspect, perhaps more accepting of life's deeper currents and wider meanings, than his publisher, the ardent preacher for moral uplift. McMurray was a disciple of God; James, of William Shakespeare.

As for the paper's "main business" of land settlement, McMurray was explicit in one issue that his paper's mission was "to bring the Free Grant Lands now at the disposal of the Government prominently before the notice of those who want to find homes. Every opportunity will be seized upon to open up and develop this Great Territory." To that end James published travel schedules, ship and train fares, and practical tips for the journey to guide those coming in search of land, as well as practical hints from those already farming in the districts.

James was in his element with that sort of thing. Hannah had shown him her treasured last letter from her father, which Joseph Boyer had written aboard the sailing ship *Webster*, telling the girls "not to wear crinolines on board ship" because it made climbing the holds hard, but to "bring pots, anything practical, and a bushel of potatoes and onions mixed in a sack." Readers of the *Northern Advocate* would now get sensible, explicit instructions like that, part of what McMurray called information from "practical experience."

All meetings of importance in the districts were chronicled by the newspaper, from reports of township council and Agricultural Society meetings, to accounts of loyalist organizations and music concerts. Week after week the columns of the *Advocate* imparted a cumulative impression to readers far away that Muskoka and the other districts were lively, cultured, organized, and engaging places to live. James rounded out current reports with accounts that suggested a rich heritage for newly settled Muskoka, publishing reminiscences of first settlers and the early history of the districts.

The editor not only contacted other settlers for informative articles and helpful tips on the successful homesteading experience. James began to write about his own lessons and experiences. Perhaps subconsciously, he was striving to create a new narrative, one that affirmed it had not been a mistake, but a stroke of genius, to open rocky and swampy Muskoka for homesteaders to settle. And most satisfying of all, he was beginning to reinterpret, in his own mind at least, his and Hannah's escape from their Brooklyn straitjacket as something grander than the desperate flight of two people in love. Their saga would always remain the love story of a man who gave up all for a woman. Yet now, seen through McMurray's exalted vision of Muskoka rather than an escape artist's desperate perspective in Brooklyn, James's view of what happened began to take on a somewhat warmer glow.

Thomas McMurray, James Boyer, and David Courtney had reason to feel satisfaction. Their efforts began attracting additional settlers, while the *Northern Advocate*'s content was helping form a sense of community among those already in Muskoka. Their broadsheet had become a community bulletin board. On the front page, in the "Business Directory," lawyers, printers, and land surveyors advertised their services. Notes about world events jostled alongside reports from the legislature, local doings, and, from time to time, an obituary or two. Weekly produce prices for wheat, oats, barley, peas, flour, potatoes, beef, mutton, bacon, pork, eggs, butter, apples, and hay were reported, when in supply. Advertisements notified readers about the latest arrivals of dry goods and clothing in local stores.

The constant work of getting the paper together made James feel at the very centre of things, running a clearing house for all that mattered.

He even took a hand in people's efforts to locate someone who'd disappeared into the frontier, running such items as this: "PERSONAL — *We copy the following from the Globe:-* J.H. Kerr, send me your address. John Bensey, Endicott & Co., Detroit, Mich. U.S. / Northern papers please copy." Men were always disappearing. The *Advocate's* editor kept a cautious eye out for any similar personal advertisement from Brooklyn.

Coverage of British and Canadian political news and constitutional events found welcome space in the *Advocate's* columns, both McMurray and Boyer being "strongly attached to the British Crown and Constitution," while the back of their editorial hand was given to pro-U.S. tendencies after they made clear that "the cry of 'annexation' shall find no sympathy in the *Advocate*, while true loyalty shall ever have a ready and willing platform." The man, who in the United States fourteen years earlier had renounced Queen Victoria upon becoming an American, lived no more. James's role in Bracebridge's loyalist societies, which had its foretaste in his involvement at Brooklyn with the Britannia

Crammed with practical information, news, advertisements for local services, poetry, and serialized novels, the paper James Boyer edited reflected the emerging Muskoka community back to itself and focused the fledgling district's activity and agenda — especially the attraction of more immigrants.

Benevolent Association, was becoming an empowering link for him as he recovered fully his British identity. The *Advocate* channelled Britannic sentiment to prospective immigrants in Britain, as well as to Americans of British stock.

As for specific issues that James championed, the newspaper, as he recorded in later accounts, "not only advocated vote by ballot, the abolition of statute labour, and a change in the system of expending money on roads, but better rotation of crops in farming."

As would be expected, the *Advocate* did a stellar job defending Muskoka against its detractors. Beside the paper's editorials and features on successful farming, James edited and published letters by prominent citizens who opined on the success that settlers might enjoy in the district, and by others who answered critics from beyond Muskoka's borders.

Those critics included some weary homesteaders in the district who, fatigued by hardscrabble farming, derided the qualities of Muskoka. Of greater concern to McMurray were the self-appointed deputations of farmers from southern Ontario who intermittently toured the district to pronounce on its unsuitability for agriculture. The partial truth of that assertion obscured the fact their damning comments were motivated by personal interests more than any altruistic concern for remote farmers. What really annoyed them was the fact that the land values of farms in southern Ontario were not appreciating as much as they wanted, because the government kept giving away land for farms in Muskoka. The more they could damn Muskoka farming, the better they believed their chances for getting the "free grants" program rescinded and seeing their own property values rise.

As a way of answering those critics, McMurray and James, in conjunction with A.P. Cockburn, cooked up an idea to bring editors and reporters from the larger Canadian newspapers to Muskoka so they could see for themselves what a grand place it truly was, and how narrow, sour, and wrong its critics were. James kept in contact with A.P. Cockburn, and saw a fair bit of him in 1872, during the federal general election, when the steamboat pioneer stood as Liberal candidate for Muskoka, and both he and McMurray did all they could to support him. The summer before the election, invitations were extended, and the Canadian Press Association's editors and newspapermen made a memorable tour of Muskoka, especially enjoying a pleasant excursion through the district aboard one of candidate Cockburn's boats. James, as an editor himself, was very much in evidence; and as one of the hosts, he was kept busy answering questions, and ensuring that the needs of each guest were provided for.

The only difficulty that arose in connection with the tour was one of McMurray's "moral" issues. Although he was not happy about it, McMurray reluctantly acquiesced, because it served his "higher interest," to serve the hard-drinking newspapermen an astonishing quantity of liquor.

Returning to their newsrooms after this well-lubricated and closely guided tour, during which McMurray and Cockburn had vied to outshine one another in their educational addresses to the visiting scribes, the men wrote articles claiming that about three-quarters of Muskoka was good for farming, and reaffirming that the place had great agricultural capabilities.

For good measure James filled the *Northern Advocate* with a highly positive account of the newspapermen's visit, further evidence of rising interest in Muskoka as one of Canada's most promising places.

15

Paper Wars

The newspaper was proving its worth, but the ever-restless McMurray decided something more was needed than a weekly sheet.

Behind the scenes, through the end of 1870 and early 1871, the men at the *Advocate* office got a new project underway. In McMurray's fashion, once he had the idea, others did the work — in this case his editor, James Boyer, and his printer, David Courtney. In late February 1871, their book, entitled *The Free Grant Lands of Canada from Practical Experience of Bush Farming in the Free Grant Districts of Muskoka & Parry Sound*, appeared in print.

Already publishing the first newspaper in Ontario's northern districts, McMurray could now claim a second publishing record for the first book printed in the north. The 150-page volume, with a full-size, fold-out map of Ontario showing the province's free grant townships, was printed in the Bracebridge newspaper's office by Courtney, although its hardcover binding was completed in Toronto.

Thomas McMurray's name rightly appeared on the book, but he'd shared his load with others and thanked, without naming them, "those persons who supplied much of the information contained in this work." Parts of the book's content had earlier been published as features in the newspaper. James wrote extensive sections of *The Free Grant Lands of Canada*, many pages of his handwritten manuscript still intact today.

"The fact of my being the first settler in the Township of Draper and first reeve of the united Townships of Draper, Macaulay, Stephenson,

&c., in the District of Muskoka, has given me considerable notoriety," explained McMurray in his preface, "hence I have received letters from all parts of the world asking for information about the country." Adding that "although hard pressed for time, I have always willingly responded to those appeals," he concluded that the time had now come "when something more than a courteous reply to letters of enquiry" was required. "There are tens of thousands in the United Kingdom, and many even in Canada, who are anxious to know whether this country is fit for settlement, or not." It was for this reason that his book was being published, he explained, to put such prospective settlers "in possession of the most reliable information."

The Free Grant Lands of Canada was jam-packed with valuable, if selective, information on Muskoka and Parry Sound districts and the conditions of settlers. It highlighted future prospects in this unique part of Ontario, from the mineral resources, to the extent and makeup of the vast forests, the quality of soils, and the types of transportation. The book updated progress on railways to the north, and the nature of services available across Muskoka and Parry Sound districts. Many hundreds had already arrived, but that was mere prelude for McMurray who now spoke of *millions* of people living in a Muskoka of the future, a vision he'd picked up from other promoters who saw a rising Ontario before them. Looking at all that open land on the map of Canada, was this so hard to imagine?

Their book was widely distributed by government immigration agents, the astute McMurray having "respectfully dedicated" *The Free Grant Lands of Canada* to the Ontario government, "in consideration of what it has done to improve the navigation, and promote the development of the Free Grant Districts." A large part of the print run was also sold by the enterprising McMurray to the railways, who distributed his book in their own efforts to stimulate settlement in the north, hoping for more passenger and freight traffic for their companies. Written with the subjective purpose of promoting immigration, the book would come to be used as an objective reference work for many researchers in generations to come.

Not all initiatives were reaping the same success. Despite the *Northern Advocate*'s campaign for temperance, people were still swallowing a lot of alcohol in Muskoka.

James did not drink, but he was not an outspoken teetotaller such as McMurray, who used the newspaper to call intemperance "the great stumbling block in the way of man's social, moral, and political elevation." The district, to the publisher's dismay, did not yet resemble his envisaged New Jerusalem. It had plenty of "watering holes" where liquor was handy for the relief of men afflicted by blackfly bites, stony fields, fatigue, despair, anxiety, a need for camaraderie, or time away from "the wife."

Bracebridge tavern keepers remained adept at relieving a workingman of his money along with his pain. Many hardware and general stores had expanded their services to include a liquor barrel at the rear, with a dipper. Alcohol was on the breath of numerous townsmen. The constable regularly dragged men before the justice of the peace on charges of being drunk and disorderly in a public place, or committing assault and battery while under the influence of liquor. Muskoka's abundant supplies of cheap whiskey caused poverty and hunger for many women and children who were its indirect, indigent victims.

None of this pleased James, but it outraged Thomas. All McMurray's advocacy, whether as a temperance preacher or as a local politician, publisher, author, and promoter of settlement, was intrinsic to the larger plan upon which he, and Boyer to a large extent, had embarked. McMurray was a visionary, still believing he could create a new and better society in Muskoka. Not just an idealistic prophet, he also had a practical program to build this new social order. He and James had created the newspaper and written the book as tangible steps to realize his dream.

It was this dream that kept McMurray going, despite the frustration he felt over the drinking habits of the area's inhabitants. He pressed on. His vision of a shimmering new community prospering on the Canadian Shield would require more if it was to become reality. So, anticipating a land boom and the influx of hundreds of thousands more settlers soon to arrive, he next constructed a large block of new stores and offices on the main street of Bracebridge.

With McMurray involving himself in other plans, James found himself busier than ever. Almost all of the newspaper work was now fully on his shoulders, in company with David Courtney. McMurray had not only immersed himself developing the main street's facilities with a major building effort; he was also engaging now in the businesses of lending money, issuing marriage licences, operating the Muskoka agency for sewing machines, as well as an agency for the sale of grapes.

He had, besides all that, built a splendid home on Bracebridge's Church Street, promptly renamed "McMurray Street" in his honour. The expansive, three-storey residence, with a stone fireplace and a two-tier, wrap-around verandah, he called "The Grove." As an enjoyable outlet for another of his talents, when at his lovely home, McMurray arranged music, and wrote prohibition hymns. James, always keen about music and immersed in hymns and choir work himself, found special joy in the times he shared with McMurray at The Grove, listening to the latest composition and making suggestions, just as he might do two blocks away at the newspaper office, for an editorial McMurray had penned.

But after 1872 a black cloud crossed Thomas McMurray's sky. It would soon blot out his sunny dream of New Jerusalem in Muskoka, and put the fate of James Boyer in peril. Were the actions of others, once again, going to determine his destiny?

—

A financial crash and ensuing recession in the United States sent Muskoka's economy, so dependent on exports of wood to the U.S., into a tailspin. This blow landed when McMurray had already overextended himself with debt to sustain his newspaper's money-losing operation, construct "The McMurray Block" of buildings, and launch other ventures to further his dreams.

His financial collapse soon gave the main street of Bracebridge a ghost-town look of deserted devastation. McMurray's fine new brick-clad block of commercial buildings, which included his own high-ceilinged office with its enormous window, apartments in the upper storey, and shops at street level, was now boarded up. Soon a number of other buildings also closed in the depression-struck community. Within two years, unable to meet his payments, with a dire slump in advertisements and newspaper sales, and no income from his newly constructed facilities and premises, Thomas McMurray's businesses failed completely. His impressive commercial building began to crumble, as its hurriedly laid brickwork loosened and fell near passersby on the sidewalk below. Deemed a hazard, it would be torn down for public safety after the mid-1880s.

The economic depression was bad enough, but James knew the end was in sight when a second Bracebridge newspaper began publication. Toronto and New York had many dailies, but in a small settlement like this, a competitor publication meant a devastating newspaper war was at hand.

The Free Grant Gazette and Muskoka, Parry Sound and Nipissing Advertiser began publication in 1872. E.F. Stephenson, who published a paper in Aurora, had become enchanted by Muskoka's beauty while touring the lakes aboard one of A.P. Cockburn's steamers. He found himself captivated by what he called the "hive of industry" still evident in Bracebridge that year. Stephenson decided to "throw his lot in" with the builders of the burgeoning town, which was ironic, since one of those principal builders was Thomas McMurray, against whom he now came to compete.

Stephenson's printing equipment suffered damage while being transported over Muskoka's wild roads on a winter sleigh from Orillia, but by May 14, 1872, the *Gazette*'s first issue was on the streets of Bracebridge and in the hands of townspeople. As a sign of just how deeply Muskoka's land settlement scheme permeated peoples' lives, the publisher of this Bracebridge start-up publication chose to identify the community his paper served by a system of landholding, *The Free Grant Gazette*, and like the paper James edited, it too identified its coverage area as the same three free grant districts.

With two papers after the same "free grant" market of advertisers and subscribers, a real publishing battle erupted between the rivals. Though James was ready for battle, this paper war started just when McMurray's financial plight made him least able to fight it. Drained financially, he sold the *Northern Advocate* to David Courtney the next year in an entrepreneur's desperate bid to keep afloat by getting cash from one of his assets. The paper, he hoped, could continue its mission, with James upholding the banner of land settlement.

This last-ditch plan ran along for only a number of months. James was no longer getting paid by McMurray, and he saw his newspaper's future dimming in the shadow of the well-financed *Free Grant Gazette*. James's prospects looked dim. Then something even more unexpected happened.

—

Part way through 1873, the career of James Boyer's replacement as Macaulay Township clerk, Richard James Bell, flamed into ruins, a result of his central role in one of the strangest election incidents in the history of Canada.

Bell was a devoted Conservative whom Prime Minister John A. Macdonald had appointed as Muskoka's returning officer for the federal general election the year before. Bell was, as well, an ambitious Muskoka settler who dreamed of one day being the district's member of Parliament himself. After voting ended Bell refused, on technical grounds, to declare Liberal candidate A.P. Cockburn elected as Muskoka's MP, despite the fact he had the most votes.

To account for his unprecedented action, returning officer Bell was summoned to appear before the bar of the House of Commons, the first Canadian ever so ordered by Parliament acting in its role as highest court in the land. The House probed Bell's poor judgment and chicanery as returning officer. Then it elected Cockburn itself, the first and only time in Canadian history an MP was elected by members of Parliament. The episode would lead to other firsts, as well, in reforms of election law.

Back in Muskoka, Richard Bell's career lay in smoldering ruins. Local fallout from the national attention paid to the district's political scandal had utterly disgraced him. He resigned as township clerk of Macaulay and in humiliation quit the Muskoka community he so loved, to live in obscurity in Toronto. A century later the story was kept alive when one of A.P. Cockburn's successors as MP for Muskoka, Gordon Aiken, retold the dramatic saga in a work of historical fiction, *Returning Office*, since republished in 2010 as *No Return*.

Richard Bell's ill-fate was James Boyer's fortune. He did not hesitate in accepting, with abiding relief and to Hannah's delight, the desperate Macaulay council's re-offer of his earlier position as township clerk. He moved back in, to help everyone quickly fill the embarrassing vacancy created by Bell's demise.

With its editor departed, the *Northern Advocate* soon suffered its final blow. In this round of Muskoka's unending newspaper wars, the end came early, in 1874. David Courtney, the printer who'd bought the business, believed he could somehow keep the publication going. It was not to be. That spring, David drowned in the Muskoka River.

The *Northern Advocate* suspended publication.

A few months earlier, in January, McMurray had run for municipal office in the annual council elections, but failed to win. It seemed that on every front, fate was against him in Bracebridge. Never daunted, he relocated to Parry Sound in 1874 and right away founded a new paper, the *North Star*. This important community newspaper became a new vehicle through which McMurray, still the true believer, continued to espouse his causes for the north country and a better society. Ever restless, he would later give up his efforts to promote a publication for a single community in order to take up, more grandly, his mission of preaching for prohibition all across Canada.

—

James Boyer's twisting, turning roller coaster ride with Thomas McMurray opened him to a wider circle of acquaintances and public activities, giving him greater self-confidence in his new identity. He gained widespread recognition among Muskokans from his important role as newspaper editor. He now possessed a much deeper understanding of Muskoka's unfolding story. He even discovered how much he liked writing articles to make sense of things, and to spread ideas and information that others should know.

As a mentor, Thomas McMurray had also imparted a sense of entrepreneurship, showing James how to turn the need for advocacy and communication into action. McMurray was a driven man, an instinctive builder and spontaneous advocate, impulsive and charismatic, who accomplished more than many men even dreamed about doing. But his intensity and zealousness had often encroached upon James's even-tempered and reflective nature.

Moving on with his life, James was glad to once again find that "balance" he'd felt he'd achieved before the McMurray meteorite blazed across Muskoka's skies. Getting back into government work as Macaulay Township's clerk shifted his perspective, returning him to the down-to-earth arena of municipal issues and provincial affairs.

As clerk James was once again working with councillors and other municipal clerks of the district on the important pragmatics, not the glorious promotion, of land settlement — and its consequences for Muskoka's steadily increasing number of homesteaders.

James Boyer, at age forty, approximately, had grown a beard as a disguise and had donned the official personage's uniform of a three-piece worsted suit, yet, still, he only managed to look authoritative in a tentative way. This picture, of a man hesitant to be photographed, is the first-known image of him to exist. James was in a bind, wanting anonymity yet needing the picture for publication in a photo-montage showing the Muskoka Agricultural Society officers.

16

Birth of a Village

After five years Bracebridge was no longer the tiny assembly of dirt-floor buildings the Boyers found in September 1869.

James tallied the population records one quiet afternoon late in 1874, immersed in the sort of things municipal clerks get curious about, measuring Macaulay Township's progress. More than 750 residents, he calculated, were now living in the Bracebridge settlement.

Ontario's government had designated the fledgling community as district capital because, being in the geographic centre, getting to Bracebridge would be most convenient for most Muskokans. That decision had expanded the place in the six years since. Providing government services and opening government offices in Bracebridge for the whole district helped boost the village and its population.

Bracebridge had also benefitted from geography in a second way. The Muskoka River's North Falls, around which the village was emerging, formed a natural barrier that made the settlement the furthest inland point of navigable water from Lake Muskoka. James, as someone who'd arrived by boat when that was the best means of getting to Bracebridge, knew first-hand about that.

At the same time, however, the river's narrowing at the falls offered an easy crossing point for the Muskoka colonization road to bridge, handily making Bracebridge the intersection of both water and land routes. As a result, the "end of the line" became instead a busy centre for transshipment of goods and transfer of passengers. The waterfalls were forcing into existence a local economy based on people switching from boats to wagons or stagecoaches, and the movement of cargoes from steamers to horse-drawn wagons, and vice versa.

Although Muskoka boasted many waterfalls, another way nature had dealt Bracebridge a good hand was that the falls at the centre of the village were large in volume and strength of flow, and relatively accessible from either side, as Henry Bird noted for building his woolen mill, and as Thomas McMurray noted with chagrin watching Bracebridge eclipse his settlement on the river's other branch. Their nature made the Bracebridge falls doubly attractive for constructing mills and generating power, adding to the village's ascendancy.

Meanwhile, because Bracebridge's scenic nature attracted visitors for pleasure, facilities to accommodate travelers and their needs were now operating on both sides of the river. Bracebridge emerged as a single venue integrating government offices and legal administration, the movement of people and cargoes by river and road, a range of manufacturing and services, and the diversified activities of providing everything in "hospitality" from hotel rooms and horses, eateries and a jail, to bars, barbers, and brothels.

Four years after James and Hannah Boyer reached Bracebridge, the emerging village was still a stark contrast to throbbing city they'd left behind, but now wood-frame buildings were replacing log structures thanks to a sawmill. The next stage in the village's evolution would come with building of a woolen mill and, after that, leather tanneries.

Bracebridge's strategic location became self-reinforcing, generating even more growth in boating, livery stables, hostelries, and allied businesses and services for travel and transport. The colonization road; Cockburn's steamers which carried passengers, freight, and mail; the *Northern Advocate* newspaper and *The Free Grant Lands* book through which McMurray and Boyer helped attract countless new settlers; and E.F. Stephenson's *Free Grant Gazette*, all combined with the provincial government's magnet of free land to bring in enough settlers so that by the mid-1870s Bracebridge qualified for incorporation as a village.

When James brought this fact to council's attention, Macaulay's councillors, most of them closely connected with the township's principal settlement, expressed keenness on municipal incorporation. It would be a milestone to mark progress, they said, a focus for civic pride. Council ordered a census to officially confirm the number of people in the village and its immediate environs. James organized the head count. When the census confirmed that Bracebridge had the population for village status under Ontario's Municipal Act, James travelled to Toronto on behalf of council and placed the matter before Ontario's municipal affairs officials. They were pleased to learn the province's land settlement policy was paying off, demonstrated by Bracebridge's ability to so swiftly become a self-governing municipality. The administrative changes were quickly put through.

People in central Muskoka had been referring to the settlement as "the village" for several years, but on January 1, 1875, that became Bracebridge's official designation under the Municipal Act, too. The place would never rival New York, mused James, but it was definitely closing the gap with Moreton-in-Marsh.

—

Bracebridge was born a pioneering village. Most Muskoka homesteaders were, like the Boyers, seasoned adults looking for a fresh start; they did not have to be told, while cutting homes from the bush and digging gardens out of the forest floor, that they were founding a new society. They implicitly understood their community's future rested in their own hands.

The small Macaulay school where James taught pupils to write, add, and shoot was not created by some remote department of government. It was built, as were other one-room schoolhouses across the district, by the settlers themselves. When families had youngsters to educate, they pooled their scarce money to pay a teacher. Around Muskoka, as in Bracebridge, mills for grain, lumber, and wool arose where determined pioneers chose to build them, and prospered to the extent locals used them. A.P. Cockburn's district-transforming steamboats were built in Gravenhurst by locally hired men, just as other vessels would later be built in north Muskoka. Thomas McMurray brought in the first printing press to publish a local paper, and even a book, with their urgent invitations to the wider world to come to Muskoka. The homesteads each settler family worked hard to create took shape to the degree they applied themselves and, of course, to the extent they'd selected good land to begin with.

It was the same with governance. Locally elected men shaped settlers' dreams into Muskoka's reality, creating structures for municipal self-government and implementing programs that advanced the community.

The inaugural council meeting of the Village of Bracebridge was held in January 1875. If the first duty of a citizen is to get a government, the first duty of a government is to get itself an administrator. James was already known as adept and reliable, experienced as Macaulay Township's clerk. He showed up at the new council's first meeting, making his appointment almost inevitable. Council's initial act, accordingly, was to appoint James Boyer village clerk. James would also continue as township clerk for Macaulay, one man in charge of administration for two municipalities.

Because Bracebridge had been born out of Macaulay, some minor technicalities of separation required attention, so the councillors' second step was to direct the village's first reeve, Robert E. Perry, and new village clerk, James Boyer, to confer with reeve James Tookey of Macaulay Township and his clerk, the self-same James Boyer, "in settling the business between the two municipalities." No unwieldy issues needed to be untangled: Macaulay's assets included $86.63 in cash and five road scrapers. The money was divided equally, a half-cent being a denomination of currency in that era. The only way to split an odd number of scrapers, however, was for the township to keep three and the village to get two.

A larger task now facing the new village council was attracting manufacturers who would create jobs and increase prosperity. In this department
everyone took inspiration from the example of Henry Bird's woollen mill.

Established at the top of the falls in 1872, Henry Bird's woollen mill
was an exceptional factor in the progress of the village and Muskoka
itself. Other towns had woollen mills, but the Bird Mill was making an
additional contribution to Muskoka's evolution in agriculture and tourism. Henry's had plenty of power from the Bracebridge falls, but needed
a steady supply of sheep wool. A rocky Muskoka farm, unsuitable for
crops, was ideal for grazing sheep. In a turn of fate, many hard-pressed
Muskoka farmers now found the booming Bracebridge mill bringing
them prosperity, too. Henry made generous arrangements with financially strapped farmers to start sheep farming, the only proviso being
that they sell their wool exclusively to his mill.

At the same time, Muskoka's vacation economy of hotels and lodges
for tourists, edging into existence, now had something distinctive and
local for their dining rooms. "Muskoka Lamb" became a menu specialty.
The rising number of sheep farmers made lucrative arrangements with
the growing number of hoteliers, supplying both fresh lamb and mutton.

Henry Bird's operation for manufacturing woollen products for the
Canadian and British Empire market inspired others to see the potential
of Bracebridge. The mill was a large employer of skilled tradesmen, a
tax-paying business, an enterprising benefactor for Muskoka agriculture
and tourism, and would remain an economic mainstay of Bracebridge
for the next eight decades, until synthetic fabrics overtook wool.

The new village status was a big help. The elected representatives
began exercising their improved ability to negotiate, officially for the
village, with any businessmen interested in establishing factories and
manufacturing shops. James arranged meetings for council with prospective manufacturers. He helped sort out tax concessions to entice new
operations to the village.

In the months following village incorporation, James began meeting
and corresponding with officers of the Beardmore Tannery on council's

behalf. Tanneries would locate in Muskoka if their industrial process could operate alongside flowing rivers and draw on the abundant tanning bark from the district's forests. The deal came together, and within three years the Beardmore Tannery was up and running, a substantial addition for Bracebridge's economy.

Despite arrival of the Beardmore Tannery, the operation of mills for grain, lumber, and wool, and the presence of a well-developing and integrated structure for its central Muskoka economy, Bracebridge at this time generally was still in a slump. The blighting downturn spreading from the American recession had already contributed to the demise of Thomas McMurray's Bracebridge businesses, along with other local concerns.

Because of this, council had mounted a concerted effort to overcome the economic stagnation, offering a five-year exemption from municipal taxes on sawmills, flouring mills, woollen factories, and foundries. That response by local government showed Muskokans really did believe their new district would be what they made it, and would not remain passive. Such extraordinary steps were needed for recovery and development, for as author W.E. Hamilton wrote when taking stock of the community in March 1875, "circumstances had knocked the bottom out of the institution of Bracebridge." Like rocky Muskoka itself, the district's economy had many ups-and-downs and rough patches.

———

In the rise of Bracebridge, creating a village library did not depend on the state of the economy, but the determination, once again, of local people willing to take matters into their own hands. In the mid-1870s, James was among those with a strong enough interest in books to have brought the library into existence.

Early in 1874, a group that included Henry Bird, Dr. Samuel Bridgeland, public school principal Tony McGill, lawyer James Browning, James Boyer, and Robert Dollar, gathered to form the Bracebridge Mechanics' Institute, the best known structure for organizing a local library in that era.

The province's first Mechanics' Institute was formed at Kingston in 1834, then more materialized in Hamilton, Niagara Falls, and other centres in southern Ontario, but the Bracebridge Mechanics' Institute was the first community library service in Ontario's northern districts. As a measure of the high value they placed on books, these leading men in Bracebridge brought a library into existence before the village was incorporated, even before locals formed a fire brigade to protect life and property. As a first item of business, the Mechanics' Institute Library needed bylaws to govern its operation, and James drew them up.

Next, books were needed. So these settlers, James included, pooled a total of 225 volumes from their personal collections, somewhat like a co-op, to start the library and expand the reading possibilities of all its members. A person had to join the Bracebridge Mechanics' Institute to benefit from its services. While legally a private organization, like a club, in democratic Bracebridge the Mechanics' Institute members themselves canvassed door-to-door throughout the village to sign up as members everybody who wanted to join, making it a "public" library in all but name. The library was housed in the top floor of the Sam H. Armstrong Building on the east side of Bracebridge's main street. The librarian, Josiah Pratt, a man described by Hamilton as "painstaking and courteous," operated his jewellery store in the street-level space below.

The Mechanics' Institute in Bracebridge was a village centre for learning and personal enrichment. Besides acquiring and lending books, it had a reading room with chairs and tables where members could find newspapers and periodicals from Toronto, New York, and London. The Mechanics' Institute offered lectures in science, engineering, and economics, providing a non-denominational and non-partisan venue to help educate trades people and interested townsfolk. Henry Bird embraced science and reading, and delighted to give talks about his own inventions, including a new generator and his "lime-light lantern," as well as on some of the latest innovations in wool milling.

Bracebridge villagers had created this library as a new institution in a building separate from peoples' homes, not part of a church or school, and independent of the newspaper office, community halls, and meeting rooms of fraternal societies, each of which had their own small book collections. The Bracebridge Library not only showed prospective immigrants pioneer Muskoka's civilizing impulse, but provided real service for those already living in and around the village.

George Kirk, a seventeen-year-old in Macaulay Township, recorded in his diary in the mid-1870s (between notations on the slaughter and butchering of pigs, the digging of potatoes in mud after an early snowfall, catching a live mink, shooting chipmunks and a blue jay, cutting logs, helping a neighbour raise a barn, and the threshing of oats and wheat) his trips into the Bracebridge Library to exchange *Gulliver's Travels* for *Cast Up by the Sea*, and later to renew the book *New Tracts in North America*.

Some wanted books, others news and current affairs from the wider world. When James Boyer visited the reading room, he first read newspapers from New York, then the periodicals from Britain. Elsewhere, such as at home, James turned to books, including the larger number now available thanks to the Bracebridge Library. He, like the others who formed the library, esteemed the transcending value of books. Whatever distractions might be occurring, from economic decline, howling winter nights, or personal setbacks, he found in books the comfort and inspiration many others took from religion.

———

Around the growing village, social life had become more organized, too. By the early 1870s, professional services available included those of a doctor, a notary public, a druggist, a music teacher, several land surveyors, and one conveyancer in the person of James Boyer.

Among the community's tradesmen could be found a house builder, carpenter, window glazier, butcher, and baker. Travellers could find a blacksmith, the stagecoach service, and hoteliers. For communication, the village had its post office, and a newspaper with print shop.

A number of retailers had opened their doors to offer specialty lines of furniture, musical instruments, boots and shoes, leather supplies, groceries, dry goods, and clothing. In the heavier end of things, still others offered threshing and separating machinery, and such services as shingle making, lime and lathe sales, grist milling, and the services of a sawmill. For those who suddenly packed it in, coffins were available in Bracebridge, "made of the latest style and on short notice."

The Boyers were members of Bracebridge Methodist Church, although by the early 1870s Protestants in and around the village had several other choices of salvation, with Presbyterian and Anglican churches in the community as well. The Roman Catholics got organized when Bishop Jamot moved his headquarters from Sault Ste. Marie to Bracebridge in 1875. The Catholics built a combined chapel and rectory on McMurray Street, which Bishop Jamot and a new resident priest, Father Nadaud, opened with their first service on Sunday, September 17, 1876, coalescing another Christian flock for the village. In militantly Protestant Bracebridge, more than a hundred Catholics attended from Bracebridge, Baysville, Germania, Bruce Lake, and Minett. Just three years later, a larger Catholic church would be needed.

Adherents not only attended worship services segregated into their respective denominations, but enjoyed community entertainments sponsored by their particular churches as well, such as tea socials, bake sales, turkey suppers, Sunday school picnics in summer, and skating parties in winter.

Members of the Orange Lodge, in which James was a very active member, had a meeting hall; the children, a school. Babies were born at home, with the help of a midwife after the late 1870s. Christenings, in cases where parents were adherents, were provided by one's church. Weddings might take place in a church, but were for more common at the bride's home. Funerals were likewise simple affairs for many, conducted from the deceased's house, although death of a prominent community member could produce a service in church to ensure more accommodation for mourners. A growing number of small cemeteries dotted the district: bodies were sometimes buried in simple wooden boxes on the deceased's homestead; sometimes in small community cemeteries at the side of township roads; and sometimes in denominational burial grounds adjacent to church buildings. Grave markers were simple wooden planks or piled stones, since nobody was yet making long-lasting tombstones.

As the recession slowly lifted, the village's patterns of general economic development created demand for labourers, millwrights, woodsmen, factory-hands, and teamsters. Several more tradesmen arrived in Bracebridge each year. Boat-building shops became important, as did furniture factories. Establishment of a brick yard provided jobs and enabled construction of buildings more permanent and less rustic than the community's initial log structures. All the while the continuing forestry work in Muskoka was keeping a few thousand men hard at logging, droving, and milling.

Hannah and James watched with delight as enterprising villagers set up stores, offices, and shops. The more the village grew, the more it secured their own future. Hannah knew most of the shops by what they offered. James in his newspaper days knew them for what news stories they created or advertisements they bought, and now in his municipal clerk's role, for the business licences they sought and the commercial issues, from closing hours to liquor sales, they caused to be discussed around the council chamber table.

—

In occupying the clerkship, James discovered a position of influence and effective power.

In New York Isaac Jelfs had registered patents that were important yet still just small details in the vast manufacturing operation of America's largest city; in Bracebridge James Boyer was playing a direct role to facilitate creation of major new manufacturing enterprises where none existed.

In Brooklyn, Isaac had participated in a British enclave society hoping to maintain an English connection fate had severed; in Canada, James lived daily in a British milieu he actively and openly promoted.

His entry into municipal government only seemed a novel departure. In reality, it echoed the career of his older brother Samuel Jelfs back in England, as clerk of the Poor Law Union at Dorset.

James's articles were no longer appearing in the *Northern Advocate*, but he was still very much in the action of public affairs. The venue was different, his role much the same. He was at a clerk's table instead of an editor's desk, writing notices, municipal correspondence, and council minutes rather than news reports or editorials, but the community agenda was pretty much the same and politics continued to swirl around him as much as ever.

The charm that James appreciated in being a clerk was that while it made him indispensable, he could remain safely out of the limelight. The clerk does the work; others get the fame. The clerk briefs elected representatives about a subject in private; they make speeches on the topic in public. The elected officials come and go; the clerk, unless immolated by scandal like Macaulay's hapless Richard Bell, stays on.

In primitive Muskoka where he and Hannah had fled in desperate hope of finding refuge, James's hand was helping shape events. The village was growing, and he with it. James Boyer was master of his own destiny more than ever. He was with the only women he'd ever loved. For the rest, he could readily escape through his cherished books.

17

———

Movin' in from the Bush

Homesteaders in Muskoka wanted fine farms, but many, finding their land so hard and their struggle so great, began to yearn for another life. The Boyers were a variation on this theme only to the extent they had come to the district together, but would not leave the land as one.

Harry was the first to break away, taking off to clear land and build cabins for others, then signing up to work at a bush camp during the winter, and taking construction jobs over the summers. Mary Ann left next, returning to the United States in 1871 once she turned twenty-one, hoping for something other than life as a homesteader's wife.

Neighbours, too, were decamping. Robert Dollar, who'd shown the Boyers how to kindle a "burn," prospered in Muskoka's lumber business and served on Bracebridge council too, where he worked closely together with James as clerk, at least until the time councillor Dollar suffered electoral defeat by three votes at the municipal elections. In the face of such voter ingratitude, he quit his nearby Macaulay farm for California, where he developed the ocean-going Dollar Steamships Line and became a millionaire.

Hannah and James, constrained by circumstances that did not bind Harry or Mary Ann or neighbours going to the U.S.A. continued at the Macaulay homestead, in no way distressed they couldn't leave. They had taken hold of their property, and it had its own hold on them. The place was, after all, more theirs than it had ever been Harry's or Mary Ann's.

During the three years James went into Bracebridge to edit the newspaper, he benefitted from balance in life many homesteaders, especially on more isolated farms, lacked. Hannah relished the season's cycles at the homestead, as they reconnected her to memories of farming adventures around Ely. She found the township pace a pleasing contrast to New York and Brooklyn, where she rushed to the millenary shops early six mornings a week. Now she was able to enjoy time with her growing girls, doing farm chores, and finding adventures in nature. Sunday church in Bracebridge with James and their daughters, and visits to the village shops for supplies and women's groups for meetings, added a balanced rhythm to her life, too.

What really kept James and Hannah content "down on the farm" was the love they continued instinctively to foster in one another. He was now thirty-seven, she twenty-nine. Feelings which had driven them to this remote sanctuary had not abated but continued to ripen, taking pleasing familiar shapes but also finding fresh expression. James's claim to be thirty-five was more than justified, because Hannah gave him energy and purpose he'd never had before. With their third winter in Muskoka approaching, Hannah was advancing through another pregnancy.

This time, Hannah did not have Mary Ann to attend her. Back in Brooklyn her younger sister had promptly found and married handsome Harry Holt and had already started raising a family of her own. Mary Ann's absence heightened Hannah's recurring apprehension about dying in childbirth. But on March 28, 1872, with a seasoned neighbour assisting, she had delivered a boy, mother and infant both fine.

A relieved and delighted James agreed to call their first son William, a name Hannah chose in remembrance of her mother's last son, her youngest brother whom she'd watched die in infancy and be buried at sea. Her own son could now carry the Boyer name in the New World that her baby brother never reached. The smiling father, in those days still editing the community newspaper, inserted a notice about the baby's birth in the *Advocate*'s next edition.

—

Despite her contentment Hannah could never rest when it came to her siblings. Caring *for* them had transformed into caring *about* them. Hardly a week passed that she did not write a letter to one or other of them. From Brooklyn, sister Lizzy was beginning to express interest in coming to Muskoka, to Hannah's surprise and delight.

Harry, already in Muskoka, was in a class by himself. Hannah's resourcefulness and determination in rescuing him from the work farm in New York was as good an example as any of their strong bond. He was the one who lived with her in Manhattan and then in Brooklyn, supported her in her complex relationship with Isaac, came with them to Muskoka, helped clear their land and build their log cabin. Harry Boyer's life and adventures became interwoven with James and Hannah's, and without his diary, much of how their saga unfolded would not be known.

After three years of unrelenting toil around Muskoka, Harry the stonecutter heard about a marble shop in Orillia, visited Hannah to fetch his tools from the barn, then headed thirty-five miles south to meet the shop's owner, Charles James Davies. Harry asked for a job, and started work the same day.

He was deeply satisfied to resume using stone-working skills, and, even more, to think he at last might have found a suitable footing for his new life as a Canadian. Charles Davies guided his new employee, picking up where American Frank Braun at his Brooklyn yard had left off back in the summer of 1869. Both masters of the craft saw in Harry Boyer not only natural aptitude for handling stone, but also intense desire to work.

Almost upon arrival, Harry was smitten with Davies's lively daughter Florence, whom he called Flora. Although she was shorter and plumper than he, Harry was attracted to her pink-and-white English complexion, dark brown eyes, and red-gold hair. She was, he exclaimed, "quick as chain-lightning. Many a time I tried to catch her and couldn't." He caught her long enough, though, when he was twenty-two and she seventeen, to marry her on May 9, 1874 at the Davies family's home, with Orillia's

Methodist minister officiating and Flora's parents giving legal consent to the marriage of their juvenile daughter. There were no attendants, but much music, plenty of food, and numerous guests, including Hannah and James who'd come down from Bracebridge. Harry, who in addition to being a natural hard worker, enjoyed life and liked a good time. He was joyously marrying into a family where partying was a normal part of living.

For the next two years, the exuberant couple lived in an apartment building Charles Davies owned on a small strip of leased land at the narrows separating lakes Couchiching and Simcoe. Harry, though more inclined to adventure than introspection, sometimes did reflect, gazing over this scene, on everything that had happened in the five years since he first saw this channel between the two large lakes, passing through it aboard the *Emily May*, going north as a seventeen-year-old to become a Muskoka homesteader.

When Flora gave birth to their first baby, a son they named Joseph Henry Boyer, the fun-loving adventurer seemed sobered by a new sense of responsibility. Harry wanted to earn more money so he could provide for his family better. He wanted a home of their own, rather than continuing to live in one of his father-in-law's apartments. Lured by big wages for stone workers on a railway being built in Tennessee, Harry went south to earn a nest egg. Bleakly, he "found the tale greatly exaggerated," and "only made enough to live on."

Next spring, catching an occasional wagon ride, he hiked back from Tennessee to Orillia to be reunited with Flora and his son, only to discover that Davies's apartment building had vanished, along with his family. Flora had been unable to reach him in Tennessee, to let him know her father pulled down the building because the land lease was expiring, and taken his boards north to a free-grant farm in Muskoka. Charlie Davies seemed to be trying as hard to get out of the stone-working business as Harry Boyer was endeavouring to get in.

Once he ascertained that Flora and young Joe were living with her parents around Muldrew Lake, he continued up to Muskoka for a joyous reunion with them. They were all living in a trim frame house built from apartment building lumber. Harry was not greatly miffed by the changes during his absence, having learned early that major disruptions in life are normal. After enjoying a festive "prodigal son party," he claimed a nearby lot. Still resolved to have his own place, Harry used his well-honed cabin-building skills to erect a rustic log abode looking over the lake. Over the next several years, he and Flora added two more children, Flo and Nan, to their family.

Meanwhile, Lizzy Boyer had arrived from Brooklyn. Hannah's sister was fourteen when the Boyer children reached New York. She had continued living in Brooklyn's Gowanus district, working as a seamstress and looking for just the right man. He had not appeared, and she was getting older. Fretful Lizzy seemed to panic, thinking she would never find a husband. She knew Harry had met and happily married someone in Canada. Perhaps Hannah had been right. Maybe the small northern community had more opportunities than she'd been able to turn up in heavily populated Brooklyn. Now ready to yield to Hannah's appeals to join her, in 1874 Lizzy gambled on trying her fortunes in Muskoka. She moved in with Hannah, James, and their three children at the Macaulay homestead. With James's help and connections, Lizzy was soon hired as a school teacher.

———

James and Hannah's son, "Billy," was a happy boy, bringing joy like the sunshine. Reaching his third year in 1875, he'd become an eager playmate for his sisters Annie, now seven, and Nellie, four. Hannah, who was again pregnant, sometime found herself pausing, her face bright with delight, just watching them play together. Being devout she would have prayed for such happiness to last.

But in late fall, a cloud came over the scene. The children became ill. The older girls recovered slowly. But on November 8, cholera took all life from little Billy. Hannah, very pregnant and inconsolable, wept for days. James stood with his distraught darling beside a freshly dug small grave, supporting her firmly with his arm across her back, gripping her shoulder. As they gazed in long silence at the small grave on their farm, he could not escape thinking about standing with Eliza, in another country, in another life, burying first one, then another, then a third of their children who perished from pneumonia, diphtheria, and cholera, the disease that had now taken into that same void Billy Boyer.

Nineteen weeks later, on March 28, Hannah delivered the Boyers' fourth child, another boy. Lizzy was on hand to assist, as best she could. What did fate have in store for this son, arriving exactly four years *to the day* after the birth of her lost boy Billy?

The parents named him Charles Ernest. This time, lacking his own newspaper, James, more solemn than before, inserted a paid birth notice in the *Free Grant Gazette*.

Talking over their plans and prospects, James and Hannah began to agree for many reasons that they were now ready for another life. It was time to move into Bracebridge.

Annie and Nellie could go to school in the village, which James believed would expose them to better teaching; Hannah welcomed the idea, too, because the girls would meet more children and make new friends, helping to lift their continuing sadness over losing their playful companion, Billy. She herself could be closer to friends. It would be easier to attend church meetings and shop for supplies. They'd fulfilled their homesteader legal requirements, including the five-year residency, and the Crown had granted the patent on Lot 14. As outright owner, James could sell it.

James himself would find it more convenient, and informative, living within the village of which he was clerk. He'd be handier, too, to deal with the burgeoning responsibilities he kept amassing in a growing number of organizations. What's more he'd no longer have to shrug and just smile in response to villagers' oft-repeated query, "When're yez movin' in from the bush?"

After six harsh, blissful, memorable years as Macaulay homesteaders, James and Hannah realized how much they were looking forward to modest comfort, closer to others. They were slightly less concerned now about being unmasked, after the passage of time and the community's acceptance of them as a married couple. Still, the possibility of James's past catching up with him would never fully disappear from their minds.

In May 1876, using money from selling "the homestead farm," Hannah purchased a small frame house at the north end of the village. The property sold had been James's, but the purchase was made in Hannah's name alone. Hotelier Hiram MacDonald, as active as ever dealing in properties, opening streets, and developing lands in Bracebridge, was once again the person selling the property to the Boyers. The house was on the west side of Manitoba Street, just a hundred yards from where the intrepid squatter John Beal had first built a humble shanty seventeen years before. Beal's reclusive effort to hide deep in the northern bush was frustrated when other pioneers followed and a settlement started, then was fully confounded when the Muskoka colonization road passed right by his front door. The roadway had since been named Manitoba Street, expressing Bracebridge's soaring patriotism at Confederation when other thoroughfares were named Dominion, Ontario, and Quebec streets. The Boyers' north-end residence was No. 2, Manitoba Street.

The land at the rear of the house, sloping gently to the west, would fill up with their garden vegetables in summer and snow in winter. The next spring James would plant apple trees to add the beginnings of a small garden orchard. Lizzy Boyer moved into the village with them, but was teaching school and did not much help out with her sister's house. Whether this was out of deference or indifference was hard to say.

Two blocks east a gurgling spring formed a pond where Hannah taught Annie and Nan how to harvest watercress in summer and fetch buckets of cold fresh water year-round. They bought raw milk fresh at a farm nearby.

A rock escarpment fell away sharply at the western edge of the property, and from its base spread out some of the fertile flat land of Monck Township, considered by some "the banner township of Muskoka District" for its sections of excellent farmland and extensive frontages on the Muskoka River and Lake Muskoka. On these fertile flats just west of the village, an area known locally as "the Hollow," farmers prospered. One of Bracebridge's brickworks nestled at the foot of this cliff. Its red clay bricks were giving local homes and commercial buildings a unified appearance that began establishing the characteristic Bracebridge look. The Boyers' frame house would eventually become a harmonious part of the redbrick town, once enough money was saved to add brick veneer.

By merely moving a few miles, exchanging their homestead and few scattered neighbours along the concession line for the now bustling village, the Boyers had begun a new chapter in their life together.

18

—

A Quickening Village Pace

A remarkable woman, strong in character yet gentle in her ways, began visiting the Boyers at their Manitoba Street house.

Mrs. Williams came from the Rama Reserve at Lake Couchiching, one of many Chippewas who journeyed north to Muskoka each summer. Most camped along the river near their former village, Obejewanung, a site now occupied by white settlers and renamed Port Carling. A smaller number, including Mrs. Williams, summered around Bracebridge and the Muskoka River.

She first came to the door to sell hand-woven baskets, high quality Native craftwork made especially appealing by its scent of interwoven sweet-grass. Mrs. Williams became friendly with Hannah, and started coming often to her welcoming house for a cup of tea and chats. Their hospitality was more than repaid, the Boyers felt, by the stories she told and teaching she imparted. Through the course of their conversations, Hannah and James learned much more about their Muskoka surroundings, from a perspective they had not before heard.

Mrs. Williams had known Chief Mesqua Ukee, from whose name "Muskoka" was derived. The chief was a renowned warrior who'd fought with the British in the War of 1812. She interpreted his name for the Boyers to mean, "Not easily turned back in the day of battle." She told stories showing them the chief's goodness to his people.

Other stories evoked harsher feelings. Mesqua Ukee had signed the treaties under which 250,000 acres of land in central Ontario were sold to the Crown. The more James learned of this land grab, the more incensed he became. "White people could hardly be proud of this transaction which gave the Indians only about eight cents per acre," he wrote, "and even then, only interest on the money was paid."

Through these conversations with Mrs. Williams, James also pieced together the mystery of the thirty-seven acre clearing where he made quiet retreats. It had not only been the site of a tent village, but the summer headquarters of a band of Chippewas. He also learned how the flat south bank of the Muskoka River at Bracebridge Bay, below the falls, had been a gathering area for Chippewas arriving by canoe over a number of days before continuing up the river together. She described the Hudson's Bay fur-trading post down the river from Bracebridge, a mile or so before it emptied into Lake Muskoka. Another time, Mrs. Williams told them about a Chippewa burial ground at the very mouth of the river, an area the Boyers knew well. They would never again pass along that shore without gazing at the low-lying soft land and be moved by the history they now knew to be hidden there.

Thanks to his understanding acquired from Mrs. Williams, James for the rest of his life took extra effort to speak with Native people and hear their stories. "When the first white people came to this District," he later wrote in his history of early Muskoka, "there were still some Indians who had camps here. They did not give any trouble, as many suspected they would, but instead were helpful to the pioneers and their knowledge of the area was of great assistance."

———

The Boyers watched Bracebridge fill up with other homesteaders who sought a change in their lives, too. Some, vexed and weary, did not even stop in the village. They wanted all the way out of Muskoka, vowing never to return.

Others caught "Manitoba Fever," as their condition came to be jokingly called in Muskoka's townships by the late 1870s, and headed west, hoping for better Prairie farms. A decade later, still more Muskokans abandoning their homesteads would head deeper into the province's interior to farm the recently discovered "clay belt" of northeastern Ontario. A farmer's paradise compared to Muskoka, the millions of flat acres of fertile soil around Cochrane, were like an oasis, surrounded by a Canadian Shield perimeter of muskeg and exposed bedrock. Over the same period, a disheartened procession of Muskoka settlers left for the United States, either returning to familiar New England or the Midwest from which they'd come, or advancing southwest to the golden allure of California.

All the while an even greater number of homesteaders gave up their struggle to farm, but would not, or perhaps could not, quit the district. These settlers who abandoned their farms but stayed in Muskoka to live and work in the villages, in whose ranks were James and Hannah Boyer, and also Harry Boyer, constituted a particular class of Muskokans. They were seasoned in rural hardships, familiar with the unique pleasures of the district, knowledgeable about farming but no longer on the land. This group, increasingly large in size and made up of many of the district's founding families, were resilient, well-rounded Muskokans.

As village clerk and a land conveyancer, James was well informed about Bracebridge comings and goings. Migration from the townships into the villages, and the continuous arrival of people looking for fresh opportunity, kept population numbers inching up. By the end of the 1870s, Bracebridge had a thousand inhabitants.

The village hummed with small factories. Many were helped in their financial requirements by Hunt's Bank. Owned by Alfred Hunt of Bracebridge, it was the only bank operating in Muskoka. All residents of the village, be they newcomers or seasoned pioneer stock, were kept up to date and politically aroused by the village's two newspapers, the *Free Grant Gazette* and its new rival, the *Muskoka Herald*.

———

The *Herald* rose like a phoenix out of the ashes of the ill-fated *Northern Advocate*.

In 1878, after the *Advocate*'s press and equipment had been collecting dust for four years in tempting silence, F.T. Graffe and Harry Oaten bought it from David Courtney's successors. The printing equipment was moved from Dominion Street into part of the Orange Hall building on Manitoba Street, where several years earlier, on its south-facing exterior, Thomas McMurray had a large sign to publicize the *Northern Advocate*. Now, using McMurray's original equipment, a revived newspaper would begin publication in this very same venue. Certainly in James Boyer's eyes, the two weeklies were closely connected. The changing of the name from *Advocate* to *Herald*, and the changed editorial policy made little difference in his eyes; these alterations were much the same as, say, a man changing his name and creating a new persona to go with it. The substance endured.

Graffe and Oaten called their new Bracebridge-based paper the *Muskoka Herald* to emphasize its district-wide focus. First copies came off the press on the evening of April 11, 1878. A large number of local Conservatives came into the hall to witness the inauguration of a paper they could believe in. Sam Armstrong, businessman and later mayor, auctioned off two or three dozen of the first *Muskoka Herald*s as they came off the press. The very first copy went to Alfred Hunt, the banker and later a Bracebridge mayor, for twenty-five dollars. Others were bid up to fifteen dollars or ten dollars, big amounts that only the bravura of an auction among close acquaintances was capable of generating. The success of the event was helped by the slowness of the printing process, which gave a dramatic interval for auctioneer Armstrong to build up anticipation and boost bids as the prominent townsmen and top Tories watched the next Herald materialize before their very eyes. Because this was no longer Thomas McMurray's show, gentlemen's flasks of whiskey were passed around to willing supporters of the newspaper. The night's haul, for a paper with a cover price of two cents per copy, provided a handsome sum to help Graffe and Oaten keep the *Muskoka Herald* afloat in its start-up year.

Although the village again had two weeklies, Bracebridge was no longer the only place in Muskoka with newspaper service. In north Muskoka, the *Liberal* in Huntsville was a short-lived paper, coming and going with a single election, more like a partisan campaign pamphlet than a proper weekly newspaper. With far better staying power, the *Huntsville*

Forester, still in operation and today Muskoka's oldest continuously operating paper, began publication in 1877. In Gravenhurst, where previously A.P. Cockburn's *Lumberman* made a brief appearance in the publishing arena, the *Gravenhurst Banner* would start coverage of south Muskoka by 1880. All these newspapers across the district took the Liberal Party's line, except one. The *Muskoka Herald* alone espoused the Conservative cause.

———

A decade after the end of the Civil War, the U.S. finally emerged from its recession, and the economic upswing steadily pulled Bracebridge into recovery by the end of the decade, enabling William Hamilton, immigration agent for Muskoka and author of the 1879 *Guide Book and Atlas of Muskoka and Parry Sound Districts,* to now report: "There was as a general thing much bustle and life in the village, owing to the lumber traffic and the large number of immigrants on their way to locate on free grants or to purchase farms." The irony was that many in this fresh wave of newcomers had learned about Muskoka's opportunities through the promotional book *The Free Grant Lands of Canada* and had been persuaded to come by the widely circulated *Northern Advocate,* but their publisher Thomas McMurray, prophet of Muskoka's future, was no longer around to take advantage of their arrival and the return of good times.

Bracebridge continued to benefit from its natural advantages for mills operated by the great waterpower of the falls, and factories like the immense tanneries dependent upon the river's large supplies of freshly running water to carry away waste. The early flour mill, lumber mills, and shingle factory, since joined by the woollen mill and leather tannery, were now augmented by a match factory, a furniture factory, another brickworks, a cheese factory, a buggy shop, blacksmith shops, and more livery stables. The village's pace continued to quicken.

The initial Beardmore Tannery, reorganized as the Muskoka Leather Company, was joined along the riverbank below Bracebridge Bay, where Chippewas once gathered, by the sprawling Anglo-Canadian Leather Company's facilities. Local tanning would continue to expand until the combined production of these companies, with Shaw's partner tannery in Huntsville, made Muskoka the largest producer of leather in the British Empire, using hides imported from across the continent and countries as far away as Argentina. This pre-eminence in the leather economy required hard work by tannery labourers, continuous harvesting of tanning bark by local farmers, and acceptance by all concerned that the Muskoka River downstream from the facilities would be outrageously polluted from emptying stinking vats of fouled tannic acid into its waters, causing fish in the river to float belly up and shoreline critters to perish.

The district would continue to receive new arrivals looking to farm, but as the general economy improved employers hired more tradesmen from the south for skilled jobs in mills and factories. In turn, as the population increased, formation of local chapters of loyalist societies and fraternal lodges kept apace. While these bodies reinforced their members' adherence to familiar causes in their strange new setting, playing the role of a cultural shock absorber, they also provided a channel for mutual support in difficult times.

James, as a senior officer of a great many of these bodies, could witness more closely than most the way Bracebridge society worked, when his central vantage point as secretary of the community's clubs and associations was added to his view from the editor's desk, then the clerk's office, and later the magistrate's bench. The overall effect was to reinforce his disposition to genial realism, taking a philosophical view of human nature, and society at large. That largely reflected the approach he wanted to take, as well, to get along so as not to create problems that could somehow bring his past into the present. Still, when James saw injustice he was forthright in expressing his opinions: on the stumpage fee double-standard that penalized homesteaders; on the calumny of governments that took Native land under treaties but did not pay as required to by their own contractual obligation; or the requirement that settlers had to provide "statute labour" without pay for road work.

As for the fact Muskoka, like the rest of Canada in this era, had no programs of government welfare or social assistance, these fraternal, religious, and patriotic entities in which James was so active were a kind of public policy program in the way they offered their members support and uplift. These societies were not outward-looking do-good community service clubs, but bodies that looked to the well-being and mutual support of their own. That attribute explained the presence of so many in Bracebridge, and why most of them enjoyed large memberships, quite apart from the grand causes they ostensibly stood for. Rudimentary "welfare" was mostly provided through local chapters of these organizations, and by local congregations of churches, which likewise looked to the well-being of their own adherents.

With the philosophy of "laissez-faire" prevailing in government's hands-off approach to society, these non-government agencies were at the fore. In many cases their philosophy was the same as the pioneers' unwritten pact of mutual self-help. "It's an honour to be able to help a man in need," was the virtuous sentiment often expressed. In the building of barns, harvesting of grain crops, and skidding of logs to rivers, neighbours pooled their labour and were repaid in kind. But a harder sentiment held just as firmly in tough-love Muskoka: "Heaven helps those who help themselves." Mutual support, whether in the countryside or the village, was rarely confused with undeserving dependency.

———

Exactly what sentiment governed land deals is harder to identify. Certainly the large volume of property transactions taking place across Muskoka fostered a climate of real estate excitement, and the quickening pace of the district's "land boom" atmosphere, all funnelled through the land registry office where James spent a great deal of time, enveloped the Boyers.

What James learned in New York at Brown, Hall & Vanderpoel about profitably buying and selling properties he had applied for his own benefit in Brooklyn. Now he and Hannah were at it again in Muskoka. This time around, an added advantage was James's awareness of possible good property deals, again due to his frequent presence at the land registry office. During their first decade in the district, when they were constantly short of money, the two acquired and sold several properties, thinking successful speculation in real estate could give them the financial boost they needed. It was an understandable inspiration, given the land rush to Muskoka then underway and the real estate boom James witnessed, and their dealings were greatly facilitated by the fact that James was the only professional conveyancer at the registry office.

James bought his first Muskoka land from Hiram MacDonald, for three hundred dollars in September 1869, and the next spring paid the Crown one hundred dollars to transfer MacDonald's squatter's rights to the property to his name, as earlier noted. But the story continues. That same spring, in June 1870, he sold the land and shanty to James Seymour for $450, making fifty dollars on the deal after the Boyer family lived in the place effectively rent-free for their first Muskoka winter.

In the spring of 1872, Hannah bought a quarter acre of prime land in the centre of Bracebridge, on the south side of Ontario Street, from Christopher Sevenpiper, paying him four hundred dollars. Described as village Lot Number 8, the land was also on survey plans as Macaulay Township, lots 1 and 2 of Concession 1. Around the same time, she acquired property from Lucy Anne Brown and William Huycke, and other property from Hiram MacDonald. That summer, in July 1872, James bought a tract of land in the core of Bracebridge, a rectangle on the east side of Dominion Street with a frontage of thirty-three feet, running 115 feet deep on each side, paying three hundred dollars for it to real estate developer William Holditch. All the documents and land transfers for these properties were drawn up by James.

For a moneyless family, it could seem puzzling how the Boyers financed these transactions. Hannah was taking out mortgages on the lands, which provided some of the funds. Also, they found another good way to get money. Early in the winter of 1872, James sold John Hunter timber rights on both his Macaulay Lots 14 and 20 in Concession 2, and on behalf of his brother-in-law sold Hunter the timber rights to Harry Boyer's Lot 14 in Concession 1. This deal had a double bounce: when Hunter and his crews clear-cut the three lots, their work helped the Boyers fulfill their land clearing obligations under the Free Grant and Homestead Act and, in the process, gain money for food and farm supplies — and buying land in central Bracebridge.

The next action, coming two years later in 1874, involved Lizzy Boyer, who had just arrived in Muskoka and was living with James and Hannah.

That September, James transferred the Dominion Street property to her for one thousand dollars, its price more than trebling in two years. This was not some effort by Hannah and James to extract windfall funds from the spinster sister. Nor was it likely that Lizzy had saved enough money during her years in Brooklyn to plunge into Bracebridge real estate. It may not even have been any reflection of real estate values rising that much in central Bracebridge, like some harbinger of the local economy edging towards recovery from the recession, either. Perhaps that one thousand dollar amount was never even paid over, from sister to brother-in-law.

What likely happened was that some cloud of uncertainty appeared over the title to the prized property on Dominion Street, which James likely became aware of in his work as clerk or conveyancer, or from vendor Holditch himself. It would be smart in the circumstances, reasoned James, to show a higher value for the property in the event it had to be forfeited or expropriated. Certainly, the land office records disclose that there were different views about title to the Dominion Street property.

On September 9, 1874, a week after that transfer to Lizzy was registered by James, William Holditch registered a *lis pendens* on title to freeze any further transactions with the property while a law suit he'd initiated against James Boyer over the title issue to the land was pending. Upon discovering James had already transferred the title before he could register his *lis pendens* to prevent it, Holditch responded by promptly adding Elizabeth Boyer as a co-defendant with James in the court proceeding, and, two days later, registering a new *lis pendens* restraint on the title, since the property was now hers.

These legal tussles were background to the main action, which was the construction of buildings by William Barker on two adjacent Dominion Street lots, his own and the one owned by James, now transferred to Lizzy. While Holditch was holding out, apparently, for some additional money, one of the contractors on the project registered a mechanic's lien on the Boyer property for his claim that Barker the contractor owed him $1,150 on the job which he'd not yet paid. While this was routine in construction projects, it further stirred up already muddy water. The Boyers extricated themselves from the mess by selling their property to William Barker early in December, for which he paid one thousand dollars to Elizabeth.

Whatever issue remained in Holditch's court proceeding against the Boyers then lapsed into a saw-off deal between he and Barker.

That was James's final appearance in real estate transactions for his own interest. He'd emerged with funds to spare, and Lizzy, who seems to have been in the deal only to provide her name and facilitate dealings, emerged unscathed. From then on, any further land transactions were carried out only in Hannah's name. It was unseemly for the municipal clerk to be so engaged, although most councillors dealt in property.

Two years later, when the Boyers sold the Macaulay homestead and used the money to buy their house on Manitoba Street, Hannah Boyer's name alone adorned the title document. When mortgages were taken out with Hiram MacDonald on the property, they were likewise in Hannah's name. When a further mortgage was taken out, to secure a one hundred dollar loan made by Marianne Cooke to Hannah in May of 1879, the dealings were in the name of Hannah Boyer. She and James discussed all these matters, but just as he often operated behind the scenes as municipal clerk, he now stayed prudently in the background on family property transactions, as well.

Hannah used the money from Marianne Cooke to pay sixty dollars to George Lee for Lots 5 and 29 on the northwest side of MacDonald Street. These were vacant lands just a short distance from their Manitoba Street house, which the Boyers would garden, still needing to grow as much of their own food as possible. Lizzy, still living with Hannah and James, witnessed her signature on the paperwork, documents all drawn up by James as conveyancer.

Compared to Bracebridge's hard core real estate players like Hiram McDonald, William Holditch, and Alfred Hunt, the Boyers were minor participants. For James the dealings were on the same scale he'd practised in Brooklyn, intermittently selling his house and buying another to net some money on the price difference. Even so, he and Hannah were in the arena and had been touched by the pace of the larger game.

The denouement of the Boyers' property activity was passive and came with the end their career as homesteaders. The other free grant lots in Macaulay claimed by James and Hannah lapsed to the Crown, since they neither lived on nor farmed them.

—

Harry Boyer's original Macaulay land claim had already lapsed, as well, but that did not mean he was, as earlier appeared, done with homesteading. While Hannah and James brought their family off the land to dwell in the village, her brother further south in Muskoka was just launching his family on a back-to-the-land escapade.

During the late 1870s, Harry, Flora, and their growing brood of children had "a wild care-free life." Around their cabin were "lots of berries, partridge, and fish — as well as an abundance of snakes, black-flies, and mosquitoes." Their land had been free, but its produce was poor. Harry did better with the "plentiful berries," which included blueberries and cranberries. They grew up on the rocks, and down around the swamps as they got drier during summer. Then the Boyers had to compete in harvesting them with hundreds of day-trip berry-pickers arriving in the vicinity from Orillia and Gravenhurst.

Much of this area around Morrison, Wood, and Muskoka townships was now devoid of pines, as a result of heavy logging and intense forest fires, leaving many "farms" almost entirely rock. The settlers' wagon route at Leg Lake was called "Stone Road" because it passed a long distance over bald bedrock. A neighbour named Pascal, a big Swede whose farm was entirely rock, only survived by practising his trade as a blacksmith. When he left in search of better land, he sold his entire lakeside place, buildings included, to a Mr. Wood for thirty-five dollars. What little the Boyers could grow they had no opportunity to sell anyway, in this hard and hard-up zone. Harry and Flora produced enough for themselves and their children to live on. Sometimes in dire need of supplies, Harry carried a load of whatever vegetables he could harvest into Gravenhurst, several miles to the northeast, to trade for goods at village stores.

—

Back up in Bracebridge, the couple whom Harry described in his diary as having been "married" in Brooklyn, had always been known to the community as husband and wife, appearances being taken as reality. James and Hannah kept their wits about them to preserve the ruse.

In New York they had contrived for their first child Annie's birth never to be registered. With the births in Muskoka of their children in 1872 and 1874, to prevent unwelcome questions or idle gossip, they gave Hannah's maiden name to the Bracebridge registrar not as "Boyer" (how to explain that?) but "Askew," a family name several generations back on Hannah's side of the family. The name also showed James's sense of humour since, if pronounced with emphasis on the first syllable (*As*-kew) it was indeed a known surname, but if on the second syllable (A-*skew*) it meant "something awry."

By the time their next children arrived, however, James was himself the local official responsible for registering births and disclosed Hannah's true maiden name, "Boyer." His newfound accuracy in recording personal information left an inexplicable contradiction on the public record, of course, solving one problem by creating another. Disclosure of Hannah's true surname did not mean that time's passage had put James at ease about his odd situation, nor had it made him careless about the risks his real identity posed. Rather, it was to support the touching story about how he and Hannah had met in New York, a tale concocted for puzzled family members to explain why the two of them had the same surname.

This story, as romantic as they come, made its way down through several generations, and was even innocently perpetrated by me in an earlier biography about my father and his ancestors, *A Man & His Words*. To recap, the tale is that when Hannah and the other Boyer children were stranded on the New York docks, officials searched city records for anyone having the name "Boyer" in the hope of matching the orphans with a relative, no matter how distant, who would take responsibility for them. Finding one James Boyer, a lawyer in the city, they sent for him, and though he was not related, he took pity on them and especially was attracted to Hannah, whom he shortly thereafter married.

James and Hannah's family grew as the years unfolded, and as their children became older and asked more questions, this saga of why their parents had identical surnames was taught, preached, and repeated until it became orthodoxy.

As for their family itself, Annie came with them from the United States, then Nellie and Charles had been born at the Macaulay homestead, where son Billy now lay buried. In Bracebridge at the Manitoba Street house, Hannah gave birth to another son on July 21, 1878, whom the couple named George. Like Nellie, the boy was given the middle name "White," to continue Hannah's mother's maiden name and renew those old ties.

Hannah and James had more children, but the next one to arrive was again the cause of heartbreak. Bertha, an infant of just eight weeks, was carried away by typhoid in December 1880. Another child, born easily on May 5, 1883, when Hannah was forty-two, would be their last. Hannah and James settled on the strong name Frederick Joseph Boyer, although the family diluted its impact, calling him Freddie, then just Fred.

When the family was feeling happy, or when they needed something to lift them to another plane, the Boyers made music. James played clarinet and flute, sang bass, and delighted to have his family sing Handel's *Messiah* as they grew older and learned their parts in this major, hallowed work. They enjoyed church attendance mostly for the music, less so for the liturgy, least of all for the sermons.

James's ever-expanding collection of books included volumes of music. First-born son, Charles, was proving to be especially musical. While he would in time become a school teacher at Ashworth west of Huntsville, then a law clerk in Bracebridge, Charles was best known and most popular as a great dancer, like his mother Hannah and her parents.

Second son, George, who in his turn would begin teaching barefoot pupils at a rural one-room Macaulay school at age sixteen, would be leading the Methodist Church choir at nineteen. George sang the soprano parts, or at least the air, until his voice changed.

All the children progressed through the Bracebridge schools, their standing reported monthly in the *Muskoka Herald*, which ran reports on each form, giving attendance reports and naming the teacher. When the paper carried results of examinations and students advancing to the next level, the young Boyers moved steadily with the ranks, about average in their marks, except for George, who was more diligent and usually near the top of his class. George was also active in the Literary Society of the

Bracebridge Model School, often giving recitations at its well-attended weekly Friday evening meetings. Annie Boyer's musical talent was channelled into the church choir, and also expressed, as the *Muskoka Herald* reported, "rendering several vocal selections which were well received" at a concert in the town hall.

In sports Charles and George were by far the most active players emerging from the Boyer household, with cricket and lacrosse two of their strongest sports. Charles was a player as well as secretary of the Bracebridge Junior Cricket Eleven, and George one of the team members. They were so good they looked for more competition, issuing a public challenge to "any fifteen or eighteen boys in the District of Muskoka under fifteen years of age to play a match at Bracebridge on Saturday." When the Methodist Sunday School held its annual excursion to Windermere, the boys formed into two sides for baseball, with Charles Boyer captain of his side.

In religion James had decided after coming to Muskoka to adhere to the Methodist Church, a consistent transition from the Episcopalian Methodist Church he'd joined in Brooklyn, and the best choice, given his views and character, among the limited options available. In addition to singing in the church choir and serving as recording secretary of the Methodist's Cemetery Board, he became a church trustee. With the shifts he'd made, it was not surprising that James told people who inquired about his denomination that he was "not a very firm believer in denominationalism." Hannah followed with him, becoming active in the Methodist church and its women's organizations, living "a consistent Christian life," as her son George put it, "doing her duty to her family and neighbours and to her church faithfully and well."

When it came to "duty to family," describing it as having been rendered "faithfully and well" was, of course, a bland understatement. Hannah's heroic determination to uphold and advance her family's vulnerable and scattered members was one dimension of duty intensely fulfilled. Another was the work that fell to her, as to all women in this era, to "keep house." First at their Macaulay homestead and then in Bracebridge, Hannah's daily life was measured out by a parade of chores to maintain her plain and frugal household from morning until night.

She baked bread and pies, cooked and served meals, and washed up. She filled lamps with oil, replaced the wicks, and cleaned the soot from their globes. Depending on the season, she kept the fire going, pickled vegetables, and made fruit preserves. She quilted covers for the bed, knit sweaters for her family, and sometimes hooked or braided rugs for the floor. She washed clothes and dried them on an outdoor line, or if it rained, indoors by the stove. She ironed shirts and skirts, using heavy cast-iron flat irons heated on top of the stove. She swept, cleaned, and polished. She planted, hoed, and harvested. She milked the cow or, after moving into the village, bought milk each day from a nearby farmer. She fetched eggs from their hens and pails of water from a stream.

All the while Hannah maintained her appearance, tended to the needs of her children, wrote to her sisters from the kitchen table, and served tea to visitors in the front room. In the evening, after she and James had shared a simple supper with the others, they caught up on news and views sitting together. Then he'd pick up a book, and Hannah, the woman who'd once crafted sensational bonnets for high society ladies in Brooklyn, settled down to darn socks, though she often couldn't for falling asleep.

"Sleep ..." whispered James, like a prayer, as he smiled upon his slumbering Hannah, "... that knits up the ravelled sleeve of care."

19

—

Powers of the Pen

James Boyer's success in creating his new Canadian identity owed much to his relationship with the pen. But even before reaching Muskoka, he advanced his career in different venues, through different jobs, thanks to pen and paper, as indispensable to him as an arrow and bow to an archer.

His first reward in the Moreton-in-Marsh classroom he attended was his schoolboy's good mark in penmanship and his teacher's smiling approbation for fine writing. His talent with a pen extended next into after-school and weekend work as a copyist in the law office of a Moreton solicitor. When it was time to leave home, he was able to use his skill in writing to land a copyist's position in a Stratford law firm, which he parlayed into work as a law clerk. Carrying his pen to New York City, his copyist talents and law clerk training got him a job at Brown, Hall & Vanderpoel, where he then became a lawyer. For Isaac Jelfs the "power of the pen" meant far more than this phrase usually implies.

In Brooklyn he discovered, when moving into the Gowanus neighbourhood and joining the Episcopalian Methodists, how organizations delight if somebody volunteers for a duty. If it is the inconspicuous and unenvied task of recording proceedings, the role is all the more readily given, with few questions asked. Suddenly finding himself the Episcopalian Methodist church secretary, Isaac found how easy it can be to penetrate an organization's inner workings. In Bracebridge he applied this insight almost from his first day of arrival.

Ability with the pen, combined with his practised skill in recording what was going on at meetings, soon made James Boyer a pivotal player as the small community's reliable recorder. Since folks feel more important when their utterances are considered noteworthy, locals welcomed the appearance of this talented note-taker in their midst. Before long James fully expected to be asked to serve as secretary of any meeting he attended, so "never went to a public event without carrying paper and pencil." His habit became self-reinforcing. In Bracebridge he found himself serving, at various intervals, as secretary of the Sons of England lodge, secretary of the Independent Order of Odd Fellows, and secretary of the Loyal Orange Lodge. He was voted secretary of the Loyal True Blue Association. He was named secretary of the Methodist Cemetery Board.

In addition to those fraternal, religious, and loyalist associations, James also became secretary of other major community organizations having a lot to do with how Bracebridge was run: the Agricultural Society, Bracebridge Public School Board, the Bracebridge Fire Company, and the Bracebridge Mechanics' Institute Library. In addition to all these positions was his influential office as municipal clerk, in which he was pen holder primo.

James shouldered these secretarial duties, not with the reluctance of those who resist clerical roles because they want greater prominence, but willingly — getting the prominence his ambition had begun to crave in New York, without the publicity that he feared because of New York.

Along the paths his pen took him, James gradually gained full understanding of the policies, problems, and personalities of these organizations, in the routine course of inconspicuously recording proceedings, receiving mail, sending out notices, and preparing reports. As time passed members and officers of these associations relied on him, amazed how he really knew more about what was going on than anybody else.

As he became indispensable, his ascent was inevitable. Over several decades James Boyer got to the top floor by coming in the back door. Just as in his prior life he'd used each advance of his career as a springboard to the next level up, James's secretary work at Bracebridge led to additional roles in these bodies. In time he would serve in the highest offices of most all them.

Between 1871 and 1873, James's crucial years for imprinting a new identity on himself and establishing his public persona in Bracebridge, his recording duties overlapped with his role as newspaper editor. At many association meetings, the indispensable secretary doubled as newspaper scribe. Because organizations wanted publicity and the paper needed news, James translated his notes of a meeting into a reporter's account for the *Northern Advocate*, satisfying two interests simultaneously. The man who was inseparable from his pen lived a seamless vocation.

By January 1875, when James emerged as clerk of both Macaulay Township and the newly incorporated Village of Bracebridge, minutes of the village and township council meetings stated alike, for the record, that the relationship between Bracebridge and Macaulay "was helped by having the same person as clerk." It was James Boyer, of course, who wrote that observation in those minutes, demonstrating how to pat oneself on the back while one's hand is out in front.

James, in his natural way, was doing what he knew best. His skill, finely honed through years of law office work and emphasized by good penmanship, was available for the asking. Respect began to accrue for the man with the pen, or pencil. Many central Muskoka organizations were doing well because he was their dependable, discreet, and diligent

Always meticulous in his record-keeping, James Boyer issued receipts for money earned in drawing up legal documents, even though he was not "officially" practicing law. This example, from late in his career, is for an 1890s bylaw and debenture for a new school section in Monck Township.

recorder. His pen sometimes brought a chance to earn money, and was invariably a vehicle for advancing his career.

—

But there was another reason James pursued these positions so actively.

Even as his experience in note-taking aided others, it helped shape and project the new persona of "James Boyer" that Isaac Jelfs was in the act of fashioning. Increasingly, the actor on stage became the character he was performing.

Not only did he create a flawless personal transformation that would survive intact for a century, he succeeded in parlaying his secretary work into positions of influence as an *eminence grise* in a fashion that is a telling study in the nature of power itself.

A more important part involved placing himself innocuously at the cross-over points between different organizations. For a number of years he was clerk of both the Township of Macaulay and the Village of Bracebridge, but for much longer he was the human link between two other parallel public bodies, the council and the school board. Although provincial policy separated politics and education by statute, with the Municipal Act and the Education Act requiring municipal councils and school boards to be distinctly separate elected bodies, Boyer himself was part of both. He simultaneously held office as municipal clerk of Bracebridge and secretary of the Bracebridge School Board. This armed him with better first-hand understanding than anyone else of the affairs and requirements of the municipal council and of the village's school. The fact he had also taught in one of Macaulay's schools, not a common attribute for a school board secretary, was further example of his overlapping knowledge from different spheres. This enabled him to better guide matters touching the school in Bracebridge because he was familiar with the needs of Macaulay's scattered one-room schoolhouses in the township. He was not a generalist, but a particularist, many times over.

As a one-person clearing house, coordinator, synthesizer, and concili-ator, James was harmoniously guiding the affairs of these various entities, both as they related to each other and as they collectively contributed to the governance and progress of Bracebridge. Imperceptibly, he'd become a powerful man in the small community.

Did this mean James Boyer secretly hoped to translate his power of the pen into power of elected office?

After arriving in the district and still cautious about not attracting attention, he identified himself as "an Independent Liberal," taking a cue from the successful A.P. Cockburn. James was not an active partisan. Living in a town rife with divisions over party politics, he astutely hewed to a line best described as *pleasant neutrality*. Even at the *Northern Advocate*, he'd been more than content to watch Thomas McMurray address contentious matters rather than push them himself.

This was prudent, because government, politics, law, and journalism were largely just different expressions of the same thing. James's was an era when newspapers were created to support a party or cause, judges appointed as reward for service to the party, and government operated to spread "the spoils of office" to deserving friends. Conflict of interest was an unknown concept. Confluence of interest was everyone's goal. Few rules prevented what, in a future era, would scandalize people. In the 1800s, overlap between public service and self-service in most cases was seen not only as appropriate but desirable.

In such a context, James's pleasant neutrality would have been instinctive for safeguarding his true identity. He kept his political views, generally, to himself. Such reticence truly set him apart, because few Muskokans hesitated to state opinions on anything, from the fence-sitting leaders of the country to the location of a neighbour's line fence. Bracebridge itself was a political hotbed. Dominion and provincial elections were frequent, council elections rolled around every New Year's Day, and townsfolk voted often on contentious plebiscite questions, all stoking the fires of political controversy.

Indeed, in this era before the secret ballot, nobody could really escape taking sides, because each man's vote was openly cast amidst spirited townsfolk thronging at public polling stations. The voter's spoken declaration, often a proud or defiant shout, named his chosen candidate. As a result everybody knew where a fellow stood, and whom he supported. As provincial and federal elections came and went, it became clear that James the Independent Liberal was voting Conservative as often as he voted for the party he nominally supported. When asked how that could be, he replied that he "judged by the principles a candidate stood for and what would be best for Muskoka." As for what would be best for voters and democracy, James felt, not surprisingly, that a secret ballot would be a good thing.

On becoming municipal clerk, James heaved a sigh of relief that his position restrained him from being outspoken, or even from taking any side at all. Conducting council elections and municipal plebiscites even required him to be *severely* neutral in the process. Using this shield James was content to be a quiet observer of controversies, fitting in so as not to stand out. He feared any animosity might trigger closer scrutiny by adversaries and betray his identity.

Even so, people continued to suggest James should run for elected office, saying he had all the qualifications, and more, of many who did. He took such suggestions as compliments, but always demurred, replying how his work in municipal government was on the administrative, not the elected, side. He could serve best by carrying on as municipal clerk to ensure stability in town, he explained, because with new councils elected every year, there was often such a turnover of members that somebody needed to remain in office long enough to ensure continuity of information about local programs and policies. That made sense. It also enhanced his power.

Such a stance above the fray comported well with James's work as municipal clerk, his role as secretary of the community's principal voluntary associations, and his instinct to keep his head down. It also served to help mould the new persona he had been working to establish since escaping to Canada.

A person can change his name more readily than his penmanship, as the slant of writing, the capital "J" on Jelfs and James, and the lower case letters "a," "e," and "s" all indicate.

He had been ambitious to improve his lot in life and render service, but to do so did not require *elected* office in government. Even though that prospect did attract him, as a further extension of service to the community, his fear of being found out foreclosed the possibility. James resigned himself to a major role in community affairs but with his head kept safe below the parapet. The truth would jeopardize everything.

The result was that James Boyer stood apart from the community, even though he was an integral part of it. He cleared his own land, but conveyanced thousands more acres for others. He took an active role in a secondary position, a more subtle form of leadership that got results without the bruising hits. He would never get real glory, but he could achieve quiet satisfaction. He was not the publisher, but the editor; not the mayor, but the municipal clerk; not the president, but the secretary. He was not Isaac, but James.

Exuding this fine balance, James had become a participant observer, a calm, reticent man whose nature suggested to others he could keep confidences. Many consulted him for his informed views on things. He became esteemed as a source for solid information, but also rose in the regard of powerful players because he was not, and did not seek to be, a contender. Pleasantly neutral James Boyer was not a threat to anybody.

———

As a pleasurable diversion, James even used his pen for the sideline of creating "illuminated addresses," written documents in fine calligraphy highlighted by artful graphic design and coloured inks.

People in central Muskoka wanting an anniversary certificate or an impressive document for a special occasion sought out his high quality penmanship, more and more as his reputation for them spread. The unique artifacts he crafted had many applications, being used for presentation of a citation, a commemorative certificate, or a civic tribute to an important official visiting Muskoka. James prepared them in his best calligraphy, using mostly red and black inks, sometimes with green and gold touches, and employed a variety of nibs of different thickness to achieve artistic flourishes.

Beyond technical skill as a writer and artisan, his adeptness as wordsmith helped convey the message that his customer, often someone with little formal education, sought to express. James was able, as Shakespeare urged, to "fit the word to the occasion, and the occasion to the word." It helped that, as town clerk, he was closely informed about Bracebridge doings and Muskoka relationships, enhancing his ability to capture just the right sense and proportion in writing these messages for anniversaries and special occasions.

There was, as well, yet another way James exercised the power of the pen. Apart from his recorder's skills, and in addition to the rich store of community information he brought with him to any meeting he attended, James was also welcomed for the practical reason that he could draft legal documents.

When establishing the Bracebridge Mechanics' Institute Library in 1874, a number of luminaries provided leadership, but it was James who drew up the bylaws. When he was named secretary of the Bracebridge Fire Company upon its formation in 1876, his first act was to write the bylaws to govern "Fire Rescue Company No. 1 of the Village of Bracebridge." The bylaws of the Muskoka Agricultural Society likewise first appeared in his handwriting.

For many of the community's various public and private bodies, and certainly for all the major ones, it was also James who reliably carried on official correspondence with other organizations, councils, and government departments. While his tasks as recording secretary overlapped with his editor's role at the *Northern Advocate*, it was a winning arrangement for all concerned. Although no longer running a newspaper, James remained indispensable to these organizations because his years at the *Northern Advocate* gave him so much direct understanding of the ways and workings of newspapers that he could arrange for public notices, advertisements, and news stories in the *Gazette* and *Muskoka Herald* in Bracebridge, the *Forester* in Huntsville and the *Banner* in Gravenhurst. Once a newspaper man, always a newspaper man.

James continued to record, report, and interpret the community to itself. The steady flow of public notices published in the newspapers over his name as an organization's secretary or as village clerk was one way of doing this. Another was that he continued to supply a reliable and steady flow of news items and articles to the *Advocate's* successor publications, the *Gazette* and *Muskoka Herald*, with whose proprietors he maintained cordial connections. A third was that, in place of his newspaper broadsheet, his minute books as clerk and bench book as magistrate became a reliable written source for specific community information, both in that era and since, for anyone seeking to understand an event. In addition to archived copies of the *Northern Advocate*, James Boyer's hand-written records have served posterity and, in so doing, preserved his scribe's place in history as well — another illustration of the power of the pen.

—

While resigned to avoiding the limelight, even while performing public functions, James nevertheless found something new occurring in his role as general secretary to the Bracebridge community. He was not only recording information. He had growing influence in how it was used by others.

On the most basic level of making minutes, he was the person who chose the words to describe what transpired. He was no stenographer making a verbatim transcript, but someone getting down the essence of what had been said. Thus, in artful and subtle ways, James rendered his own interpretations as he recorded things. As well, because writing is always a process of selection, he decided what got into the official account, and what was omitted. The man who'd made sure the birth of his first child with Hannah was never recorded knew the value, even the necessity, of occasionally omitting information from public records.

But his secretary's role involved more than deciding what narrative to create as Muskokans deliberated, reached decisions, and made their progress. Because he knew so much about the community's organizations, thanks to keeping the records of their every endeavour, James's specific knowledge increasingly made him an indispensable advisor.

Being the secretary for so many organizations, he also became the reliable source to those in senior positions for a sound, integrated interpretation of events across them all. Increasingly, it was hard to find any entity in the village of Bracebridge to which he did not belong, other than churches of other denominations. Beyond the village he also participated as secretary in district-wide fraternal, religious, and agricultural organizations. As Muskoka magistrate he gained an even wider perspective and a great deal of detailed information. He even became involved in private companies, such as Bracebridge & Trading Bay Railway Company, as secretary and a director.

The consolidated understanding he could extract from all these positions meant that pleasantly neutral James Boyer now wielded significant influence over the direction of community affairs, and the interpretation of who Muskokans were becoming as a people.

20

A Patriot's Refuge

If Isaac Jelfs had been able to live out his life in England, he would not have become the excessively zealous Englishman he created as James Boyer in Bracebridge. The more he was driven to reinvent himself, the more he sought reassuring refuge in patriotism.

At first, forced by fate to become an expatriate, and then an American citizen who renounced the great Queen Victoria as his sovereign, Isaac sought to retain some vestige of his birthright by joining the British Benevolent Society in Brooklyn, where his noticeable enthusiasm for the cause soon propelled him into a leadership position. Had he not decamped for Canada, he doubtless would have advanced from vice-president to president of this assembly of Brits trying to hold onto their identity rather than fully assimilate into American culture.

In Canada, though no longer facing fetters upon being British, he still found himself in a colony rather than the mother country, some kind of copy of the original. He suffered the curse of many whose identity comes from being born within an imperial power: a sense of superiority to the foreign land in which they found themselves. When his dilemma drove Isaac from New York, Canada beckoned because it offered free land, a remote hideaway, and relative safety as a place to reclaim his Britishness without the risks of returning to England itself. So the zealousness James Boyer displayed at Bracebridge in re-embracing his Britishness was the passion of a man trying to elevate himself out of the colony, the part of him seeking some kind of personal vindication.

Cloaking himself as a fervent British patriot was connected, at levels he did not even fully understand himself, to his new persona and the struggle, not of James Boyer, but of Isaac Jelfs. It would still require, as we shall see, remarkable development for this to be revealed.

In Bracebridge he promptly joined the Lancaster Lodge, a local chapter of the Sons of England. Later he enlisted in the Loyal Orange Lodge. In the interim he became a member of the Loyal True Blue Association.

Not only did he carry his note-taker's supplies to these organizations' meetings, since he'd become the secretary of each, but brought positive energy as well. Newspaper reports about James's involvement with the Orangemen, whom he joined through Bracebridge Lodge No. 218, made a point of referring to his "enthusiasm." He might be reticent about debating politics, but in the meeting rooms of these patriotic associations he freely expressed emotions of British pride. James was not just seeking personal fulfillment, but a measure of community respectability with the Orangemen, the True Blues, and the Sons of England.

The presence of so many loyalist organizations in the small community underscores just how British-minded Bracebridge was becoming. These groupings of the like-minded had a powerful reinforcing effect for their members, as well as within the village itself.

Like the Boyers, many British-born homesteaders resettling in Muskoka from the United States had only been in the New World a few years when they responded to the appeal of free land from Ontario's land agents and the allure of living in a British rather than American version of the New World. The upshot was that Muskoka had far more British-minded homesteaders than was disclosed by statistics on the number of arrivals from the U.S.A. Many emigrating north were, like James, not Yanks but hard-core Brits.

Hannah never doubted that she was a loyal British subject, regardless of where fate or love took her. Canada, being an integral part of the British Empire, gave her a sense of belonging, despite everything that was new and strange in Muskoka's pioneer frontier. Although Hannah willingly participated in Bracebridge's patriotic leagues for women, she was not as consumed as James by the importance of it all. She had not renounced her birthright so had nothing to prove by making amends, the way he now seemed to be doing. Hannah thought James was displaying uncharacteristic zealousness, but did not question the ardour he devoted to his new patriotic work. The man she loved now had full scope for impulses that in Brooklyn had been confined, and she was just happy that he seemed enthusiastic and self-assured.

———

A fine speaker with a warm style, James enjoyed holding forth in front of an audience.

The shyness he experienced early in life, and that had once made his solitary work of a copyist comforting, had been obliterated by years of soldiering, lawyering, and living in the United States. Whether he was in Brooklyn addressing prominent members of the Britannica Benevolent Association in their fine new Brooklyn hall, or speaking before homesteaders crowded on hard wooden benches and chairs in the Orange Hall beside the dirt track that was Bracebridge's main street, he was in his element facing an audience. James Boyer, others had noted, could always "rise to the occasion" when talking about Britain's glory.

The concept was real to him. Britain *was* glorious, provided he could forget the injustice of being made a scapegoat for a lawyer in Stratford, or the madness of a war fought in Crimea, or the poverty of back-alley children in Birmingham. Ignoring such gritty scandals, James lifted his eyes and his audience's mind to loftier themes: the democratic institution of British parliamentary government; the civilizing role of the British Empire in the world; the engaging playwrights and sensitive poets and, above all, the charm and genius and wisdom of William Shakespeare; the historic turning points in battle on the fields at Waterloo and the seas at Trafalgar; the resplendent Rule of Law; and of course Queen Victoria's ground-breaking reign.

James Boyer's relationship to Queen Victoria was emblematic of his real problem. In New York he renounced her, but now in Muskoka he reclaimed her. Both times it was because he sought to make a new life, in different countries, to overcome the calumny which had ruined his life in England and whose impact he could never escape, no matter where he fled. Denial had not helped much. Now he was embracing acceptance.

As his Muskoka years unfolded, James rose to senior ranks in all the patriotic and British loyalist societies he'd joined, and participated as well in other fraternal associations, including the Independent Order of Odd Fellows and the Independent Order of Foresters. All these entities — Sons of England, True Blues, Orange Lodge, Foresters, and Odd Fellows — were serving, in their particular way, to knit together the social fabric of Muskokans and create a bellicose culture that expressed itself with militancy in commemorating the Protestant victory at the Battle of the Boyne every July 12; embracing with vehemence the armed suppression of the Riel Rebellion; sending with enthusiasm young Muskoka settlers to their deaths in Britain's war against Dutch settlers in distant South Africa; and raising with deadly resolve an entire district-wide battalion of soldiers for the four-year massacre in Europe that awaited with the First World War.

Although he now seemed to cleave to all things British, James did not go so far as to rejoin the Church of England. He and Hannah had friends in the Bracebridge Anglican congregation at St. Thomas Church, but, not putting much stock in denominationalism anyway, he chose to stay with the church he'd joined on arrival in Bracebridge, the only one with a local congregation at the time, the Methodist Church, where he was fully engaged with choral work and also in charge of cemetery adminis-tration. Methodism was also of British origin, but more in keeping with his down-to-earth outlook.

———

James worked hard to contribute to the vitality of all these loyalist associations.

At Bracebridge's Lancaster Lodge, he and fellow members heard talks on important Anglo themes and got news about developments from across the British Empire. Some addresses were given by know-ledgeable English travellers visiting town; others were made by Lodge members taking turns. James felt the urge to step forward in these ranks, and decided to talk about the Battle of Trafalgar. He read and studied all he could lay his hands on at the Bracebridge Library, then gathered up his research, prepared his notes on this epic naval battle, and delivered a moving speech about its significance.

Beginning with the attention-getting conclusion that the engagement on October 21 in 1805 was the most decisive British naval victory in the Napoleonic Wars, he noted that the Battle of Trafalgar came early in the long war, which had begun two years earlier and would drag on until 1815 and that year's decisive victory over Napoleon's army in the Battle of Waterloo. James described how Admiral Nelson led twenty-seven ships to face the combined fleets of the French and Spanish navies off the southwest coast of Spain, near Cape Trafalgar. Then he reported how the Royal Navy destroyed twenty-two of the enemy's thirty-three ships, without losing a single British vessel.

"Hear, hear!" interrupted several voices from the militant Lodge audience, expressing patriotic approbation.

James added that the one-sided spectacle confirmed to the world the naval supremacy Britain had established in the 1700s, then stressed how the British victory in part was due to Horatio Nelson's departure from orthodox naval tactics. The prevailing method for engaging an enemy fleet involved presenting a single line of battle, parallel to the enemy, to facilitate signalling in battle, maximize fields of fire on target ships, and permit ready disengagement should retreat become necessary. Nelson gained the all-important element of surprise, however, when he instead divided his smaller force into two columns and ordered them to attack the larger enemy fleet, not frontally but on a perpendicular angle. "The results," James explained, "were decisive."

He hardly needed to add that Nelson was mortally wounded during the battle, becoming in death one of Britain's greatest war heroes, because every Son of England in the hall, just as each child in school, had been taught about Nelson's valiant death as bedrock history, just as the lesson was known, though James repeated it anyway, that after the Battle of Trafalgar, the Royal Navy would dominate the world's seas.

James relished the applause, and suggestions that he print his address in the newspaper. Thomas McMurray was delighted with such content in for the *Northern Advocate*. It would augment his paper's appeal to potential immigrants from Britain, portraying Muskoka as a place where British values and knowledge were at the forefront.

A full decade later, still enthralled by the saga of Nelson's heroic venture, and impressed most of all because of the commander's intelligence in doing something unorthodox to prevail, James was delighted to find in a Toronto book and art shop a large-scale dramatic presentation of the admiral's triumphal moment. He bought one, and in Bracebridge had the five foot by twenty inch engraved print framed in dark mahogany and covered in glass. As such a patriotic Brit, James said it was the least he could do to honour the man who stood in marble atop a stone column on Trafalgar Square in London.

In his home the engraving had pride of place, and James delighted when patriotic visitors admired this rendition of mortally wounded Admiral Nelson, prostrate on the deck of his aptly named ship *Victory*. They saw the dying commander's head, held upraised against the thigh of one of his officers, steadied while looks of awe and dismay mark the expression of all others around their fallen commander. The battle raged on, cannonballs ripped through sails nearby, but Nelson's calm face remained as fearless of Death as of the Spanish Armada.

———

In addition to wrapping himself in the Union Jack, Isaac fleshed out his new James Boyer persona in other ways, too.

Being constantly drawn into activities that required close attention to others, James craved solitude for balance in his life. He could even get that quietude in the presence of others. As clerk and secretary, he often sat calmly recording proceedings as storms of contention raged around him. Even as he interacted with others, he maintained a sphere of privacy and professional remoteness, his serious conversation and mild humour becoming an effective buffer to shield him. Not one to share intimate companionship with other men through fishing, hunting, or sports, he relished the quiet joys of being alone, interacting with himself, not having to explain anything to anybody. His thoughts drifted by free association into creative daydreams, helping James rebalance himself between public affairs and his inner devils. Reading books was another avenue, available even in the presence of others, whether in a crowded train compartment to Toronto or in the company of his family, he would sit resolutely facing the pages of a book to deflect interruption. A companionable book was James's passport from the daily moil to places where his true self found stimulation and refreshment, entering a larger universe where his private misgivings submerged in the flow of humanity's deeper, wider currents.

James's ability to retain his equilibrium through setbacks and difficult situations sprang from his own awareness of his emotional limits and his capacity to overcome fatigue or dispel anxiety. One way was to retreat to the Chippewa clearing in the woods, or a pristine place like it, and simply see himself as a small speck in the vast timelessness of nature, giving his current "crisis" its due proportion. Another route to renewal for James was music, playing or singing to ease tensions and provide an outlet for frustration or anger. Still another, as noted, was the handiest, picking up a book and transporting himself through its pages to somewhere else. He found novels an easy escape, but his deeper form of respite came through more serious works, such as a familiar drama of Shakespeare, in which joy and sorrow commingled and pulled his feelings and thoughts into a different channel altogether.

James's refuge in a glorified interpretation of his birthright stood in contrast to all these other ways he coped. His exuberant pro-British sentiment, when viewed in relation to the balanced, detached, stoic, and philosophical manner in which he generally lived his life, seemed out of character, Hannah noticed this. The artificiality of intense patriotism was different because it was a mask covering Isaac's deeper conundrum.

Hannah's love was the most enduring and truest thing in his life. It could make him sail up into heaven and still be anchored to the strongest rock below. He was more natural when he wrapped her in his arms, than himself in the flag.

The loyalist societies in Bracebridge esteemed visible patriotism. As Bracebridge clerk James ensured that council voted money at regular intervals to buy a crisp new Union Jack for the municipal hall. An unostentatious man he never wore a flower, except once each year, when he fastened a rose in his lapel on St. George's Day to honour the patron saint of England.

Wrapping himself in the Union Jack and re-embracing his Britishness with profound intensity enabled Isaac Jelfs to reclaim something of his real self and the world he'd lost, though it was a distorted version of how Isaac would have been if able to continue simply as a law clerk in some English county town, living out his time in the prosaic Englishman's way of life. In Canada, being a red-blooded Brit was part of the character "James Boyer" acted out, which had the irony of being how Isaac Jelfs helped retain something of himself even as that reality became distorted.

Though restored to his British birthright by emotion, he had not reclaimed his British status in law, for Isaac remained a citizen of the United States. He expediently reassumed, on his own, his legal status as "a British subject" in Canada, as if the New York chapter of his life had never been written. Aided by his English accent, he was never challenged. As an American, he voted in Canadian elections and held offices as municipal clerk and district magistrate that required him to swear allegiance to the Queen.

Though without his original name, and no longer clean-shaven but wearing a masking beard, Isaac Jelfs, "the lost one found," had resurrected himself in James Boyer, ardent patriot.

The continuous interactions and changes between these two versions of the same man assumed the mind-bending complexity known to a double-agent or someone lost in the Hall of Mirrors.

21

—

Upholding the Rule of Law

Just as James Boyer's life was created by Isaac Jelfs, so in turn Isaac's life had often been shaped by others.

As a boy he was sent by his parents to Moreton solicitor Edwin Tilsley's office to earn money for the family as a copyist, which he did. When they told him at age seventeen it was time to leave home, he did. When his employers in Stratford sent him away saddled with blame, he was propelled in a fateful new direction. When Elizabeth Heath and he married, it appeared to have been a bond more of her making than his. The British government got into a war that swept him onto a new course. Its trajectory propelled him, via Crimea, to the New World.

In Muskoka his destiny continued very much in the hands of others, in particular Thomas McMurray and A.P. Cockburn. Both men shared many attributes. McMurray promoted Muskoka's development through land settlement and moral uplift; was elected first reeve of four combined townships in the centre of the district; erected office buildings; and operated a number of commercial services. As pioneer publisher in the north, he advocated growth and development, and became a prophet for building a better society. Cockburn, just as entrepreneurial and visionary, promoted Muskoka's development through land settlement, logging, and tourism. He'd started a grocery business in Gravenhurst, begun the village's first newspaper, and emerged as Muskoka's pioneering steamboat operator with the district's first fleet on the lakes. Both men worked through political office, McMurray at the municipal level, Cockburn graduating from local office to become Muskoka's representative in both the provincial and federal legislatures.

Cockburn and McMurray were two of the most influential men in the district's opening days. As catalysts in Muskoka's progress, each was astute enough to entwine their causes with James Boyer's malleable life. They found in him an alert, informed, and deferential man who applied himself diligently in ways that advanced their own causes and careers.

For James's part, while his life had indeed often seemed like a cork bobbing on waves stirred by others, he was not passive about accepting the new directions proposed for him, first by McMurray, or later Cockburn. He became a willing voyager because their visions inspired him to see Muskoka as something much grander than his initial view of the district as his last, best refuge. And the roles they led him into as newspaper editor, then as magistrate, gave larger importance to the new persona he was striving to create in Canada than anything he could ever have fashioned on his own.

—

Cockburn enjoyed boasting that he was the man who'd "introduced James Boyer to Muskoka," referring to the coach ride he shared with the Boyers, and his commentary, as they crossed the Severn River together, when the party from New York entered Muskoka for the first time in September 1869.

After that first encounter sharing a rough coach ride, the two men kept in contact. Cockburn was a shrewd man who advanced his interests through politics. That required keeping friendly with someone who, at turns as newspaper editor, school teacher, municipal clerk, and officer of more than a half-dozen church, fraternal, loyalist, and agricultural societies, could influence countless others.

Whenever occasion permitted, the two enjoyed free-booting information and ideas, finding their exchanges stimulating as well as informative. Each operated for Muskoka's interests, but in different arenas, so each was able to illuminate whatever topic was under discussion from different angles. They shared a wily, hard-nosed outlook about the workings of government and politics. Although both were Liberals, each was also his own man. If James voted for Conservative candidates when he agreed with their stands, Cockburn voted with Conservatives in Parliament or the legislature if it helped install locks on the Indian River for his steamboats, get Crown timber concessions to log Muskoka's forests, win government grants and mail contracts for his pioneering steamboats, or get people he recommended appointed to public offices.

One day Cockburn suggested it was time for James to become a justice of the peace and serve as magistrate of Muskoka. He would recommend the appointment. James was flattered, but astonished. He'd first become familiar with the role of county magistrates in Moreton-in-Marsh, where effective local government was principally in their hands. Then he had some dealings with the magistrate as a law clerk in Stratford-upon-Avon. But in those English settings, and given the prominent social standing of Britain's county magistrates, he never imagined occupying such a role himself. He became distracted thinking about the implications for his hidden identity.

The rules governing appointment, Cockburn continued, because James remained silent and appeared somewhat stunned, stipulated that a JP could not be a practising lawyer. Another shock. Suddenly, the very circumstances that had precluded a chagrined James from formally practising law in Ontario turned out to be an advantage, an ironic twist of fate of which his friend Cockburn was, of course, unaware.

Alexander Cockburn, a dynamo in Muskoka's early development, and active in lumbering, retailing, shipping, and politics, knew how to meld his advancement with the district's progress. In 1869 he'd accompanied the Boyers into Muskoka, and within the decade he had helped his friend and protégée James become magistrate.

The provincial government, Cockburn continued in his monologue, liked to appoint someone of "standing" in the community, which James had achieved in less than a decade as editor of the district's first newspaper, clerk of the district's capital municipality, and a senior officer of many community organizations. If a Liberal, even an "Independent" one, Cockburn concluded with a grin, better still. Eventually, James must have said "Yes," or else Cockburn just took his dazed silence to mean consent.

Oliver Mowat, a mutton-chopped man with poor eyesight and thick glasses, was leader of the provincial Liberals and the successful head of Ontario's government, serving as both premier and attorney general. His success was due in part to the close attention he paid to political patronage. That included whom he appointed as local magistrates. In 1878, on the recommendation of Muskoka's Liberal member of Parliament, A.P. Cockburn, Mowat appointed his fellow Liberal "James Isaac Boyer" of Bracebridge as Magistrate for Muskoka District.

———

In shouldering his duty to uphold the "Rule of Law" in Muskoka's rugged 1870s frontier society, James at age forty had become the magistrate, a personage he could not have contemplated during his days in England.

Cockburn understood enough about his friend to know that a position with some remuneration would help. But James's appointment did not come through as a "stipendiary magistrate," which would have included getting pay from the provincial government. Instead, James found himself in the same dubious position as most Ontario justices of the peace, having to pay himself out of the fines he levied. It was a process subversive to the administration of justice. The greater the number of convictions, the larger the pool of individuals on whom to impose a fine. The higher the fine levied, the more money flowed into a JPs' court from which he could pay himself, a system so tempting it required men as virtuous as angels to hold the office.

Not all were. A few avaricious justices of the peace in Ontario became so zealous in executing their duties that they travelled around with constables, helping them find infractions to prosecute, boosting their self-generated remuneration. Even the most ethical and public minded JPs, working hard to provide justice, still had to use this system, or else get no payment at all.

A number of municipalities mitigated the bad effects of this slice-back system by paying the local JP themselves. In Bracebridge this was an on-again, off-again arrangement, fluctuating with changes in town council's attitude and the state of municipal revenues. James strongly advocated the principle of remunerating JPs from public funds, arguing that for proper administration of justice and to create respect for the rule of law, a public official such as Muskoka's magistrate should not be paid from the fines he himself levied.

A second feature James faced in the operation of his court, which would also surprise many today, was the use of "moieties," a sort of finder's fee for people bringing cases to court. Canadian legislators had imported this practice from English courts as a reward to individuals for prosecuting public offences. Anyone could make "a citizen's arrest." Known in the 1800s as "common informers," these individuals initiated court proceedings for any breach of the law they saw, in exchange for getting a share of the fine, provided they had enough evidence to convict

His beard trimmed more neatly, James Boyer appears to have hit his stride as Bracebridge municipal clerk, magistrate of Muskoka, senior officer in many organizations, and head of a growing family. Yet his solemn reticence endures.

the culprit. Usually they did, with evidence of deer killed out of season or ducks blown out of the sky on the Lord's Day, but sometimes James would dismiss a case when the self-designated enforcer had no evidence to disprove an accused's assertion that he wasn't deer hunting out of season but "only shooting a squirrel to feed my dog."

James recognized the strengths and weaknesses of the moiety system. The odd word *moiety* itself was a bastardized English version of the French word *moitié*, meaning half. Originally, this rule authorized a judge to pay half the convicted person's fine to whoever had prosecuted him, but over time moieties came to mean *any* fractional part of the fine, and James sometimes awarded only a third, or sometimes even a quarter, of the fine to the private prosecutor. He did this to balance the system if he deemed the common informer too zealous arresting men and boys who, though in technical breech of the Game Act, were just trying to feed their hungry families. James himself had hunted to prevent the Boyers starving, sometimes with his eye on the woods rather than the calendar and statutory hunting seasons. He wanted to uphold the rule of law, but appreciated that he had to be realistic about doing so in a frontier society where sometimes the law of survival trumped all others.

Yet, precisely because Muskoka was a wilderness, James also felt moieties did have a useful role in helping uphold the rule of law. Paying them cost the public treasury nothing. It was an easy way to increase law enforcement, far beyond the limited number of constables and provincial game wardens. Isolated hunters deep in the woods shooting deer out of season contrary to the Game Act, or a lone angler catching fish up some obscure stream on Sunday in violation of the Lord's Day Act, were paraded before James Boyer in court by alert informers who'd done it for the money.

James usually heard the cases in the town hall, where he could convene court on a moment's notice. As municipal clerk he was already handy in the same building. On occasion he travelled to other communities, such as Falkenburg and Port Carling, for trials there. Sometimes on weekends and occasionally at night, he'd answer a knock on the door to find a constable with an arrested man, and provide speedy justice on the spot. The rule of law took no holiday, so neither did the constables nor the justice of the peace.

For every case, James recorded the particulars on the glossy pages of a leather-bound volume he purchased from Eaton's department store during a visit to Toronto. This "bench book" became the only record of what transpired. In addition to the style of cause, names of the parties, and crucial statements of testimony, James recorded at the end of cases whether the result was a conviction, dismissal, or, on rare occasions, an appeal of his decision. If the guilty party was sentenced to serve time, that fact and confirmation of his committal to jail were recorded. Entries were also made when a convicted person, unable to pay his fine, was put in jail instead.

The "Bracebridge Rock Cut" was blasted out of the Canadian Shield for railway tracks in 1884. When this work gang had gone unpaid for weeks, they rioted in town. James Boyer had seen riots in New York and Montreal, and moved quickly as municipal clerk and magistrate to face down the men, reading the Riot Act to them in his successful bid to restore order.

These informative records owe much to the fact James was adept at getting down important points, and recording a witness's telling phrase. He wrote with pen and ink, quickly taking down basic details and essential evidence as it was being given. Short forms and abbreviations he'd learned as a law clerk in England and a lawyer in New York helped him keep up with the rapid flow of testimony before him in Bracebridge. His knack for summarizing events had been further polished writing succinct accounts of lengthy community meetings for the *Northern Advocate*. For James, making a good record was an ingrained skill and a valued exercise in its own right.

Sometimes documentary evidence was presented in court. These records ranged from a township's licensing bylaw, under which it was prosecuting a farmer for selling vegetables to cottagers from his boat, or Bracebridge's restrictive bylaws on closing hours for stores or cows wandering at large on the streets, to a newspaper advertisement of a local "doctor" whose remedies promised amazing cures when he was not in fact a qualified medical man at all. Other evidence came as objects produced in court. When James examined exhibits of animal parts, several fowl that had been stolen, confiscated guns, a distiller's illegal bush-lot still, sticks, axes, and stones.

The dilemma facing him each time was how to dispose justly of the contentious matter before him. At this stage of the proceedings, James pondered awhile and then, unless dismissing the case, announced his sentence, usually choosing between a fine or a period in the lock-up. If the latter, the prisoner was escorted to the squat stone structure right behind the town hall, or in the late 1890s, cells in the stone cellar of the Muskoka Herald building next door. If a fine, he then had to decide how much money the guilty person should forfeit to make the punishment fit their crime. Prostitutes got hefty fines, although the sentence was sometimes coupled with the proviso that they need not pay if they left town. Stealing a silk scarf, breaking a window pane, or absconding with some else's chicken brought fines so high they seem outlandishly harsh by today's standards.

Usually the person who was fined would be given a backup sentence of time in jail, in the event of non-payment. Sometimes the fine was supported by a distress order, meaning James empowered the sheriff to seize the person's assets if he couldn't pay the amount, to sell them and use the proceeds for the fine owing to the court. No reasons had to be given for any judgment in a JP's court, and none were. The penalty spoke for itself.

James had no court clerk to record the proceedings, register the verdicts, or administer the fines. He did it all. His bench book served as official ledger for payment of fines and costs. He'd note the amounts of fines levied, of payments received, any payments made to constables and witnesses or allocated to court expenses. If it applied he also recorded the amount of a moiety paid to a person bringing the charge. He glued in receipts. Where fines were paid off in installments, his series of entries tracked the gradual reduction of a convicted person's debt. James made these financial and administrative entries directly in the bench book, at the bottom of the case in question, having no other system for keeping such records.

When it was necessary to update his records of decided cases — for instance when a garnishee had finally produced money for a fine, or when a convicted person who'd absconded had been tracked down, arrested, and brought back by the sheriff to face justice in Bracebridge — James normally turned back several pages to the relevant case and added a notation, sometimes weeks or even months later. But he was a busy man and sometimes got behind in his work. Then, he'd just make a cluster of entries for several different cases, all at one time and on a subsequent page, hurriedly catching up. One way or another, James's meticulous nature resulted in all key information in the same convenient volume. James sometimes noticed periods of several calm weeks between cases, as if all was quiet in law-abiding Muskoka. Other times he faced a flurry of prosecutions, as if the district was being overrun by a crime wave. The difference, he soon realized, was that a particular town constable had been feeling public pressure to crack down, or a newly hired hygiene inspector was out to prove his mettle, or a hard-up individual learned he could get money through moieties and went around laying charges for public offences against his errant friends and wayward neighbours, or sometimes even his own relatives.

Every case heard by James Boyer was carefully recorded in his clear handwriting, as seen from this typical page of 1890s cases in his "bench book."

In bleak Birmingham, then in the Crimean War, and after that in rowdy, corrupt, filthy New York, James had already seen a lot of life's rawness. In the coming three decades presiding over Muskoka Magistrate's Court, he would peer still more deeply into causes of hardship, and witness more sharply the unending varieties of the human dilemma.

Whether hidden beneath a carapace of pride or behind a cloak of shame, many of the individuals arraigned in court before James Boyer had secrets about what caused them to be on trial. The man who sat before them in judgment had secrets about why he was there, too.

22

Bound Up in Farming

James proved, after coming off his township farm to Bracebridge, that while a man might leave the country, the country will not let go of the man. Even a quarter century later, James would write Hannah how he was still "terrifically bound up in fall fair work."

One reason was that farming had always been a deeply ingrained aspect of his makeup, another that the traumatizing impact of farming in Muskoka stayed with him, and a third that it was one of the most natural and therefore wholesome aspects of who he'd become in his new Canadian life. Where his exuberant embrace of old Britishness in the fresh setting of Canada was not uncommon in this colonial culture, it was still highly artificial. Everything about farming was real.

Unlike some settlers arriving in Muskoka with a lot of hope but little or no farming experience, the Boyers were already quite familiar with rural life.

James had soaked up farming's needs, seasons, and practices at Moreton-in-Marsh. Hannah and Harry, growing up on estate farms in England, had been taught by the fen master, their father Joseph, to remain attentive to everything happening in and around the fields. Harry's year on the Farm School for Boys at Westchester underscored the lessons about farming's long hours and hard work, but also imparted practical know-how for picking fruit, digging potatoes, minding hens, milking cows, and churning butter.

Like most folk from small 1800s villages, the Boyers were also adept at saddling and riding a horse, harnessing horses and driving wagons, and knew basic horse-care from feeding to brushing down. They understood first-hand how chickens, hogs, and milk cows fitted into the picture. As they headed into Canada in autumn of 1869, the Boyers believed that, together, they could prosper on their farm.

Before arriving James pictured what their new farming life would be like, but two aspects were beyond envisaging. The first loomed when they crossed the Severn River and came smack up against the rising rock face of the Canadian Shield. This irregular terrain of lakes and rock, catchments of good soil interspersed with large stretches having only a thin overburden, bottomless swamps and high waterfalls, was the unexpected face of Muskoka's agricultural lands greeting them. It was unlike anything in other farming regions. From the time they scratched the first seeds into patches of exposed dirt around stumps during the opening spring of 1870, James and Hannah, as well as Harry, discovered through one shock after another how Muskoka's geography forced farming to be different.

The second thing James did not envisage was that he would become not only a farmer, but a farm leader. His self-descriptions in his early Muskoka years changed from "gentleman" to "yeoman" to "farmer," as he re-defined himself through the lens of his Macaulay farm. He remained devoted to Muskoka farming because this identity was essential glue holding together the new man James Boyer had become.

A founding member of the Muskoka Agricultural Society, he'd happily written the bylaws setting out the organization's goals, a felicitous blending of his desire for Muskoka farmers to prosper and his lawyer's interest in structure, form, and clarity.

A principal object of the Agricultural Society was holding a fall fair. These events thrilled James. The boyhood excitement he felt Tuesdays when farmers brought fresh produce into Moreton and the town filled with a festive "market day" atmosphere was rekindled at every fall fair he attended in Muskoka. The memory of the country competitions and loud cheering at the Cotswold Games was another joyous connection to his youth, triggered when the fall fair races began. The joy in seeing friends and renewing acquaintances from the countryside gave a comforting reassurance he'd never known in his life, except in Muskoka.

The fall fairs, by establishing well-attended public venues for farmers to display their animals and produce, and farmwives their baking and sewing, encouraged higher quality produce and better bred livestock. By fostering competition the fairs also advanced household arts in baking, pickling, making preserves, churning butter, sewing, quilting, and knitting. Not only in Bracebridge, but in Severn Bridge, Gravenhurst, Baysville, Huntsville, and Rosseau, excitement built as judges made their rounds, examining entries to award red, blue, and white ribbons for first, second, and third prize, along with the all-important cash that accompanied them. Fall fairs became a Muskoka venue for fun, learning, pride in prizes, and camaraderie between farm folk and townspeople. James was in the middle of it all, because a fair focused the entire community's attention on the importance of farming.

He continued as the Agricultural Society's secretary, became a director, and in 1884 served as president. Although he was but one leader among many in Muskoka's farming community, James Boyer was among the most willing in his steady, quiet way.

—

His emergence into a prominent role with Muskoka's farming community also stemmed from how James, inspired by Thomas McMurray, had himself become a promoter of agriculture in the district. From the front lines, publisher and editor boosted Ontario's free grant territory with enthusiasm and to good effect. In Muskoka's important settlement years from 1871 to 1873, James was in regular contact with farmers across Muskoka, looking for "practical tips from experience" for readers of the *Northern Advocate*. When a farmer couldn't write copy himself, James penned accounts from information gleaned from his rural contacts.

The district's free grant opportunities were simultaneously being advanced further afield by zealous railway companies, land companies, the government's own overseas immigrant recruiting agents, and even religious leaders like Reverend Styleman Herring in England, who organized his parishioners to colonize Muskoka. Their combined effort was filling the district with pioneer farmers. By 1877 the whole of Macaulay Township was taken up, including lots held by a number of squatters. All but five of the most marginal lots in the township were occupied. As James witnessed all this from the Muskoka end of things, he could not help but feel vindicated, both as one of the very early settlers and as one of the very strong advocates for farming in the north country.

James travelled far and wide, usually with a fellow officer of the Agricultural Society, to display Muskoka's prize-winning produce after it had been judged at the Bracebridge Fall Fair or similar fairs around the district. In successive years he appeared with bushels and baskets at the Canadian National Exhibition in Toronto, the Central Canada Exhibition in Ottawa, and the fall fairs at Owen Sound and Barrie, putting on show Muskoka farmers' best products. This was important, he believed, to counteract the bad press Muskoka was getting as a stony nightmare for luckless farmers.

Getting good press, though, was not easy. In a letter home to Hannah from Owen Sound, James related how a reporter looked over the exhibit of Muskoka produce with favour, then propositioned him: "Good exhibit. If you pay me, I'll write it up in the paper." James was indignant, and "did not pay." It was no different in Toronto. In the autumn of 1887, the Agricultural Society sent president Peter Shannon and secretary James Boyer to exhibit produce at the Canadian National Exhibition. Both men were keen to show that Muskoka had become an agricultural contender, despite what critics said. Described by James as "a splendid exhibit," their prized entries came from farms in all sections of Muskoka.

"It was difficult," he wrote Hannah from Toronto on September 12, "to make some of the visitors believe that grapes (Lindley or Rogers No. 9), some bunches of which weighed 1¼ pounds each, were grown in the open air of Muskoka." One of the samples of wheat grown on light, sandy soil in Macaulay was sold at the close of the Toronto Exhibition to an American for one dollar, a very good price. James described the praise Muskoka's exhibit received. "Our Duchess apples are not beaten by any that are exhibited prizes. Both the *Globe* and the *Mail* wanted to be paid to puff our exhibit, but Shannon and I refused to pay them one cent."

Muskoka's valiant farmers faced not only hard land, but hard-bitten newspapermen as well.

Some fortunate settlers, winners at land grant roulette, had discovered pockets of fine Muskoka soils in the district's scattered valleys and flats. Priding themselves on good farming practices, their crops and produce compared advantageously when put on display at major fall fairs in the populous southern parts of the province. That is how James sought to show that Muskoka was no forlorn wasteland for farmers, even without paid articles in the daily papers' news columns.

———

The Ontario government, in opening the northern districts of Muskoka, Parry Sound, and Nippissing to settlers, sought to create another region of self-sufficient farmers in the province. It had only taken a few years for the government's settlement policy for Muskoka to get results, but they were mixed — reflecting the variable terrain of the district itself.

Harry Boyer was one of those who decided, in township terminology, to let his lot in Macaulay "run out." He just let the five-year limit expire, without fulfilling the requirements to clear, build, and live on the land he had "located" by making his claim in 1869 with the government's land agent. Because a homesteader's claim lapsed for non-fulfillment, the property simply remained with the Crown.

Farmers who had been unfortunate in their choice of lots had no hope of winning prizes at the fall fairs. Getting food enough to survive off their rocky land was difficult enough. By 1886, although 133 new settlers located on lots in the district's townships that year, the government at the same time cancelled ninety-nine grants for non-fulfillment of settlement duties. Many farms were deserted. Some families stayed in poor locations on scrub land and sank to poverty living.

The agricultural experience in Muskoka was gradually producing, in addition to its success stories, an economic underclass of families whose farms were marginal, or worse, but who remained on them just the same, because they had nowhere else to go. They had escaped to Muskoka, but could not escape from it.

From James's various vantage points — working his own farm, at the *Northern Advocate* editor's desk, in the Bracebridge town office, on the magistrate's bench, conveyancing homesteaders' properties at the land registry office, interacting with other municipal clerks across the district, and as an officer of many community organizations including the Agricultural Society — he took stock. It was time for reappraisal. He began to see Muskoka agriculture with new eyes. Farming was not what had been expected, either by most settlers or by the Ontario government itself. It had changed, becoming remade in the image of Muskoka itself. Therefore, a farmer's role in this district had to be understood in quite different terms than applied in southern Ontario, if it was to be understood at all.

From the outset the province's action in granting timber permits for logging the district while simultaneously issuing grants of land for agricultural settlement guaranteed that farming in Muskoka would be unlike the experience elsewhere. James had encountered the results of that directly, when the government wanted the Boyers and all other homesteaders to pay stumpage fees, the same royalties the loggers paid, as if they were logging rather than clearing land for farming.

James saw a second example when government policy created incompatible uses of navigable waters. Litigation came before Bracebridge courts about log booms blocking the river and preventing settler activity, impeding steamboats, and even denying resupply of the Bracebridge settlement on which farmers in central Muskoka, as well as villagers, depended.

James accepted that agriculture in Muskoka was on a different course from that envisaged by the government in its promotional brochure about free grant farming that he'd first read in Brooklyn, when he saw how the district economy was evolving in totally unexpected ways. Local manufacturing and hospitality services for vacationers, which nobody contemplated when opening the territory for homesteaders to farm, not only emerged but had done so in a way that most Muskoka farmers were now part of this new economy. While "mixed farming" was the term to describe small subsistence farms combining cultivation of crops with raising of livestock, James recognized that in Muskoka "mixed farming" had an expanded meaning because it entailed a far broader range of broadly defined "agricultural" pursuits.

This unanticipated reworking of farming in its Muskoka context began simply enough, when loggers and homesteaders discovered their mutual dependence. The men whom logging companies hired needed to eat; Muskoka farmers sold them food. The companies needed men in the bush camps felling trees during the winter; strong-backed farmers worked for them in the off-season while their wives and children milked cows, gathered eggs, and did other chores back on the farm. Farmers who felled trees while clearing the land could get money for logs they got to a lumber mill, and so they stopped the wasteful practice of burning them.

James realized, as he evaluated this evolution, that not only did traditional idea of farming not much apply in Muskoka, but more crucially, other farm-based activity, which nobody talked about, did.

In Muskoka some marginal rocky farms, instead of failing by following traditional farming patterns, evolved successfully into prospering operations because their entrepreneurial owners began doing things differently. They became integral to Muskoka's new "mixed farming" economy, in many ways.

A number began raising sheep to supply wool to Henry Bird's vast woollen mill in Bracebridge. Other farmers, who'd already learned to supplement their meagre incomes from crops, milk, eggs, and livestock by cutting trees in the winter to supply the sawmills, found with the new leather tanneries in Bracebridge and Huntsville that it paid to specialize, when it came to felling trees, on their stands of hemlock. By supplying vast quantities of hemlock bark, or the bark of other trees rich in tannins, to the insatiable tannic acid vats of Muskoka's sprawling leather tanneries, they had a new year-round source of income. Both the leather tannery and the woollen mill gave a surprise boost to local farmers that, as James realized, "put a very different face on 'agriculture' in Muskoka."

Lucrative harvests could also be produced from a farmer's forests in the form of maple sugar and maple syrup, and production across Muskoka soared. For still other farmers, if they had claimed lots fronting on lakes, new income from the land could be derived from a two-legged cash crop: the human visitors busy creating Muskoka's rapidly emerging vacation resort economy. By the late 1800s, more farmers with land that was too uneven or stony to plow for crops could seed it with grass and populate their spread with herds of milk cows, earning good money supplying many gallons of milk daily to the cheese factories at Rosseau, Watt, and elsewhere in north Muskoka, and Bracebridge.

James was no mere observer, but an active participant, in many of these changes. In the case of the cheese factory, for instance, his role as clerk of Bracebridge was important. In 1898 William Spencer, who'd arrived with the first settlers in the 1860s and operated a dairy herd at his Monck Township farm, was approached by Alex Anderson, operator of cheese factories in Rosseau, and other places. Spencer listened as Anderson proposed the building of a cheese factory in Bracebridge if local farmers could guarantee milk from two hundred cows for five years, then convened a meeting, took the chair himself, and directed proceedings as his fellow milk producers thrashed out Anderson's proposal and accepted it. Nine of the farmers, including Spencer, whose dairy operations all lay around Bracebridge in Draper, Muskoka, Macaulay, and Monck townships, were elected directors for the new cheese factory. After touring possible sites with Anderson, they selected land for the facility atop a hill on the dividing line between Monck and Macaulay, at the north end of Bracebridge.

As Bracebridge clerk, James, who knew each of these farmers personally, was kept fully abreast of the cheese factory developments. He informed Bracebridge councillors, helping ensure the project received the town's co-operation. Construction of the cheese factory began a few days later, all needed permits promptly issued. Soon production of Made-in-Muskoka cheese met, and then boosted, local demand, as the people of central Muskoka developed a taste for the factory's savoury output. Dairy herds were expanded. The milk-producing farmers prospered. The promontory on which the building stood was soon known as "Cheese Factory Hill." The definition of "mixed farming" in Muskoka had once more expanded.

Another way agriculture was "mixed" in Muskoka was that no distinct line separated "urban" from "rural." On one hand, most township farmers did not depend on agriculture alone; on the other hand, many people in town engaged in farming pursuits. When the fall fair rolled around each autumn, entries flowed in from the centre of Bracebridge as well as from the furthest back-concession homesteads. The Boyers had placed exhibits in the fair when they lived on the Macaulay farm, and continued to do so now that they lived on Manitoba Street. The agricultural experience had become woven into the very fabric of all Muskokans' lives and the district's culture. Farmers brought grain to the grist mill in the centre of Bracebridge, and it was here they also came to buy farm implements and hardware, or exchange produce for goods in barter.

Keeping poultry provided another example. Eggs were a mainstay of pioneer cooking, and the chickens themselves sooner or later became a meal as well. But the work of fetching eggs, or beheading a chicken, then plucking and cleaning it, did not require being out on a countryside farm. Many people in Muskoka's villages and towns had chicken coops in their back yards, just part of the picture of townsfolk producing their own food. At numerous houses along the streets, backyard vegetable gardens grew rhubarb, carrots, potatoes, beans, squash, corn, and turnips. Many people in town also had a horse, kept either at a livery stable or a small barn on their property. The barns often accommodated a milk cow, and perhaps a few pigs or goats, too.

As magistrate, James heard many cases of cow owners charged under a Bracebridge bylaw prohibiting the animals from being at large in the streets, grazing on people's flower beds, and defecating in the roadways. In one case, the stench from a pig sty in Bracebridge was an issue because liquid manure flowed down a slope, and the breeze from the filthy pens made people gag. For better and for worse, he knew, town and country blended as one.

Alfred Hunt, owner of Muskoka's first bank in Bracebridge, and a big property owner in the settlement who would serve as Bracebridge mayor, and manifestly a townsman, provided another picturesque example of agriculture and town life blurring. He kept poultry in a large shed behind his home in central Bracebridge, just east of the river atop "Hunt's Hill." His husbandry gave a steady supply of eggs and chickens for his own eating, while enabling him to also display his considerable talent as a competitive breeder — all within town boundaries. Under Alfred Hunt's leadership, the Bracebridge Poultry Association became an active concern and held its annual bird show in December, right inside Bracebridge Town Hall.

In a flash the Poultry Association members could transform the place into a barnyard scene of feathers, sawdust, straw, cages, prize ribbons, crowing, and loud clucking. Into the midst of this gaggle of local exhibitors and their birds soon arrived from Midland, Orillia, and Huntsville many additional poultry men, adding higher levels of excitement and noise, with caged poultry of many varieties. Hunt, instigator of it all, was a true competitor in this field, always entering far more birds than anyone else, which was not hard because his hatchery and hen house were conveniently close to the town hall. One year he had forty-three birds in the show.

Municipal clerk Boyer chuckled for weeks after when he still found feathers around his desk and in the council chamber.

———

James knew Muskokans further blurred traditional definitions about "agriculture" by what they brought to the table at mealtime.

Agriculture's formal distinction between domesticated and wild animals certainly got lost north of the Severn River. Beef, pork, mutton, and chicken were expected items to enjoy for supper. But being unavailable, their place was often taken by bear, venison, fresh fish, wild duck, and partridge. In south Muskoka the widow of a Civil War soldier, at her cabin deep in the woods, even served youngsters Fred and Emily Penson "prepared, stuffed, and roasted robins."

With many homesteaders living near starvation, Muskoka's "mixed farming" necessarily included the district's abundant wildlife, an ever-ready food source for a hungry frontier society. Fish was caught year-round from boats and in illegal nets during spring, summer, and fall, and through ice in winter, regardless of catch limits or seasonal restrictions in the Fish and Game Act.

In Franklin Township east of Huntsville, homesteader Thomas Osborne made nets to catch fish overnight during the 1870s. Eating his illegally caught fish kept Thomas, his younger brother, and his father from starving to death. For weeks on end, that's all they had to eat. One evening, after a turn of good luck and better hunting, Thomas, a seventeen-year-old who'd mastered back-bush cuisine, served a roast "beef" dinner to a Muskoka game warden who chanced to come by, hungry, around supper-time. The officer of the law enjoyed the special way Thomas cooked bear meat, though it, like the fish, had been taken in violation of the law. When he departed next morning, stomach again full, the game warden mumbled a mild warning about "next time."

Not every game warden, evidently, could be bought off for a tasty meal of "beef." Other cases did get to court, and from the late-1870s to 1900, James would try dozens of men charged with hunting ducks and deer out of season, often to feed their families. James himself had helped his own family survive by "living off the land." He had even been inspired to teach his Macaulay students to shoot a rifle, not so they could fight on foreign battlefields or kill fellow pupils, but to survive on a Muskoka farm.

Yet another feature of animal use that caused James to reinterpret "agriculture" in Muskoka's harvesting economy was the widespread practice of trapping. Trapping animals had been important in Muskoka long before settlement days, with "Trading Lake" (later, Lake of Bays) being one venue for exchange between fur traders from Montreal and trappers, while down towards the mouth of the Muskoka River where it emptied into Lake Muskoka, the Hudson's Bay Company ran a trading post as well. Once homesteaders arrived, a number began trapping animals as part of their livelihood. Fur pelts, used for rugs, blankets, and clothing, were also bartered for money or goods; the carcass often provided another source of food.

Though use of animals in this way was not officially part of "agriculture," it was hard in Muskoka to distinguish this activity from that of a farmer slaughtering animals in his pen, selling the hide to a local tannery for leather, and eating the meat. Certainly, most Muskoka homesteaders didn't make the distinction. However the Department of Agriculture down in Toronto might classify production according to categories distinguishing wild from domesticated animals, on the ground in Muskoka it was all part of the district's single integrated farming life, two faces of the same thing.

Trapping, as a major part of Muskoka's "rural" economy, generated work for the district's magistrate. In one case James took pity on a trapper charged with unlawfully having over one hundred muskrat pelts, because of his age. So he sentenced the frail seventy-two-year-old to seven days in the town jail, a lenient penalty. By bizarre coincidence, just one week later a healthy young trapper with an equally illegal large haul of muskrat skins was brought before him. Stuck with his own recent precedent, James had no choice but to sentence him to a mere week in jail, too.

Everything he saw taught James that categories applicable to farming and agriculture, developed outside Muskoka, did not much apply inside the district. Had the place resembled the interminable flat fields of southwestern Ontario, the rolling farmlands of central Ontario, or the extensive clay deposits north of Temiskaming and around Cochrane, Muskoka might have been subject to a much clearer verdict on its success or failure as a farming community, in traditional terms.

But comparisons were invidious because Muskoka was unique. Even the Department of Agriculture's annual farm statistics measuring production of apples, wheat, and grapes; milk, butter, and cheese; pork, mutton, and beef, showed how Muskoka was not the same. While southwestern Ontario farms grew far more tomatoes than those in Muskoka District, Muskokans produced staggering quantities of maple syrup and sugar, while farmers in Middlesex County made almost none.

—

Understandably, farming was something James and Hannah raised their three sons to value.

Fred, who never lived on their homestead farm, liked it so much that, after first trying his luck on a spread further north at Magnetawan in Parry Sound District, moved to southwestern Ontario, where arable land was widespread and he could enjoy productive farming of the traditional kind. He never returned to Muskoka, except for command performances such as attending family funerals. On the other hand, Charles, seen by his father as the son most resembling him, did not have much aptitude for farming, being more interested in law office work, teaching, dancing, and patents.

Son George fell between his two brothers, not only in age but in his balanced relationship to agriculture. While he fully enjoyed teaching, sales, printing, and writing, George was equally interested in farming. As a boy he took pleasure growing apples in the small orchard at the back of the Manitoba Street house. There were four or five varieties, he recalled, one called "Duchess of Oldenburg," another, with a green skin, "known by the name of Delicious," and small crab apples with dark red skins. George would spend all the time needed to select good-looking specimens of each variety, polish and arrange them, then take them to the Agricultural Hall and enter them in competition, often winning some prizes. As an adult he would relish following his father's footsteps as president of the Muskoka Agricultural Society.

For his part James would continue to delight in the elixirs of a farmyard, a whiff of Moreton in his nostrils that triggered immediate memories. He lived for the smells and sounds of Muskoka's fall fairs: the wafting scent of pungent cow flaps on rough grass, horse manure trampled into fresh hay, or sawdust in weathered board stalls; or, on a tour through the Agricultural Hall, the aroma of baked goods filling the air. He listened with joy to the high-pitched crowing of prize roosters, the frenetic bleating of crowded sheep in pens, the laughter and squeals of children, and the galloping rhythms of horse hooves pounding out an oval dirt track and kicking up clumps of earth behind them while townsfolk and farmers watched and placed small bets on the outcome.

23

Muskoka's Magnetism

As Muskoka evolved with the passing decades and the district acquired a renown that exceeded its geographic size and level of population, the mystique of Muskoka imprinted itself on people far afield. The place had a definite magnetism.

The Boyers had been enticed to Muskoka by the tantalizing pull of free land and, with it, the vision of a pastoral life as a country squire as Isaac had "seen aplenty back in England." Harry Boyer described him as "entranced" with free lands while still in Brooklyn.

While free land was the initial draw, it had not taken long to realize that this incentive was akin to a merchant advertising a door-crasher special. The appeal serves to attract people, but once in, they seldom get just what they came for. Once in the district, Muskoka's new arrivals discovered the natural appeal of the waters, forests, and rocks. If not trying to farm the land but enjoy the scenery, one saw a quite different Muskoka. That was becoming a new draw.

When Hannah began writing to her sisters who'd stayed behind around New York, urging them to join her, she pointed out that more and more people were coming up from the United States for the curative powers of Muskoka. She did not hold out free land as an enticement, but the "Muskoka Cure." In doing so, she registered the major change underway in the district. The allure of free land was being matched and would increasingly be superseded by the new magnet of a Muskoka vacation.

Permanent settlers in Muskoka, as Hannah and James witnessed, were being joined by people spending time in the district on a seasonal basis for pleasure. They came to the north, not to start a new life, but to refresh the one they already had. They did not seek to clear the land and farm it, but to hunt its woods for game and gaze upon its scenic splendour. They would not use the lakes and rivers to transport logs, but to fish and boat their waters for pleasure. The magic of it all was that they came, not to try to make money, but to spend it.

The Ontario government's homesteading project, aimed at filling Muskoka with farmers, was taking a surprising turn. This presence of vacationers was putting Muskoka on the map in an unanticipated way. Situated at the gentlest and most southerly edge of the Canadian Shield, Muskoka offered people the experience of a natural northern setting that was conveniently close to the cities in the south. With the eventual extension of railway service north and the gradual expansion of steamboat service on the lakes, the district had become open to people who wanted "a Muskoka vacation" and could reach the place with what was, for the era, relative speed and convenience.

—

The pattern for Muskoka's vacation economy had long existed. While some Chippewas had settled into permanent cabins and tended their planted crops at Obejewanung, others canoed into the district from farther south to enjoy the place only in summer. The local and visiting Natives engaged in barter for their respective needs.

The pattern continued when non-Natives began arriving. At the time the Boyers arrived in 1869, adventuresome non-Native visitors had been coming from Toronto, exploring the contours of a Muskoka vacation, for almost a decade.

As the magnetism of Muskoka grew, with influx of more people and advent of new holiday activities, this interaction of summer visitors and permanent residents added a fourth pillar to Muskoka's economy, now supported by lumbering, farming, manufacturing, and *vacationing*. More public resorts and private cottages began to dot the district's landscape, and the expectations of those who patronized them harmonized with the urgent needs of Muskokans to earn a living.

Locals who had come to farm but now set themselves up to facilitate the Muskoka Cure soon found not just economic opportunity, but a different way of life. Muskokans would increasingly come in two basic categories: seasonal vacationers and permanent residents. Their symbiosis would be a nuanced mixture of mutual dependence, friendship, and antipathy.

The magnet pulling this all together and holding it in place was no longer free land but freedom itself. A "Muskoka vacation" would be called by some, a bit simplistically, "tourism." But there were no pyramids, ancient ruins, or other spectacles of the sort that give rise to "tours"; the draw of Muskoka was the absence of the human imprint, the natural beauty of the place, the opportunity it afforded those who came to the district to "vacate" their minds of the worries left behind, even if just temporarily — the true meaning of a vacation.

A.P. Cockburn would be called "the father of Muskoka tourism" because his steamboats made vacationing at summer places on three of the district's major lakes possible. Yet again, that was an over-simplification. The men and women who created those lakeside lodges could also claim some credit for Muskoka's new vacation economy. So could the homesteaders who opened roads and built up settlements with stores and services, because second-wave vacationers could not have readily visited the district until first-wave settlers colonized it, even if just a few scant years before (or in some cases, even simultaneously) with mills, hotels, livery stables, boats, food supplies, and taverns.

Muskoka's new vacation economy was not being built from a single blueprint. It was under construction, piece-by-piece, devised in common by Muskoka's permanent residents and their visitor guests. Homesteaders with disappointing crops found that, if their rocky fields backed onto a major lake, they could make a livelihood by opening their log homes to parties of fishermen and hunters. Rustic homesteads were transformed into summer resorts in a mutual exchange benefitting both backwoods cabin dwellers and the wealthy urban sportsmen staying awhile in their accommodation.

Families would vacate their beds, put fresh straw ticks on them for the guests, and move into a shed to sleep. The small parties of sportsmen were content with a couple of square meals at the family table each day. Each adjusted to the other, and learned from the other, as their standards and expectations evolved. The next year, the homesteader might advertise in southern newspapers that he had accommodation available for sportsmen. When they'd return, they would find that an addition to the original log cabin now offered more space.

The names of some of these evolving early lodges epitomized their character of domesticity, from "Cleveland's House" and "Windermere House" to Francis and Ann Judd's cabin "Juddhaven" and John Montieth's place, "Montieth House." Over several decades the range of accommodations was constantly upgraded, and Muskoka's dozens of resorts would become hundreds.

———

When Lizzy Boyer responded to her sister's appeal and in 1874 came to Muskoka from Brooklyn, moving in with Hannah and James at their Macaulay homestead, she was looking for neither free land nor a northern vacation but a very specific form of the Muskoka Cure. Yet, two years later, when she moved with them into Bracebridge, Lizzy still had not found a man suitable to marry and who wanted her. A woman who could not attract a husband had merely relocated to a different venue.

As a school teacher spending all day with youngsters, she was not of course in circulation with marriageable males. The better arena offered by attending church and community events with Hannah and James did nothing to overcome her lack of appeal to any eligible man she did encounter. In exasperation James eventually suggested she might want to meet Thomas Aitkin, of Windermere.

Aitkin, still in the early days of parlaying his humble homesteader's cabin on the shore of Lake Rosseau into prestigious "Windermere House," was coming into Bracebridge to complete a land transaction. James was handling his deeds and paperwork to buy additional land for a new building Aitkin was constructing. Months earlier the two men met for the conveyancing land, then found enjoyment in one another's company talking about local developments and Muskoka's future prospects.

A Scottish settler from the Orkney Islands, Aitkin was already a widower when he arrived in Canada in the 1860s, accompanying his sister Ellen and her husband, David Fife. The trio first found land near Peterborough, east of Muskoka, where Thomas met charming Mary Traill, a widow with two children. Her warm, outgoing manner provided a pleasing counterpoint for the taciturn Scot, and soon they married. But Aitkin and Fife, being clear-headed Scots, figured they would have better prospects if they relocated to Muskoka under the new Free Grants and Homestead Act, which was being much talked about. In 1870 they left Peterborough with their wives, chose lots in fertile Watt Township, and began clearing land beside Lake Rosseau.

Soon A.P. Cockburn's new steamer *Waubamik*, plying the upper lakes through the recently opened Indian River locks at Port Carling, began making calls along Rosseau's shoreline, using Aitkin's wharf and lakeside clearing as its main place for connections on the east side of the lake. The little cluster of houses was now designated "Windermere" because, for the tiny community post office Aitkin operated, Ottawa needed a place name. In the mid-1870s, Thomas Aitkin and his hospitable wife, Mary, began boarding sportsmen, who'd come to fish the lake, at their Windermere house. They were following the lead of other homesteaders who'd discovered that offering a Muskoka vacation to visitors was their ticket to a more prosperous future.

Although Thomas was not a natural hotelier, Mary's friendly manner, combined with the fine breeding that contributed to the renown of all the Traill sisters, contributed a welcoming character to the place. To his delight her charm was matched by practicality. Soon Mary's cooking of tasty meals, her attentive making of guests' beds, and her relentless cleaning of the premises helped their small resort emerge as a special destination for vacationers.

On a higher plateau, Mary's refined tastes also resulted in more elegant designs for the structures Thomas was adding to Windermere House. The first resort houses had been decorated, in keeping with the ambiance enjoyed by hunting party guests, with stuffed heads of trophy moose and deer. Under Mary's influence, the dead animals disappeared, replaced by fine paintings.

With such steps, large and small, Muskoka's vacation economy was emerging. A new class of visitors began coming to Windermere House, expecting more and paying more. The couple's future looked bright, for not only was their resort expanding, but in 1876 Mary and Thomas were about to add another child to their family as well.

In their home at Windermere, Mary died giving birth to their daughter. Thomas was devastated. She had become the new centre of his life, after he'd left Scotland, heartbroken, when the first woman he'd ever loved, his cherished first wife, Janet, had died in childbirth, along with her baby, in 1859. Thomas was left reeling after fate dealt him the same blow a second time.

His face to the world remained taciturn because that was his nature, but inside he churned. The progress of Windermere House, his joint project with Mary that bore the imprint of her enlightened thinking about what vacationers really sought in a Muskoka holiday, seemed stalled without her. Alone, Thomas pressed on, but his heart was not in it.

———

After completing the transfer of Aitkin's property, James offered his forlorn client a friendly family meal at his Manitoba Street home. Hannah and he had already discussed his plan. She took pains to ensure the food was plentiful and tasty, and that Lizzy spent the entire afternoon preparing herself.

Over dinner a spark ignited. James that day not only conveyanced land for Aitkin, but also conveyed his live-in sister-in-law, now thirty-four, to the arms of this needy man, a prospective husband.

Lizzy and Thomas shared a bond of mutual sympathy, her feelings real because she had lost her mother in childbirth and could understand his emptiness. And if Lizzy craved a husband, Thomas's urgent requirement was a wife who could help him with his growing children and expanding hotel. Their wedding took place in Bracebridge on July 4, 1883 at the Boyer house, the much relieved bride not only acquiring a husband but getting a Muskoka resort in the bargain.

Now it was Lizzy's turn to step forward, next woman up. She would give Thomas two more children, without complication, but on the hospitality side, the Brooklyn seamstress lacked Mary Aitkin's human lustre. Villagers soon nicknamed her "Queen Victoria" because of her haughty ways. Her husband, Thomas, was considered "dark and taciturn" by Muskoka artist and diarist Seymour Penson. Together, they made an odd couple to run a hospitality business.

Still, the fated pair seemed to be doing something right. With continuous additions to the premises, Thomas and Lizzy took in more summer guests each succeeding year, with capacity jumping to thirty-five, then one hundred, then over two hundred. They and the next generation of Aitkins continued to expand the facilities of Windermere House with a spacious ballroom, tennis courts, bowling greens, and larger gardens to provide more fresh flowers and vegetables for the elegant dining room. While fishing was still on offer, so was golf. Windermere House opened Muskoka's very first golf course on what had been Thomas Aitkin's free grant "back forty" fields. Conversion of these rough acres to accommodate sport for the leisure class epitomized the transition overtaking Muskoka's economy.

In time Lizzy and Thomas installed pumps to lift water from Lake Rosseau, and acetylene gas jet lights to illuminate the wide corridors, giving the place an enchanting appearance across the darkened nighttime lake. Their addition of wrap-around verandahs and upper balconies heightened the sense of opulence. Live orchestras played dinner music for the guests, and then switched to dance music as the evening progressed at the posh "lady of the lake."

Hannah was happy. Lizzy was now set for the rest of her days, living in a Muskoka village less than twenty miles away. Hannah also had her house back again, and with it, better days with her beloved James. He no longer felt crowded by a woman he cared not much for but who had become a fixture for too many years, occupying the small Manitoba Street home as if the place where her own.

Hannah's brother Harry, meanwhile, was showing how differently Muskoka's draw could rearrange peoples' lives, even in the same family.

Harry had been pulled as strongly as James by the original magnet of free land. After some major detours away from farming, he'd taken a second shot at homesteading with Flora and their children around Muldrew Lake, in a southern section of the district. But his idyllic carefree life had become humdrum, and by the late 1870s, Harry was tired and floundering as a lacklustre farmer. He was again struggling to find his real purpose in life. Deeply restless for work, he was annoyed there was none to be had down at Charles Davies's all-but-abandoned stone finishing shop in Orillia.

Once again, to relieve Hannah's anxiety about one of her siblings and because he thought it good for Bracebridge, James came to the rescue. As secretary of the school board, he knew of plans for Bracebridge to build a public school. As clerk of Bracebridge, he also knew about the

School children donned hats for their picture at Bracebridge Public School. Built in 1880 the school boasted stone lintels, sills, and steps, all cut by Harry Boyer. Once, the bell, while being rung to call in the children, broke free and plunged heavily to the ground, landing just two feet from James and Hannah Boyer's son George.

municipality's intent to build a town hall. Two new public buildings would generate a lot of work, he informed his brother-in-law, including stone-cutting. Cheered by this ray of light, Harry told his father-in-law the news. Charles Davies won the contract to cut the stone sills, for both buildings.

Snow was still on the ground in early 1880 when Harry and Flora moved their children Joe, Flo, and Nan to Bracebridge so he could start on the stone work. His father-in-law joined him for parts of these major projects, but it was mostly hard-working Harry's chisels and mallets that got the job done. Charles Davies, with his share of the proceeds from the two Bracebridge jobs and sale of his premises in Orillia, moved his family to Chicago, but Harry and Flora would stay in Bracebridge the rest of their lives. He was happy to be back near his beloved sister, Hannah, and she was unspeakably proud of Harry when he announced he was going to start up his own business in town.

Bracebridge town hall, also built in 1880 with Harry Boyer stonework, became James Boyer's headquarters for the next two decades, housing both his town clerk's office and magistrate's court. The registry office next door was convenient for land conveyancing, while the cellar in the Muskoka Herald building to the left briefly served as a town jail for those he sentenced.

The Bracebridge Town Hall and Bracebridge Public School were imposing buildings, showing townsfolk a handy and prominent example of the quality of Harry's stoneworking talents, the best kind of advertisement a tradesman could proffer. That same year, he opened "Bracebridge Marble & Granite Works" on Bracebridge's main street.

Soon his monument and stonecutting factory had all the work Harry could desire, and he now had a real purpose in life. Having begun his trade in Brooklyn, learning to rub stone until his fingers bled, he'd finally emerged in Muskoka a master stone carver, operating his own business. When he began to teach his boys the skills so they could help him with the growing orders for cut stone, he told them he was their age when he'd started learning the craft.

Many people were soon calling the Bracebridge Marble & Granite Works simply "the tombstone factory" because grave markers were a main line of business. Complete strangers were assisting Harry, dying off so he could make their tombstones. Muskoka's cemeteries filled, in an unbroken pace, with handsome grave markers at the base of which appeared the discreet words, "Harry Boyer Monuments, Bracebridge." His renown was spreading as the best, if not indeed the only, stonecutter in the north. Before long Harry was shipping monuments up to Rosseau, then as far away as Temiskaming, "made of St. Lawrence marble highly polished and of very neat design."

The man who wanted work was busy now, supplying far more than tombstones. He crafted cornerstones and stone nameplates for public buildings and office blocks rising in the district's towns. He made stone sills, lintels, and steps for the community's more substantial new structures. He landed lucrative work from millionaires building grand summer residences west of Bracebridge around Beaumaris on Lake Muskoka. Harry prospered in Muskoka's vacation economy, whether serving those who wanted to holiday at a palatial summer estate, or those gone on permanent vacation above.

Harry and Flora rolled along, blissfully adding more children to their brood. Although Philip died in infancy, and the last baby was stillborn, all the others — Tom, Lydia, Sam, Harry, Pearl, Ruth, Joe, Flo, and Nan — were healthy and, while a couple never married, the rest did and ensured there would be plenty more Boyers in Muskoka for generations to come.

With his family expanding and his stone business flourishing, Harry had at last reached the stage he'd dreamed about during his harrowing years and risky adventures. He'd become a secure provider for his family. And, like his own destiny, Harry believed Muskoka itself would be what he and others made it. This was not abstract idealism, but practical observation from the changes he'd seen taking place around him.

With his newfound security, Harry Boyer began to take a keen role in local affairs, winning election to the Bracebridge school board, volunteering as a member of the Bracebridge fire company, and playing trumpet in the Bracebridge Citizens' Band. He was active with the Conservatives, and won appointment from the Ontario government as licence inspector for Muskoka District. The youth who'd once helped a brawling man escape the police was latching onto respectability, even serving as a lay preacher for the Methodist church, where Hannah's family now paid more heed to the sermons, if only out of curiosity.

Harry Boyer's marble and granite factory on Bracebridge's main street, known to one and all as "the tombstone factory," provided steady work for Hannah Boyer's brother. Harry, standing left, taught two of his sons the stonecutter's craft. His name endures today, chiselled discretely onto hundreds of Muskoka gravestones.

With his fellow musicians in the popular Bracebridge Citizens' Band, trumpeter Harry Boyer sits in very front, second from left, obscuring part of the town name on the drum. In the back row at left end is Harry's tuba-playing son, Sam Boyer.

James Boyer followed these developments closely. He learned what was happening around the lakes with Lizzy and Thomas Aitkin's progress at Windermere House, and the lucrative contracts Harry Boyer was getting at summer residences being constructed for American plutocrats. At the town office in Bracebridge, he saw many aspects of Muskoka's rapidly evolving social order when dealing with local merchants and resort operators on a wide range of municipal matters. Then there was Magistrate's Court, yet another vantage point on how the economy's fourth "vacation" pillar was shaping up. One of James cases illustrates how dynamic this scene was.

As the 1800s advanced, farmers found a novel way to service the needs of cottagers and summer resorts in a convenient manner, by selling produce and other food items to them from supply boats. These vessels, although licensed for navigation and passed for safety inspection, ran aground on the hidden shoals of a new municipal licensing requirement of the United Townships of Medora and Wood, whose jurisdiction included much of central Muskoka's lake land.

Most farmers and boat operators did not even know about the new law. Yet that did not stop the township council, seeing a new source of revenue in licence fees, enforcing it, and they began to charge people who'd been in the summer supply business for several years. At Magistrate's Court in Bracebridge, James prepared to hear the charges brought by the municipality.

With summer tourism now a key part of Muskoka's economic life-blood, he appreciated that these enterprising farmers and supply boat operators were doing their best to cater to visitors' needs by bringing fresh produce from their fields, orchards, and berry patches right to the docks of summer cottages and resort operators around the lakes of central Muskoka. They even made the extra effort of bringing in bananas and canned goods to supplement what they grew themselves, thus providing even greater benefit and more convenience to summer residents, at least one of whom, according to evidence in court, was a judge. But the township now wanted a large fee for allowing them to do this, and fines levied against those charged for operating without a licence. Where was justice to be balanced?

James weighed the matter in light of his own experience with licensing bylaws as clerk for one of Muskoka's largest municipalities, his ongoing efforts through the Muskoka Agricultural Society to encourage local farming, and his remembrance of Moreton-in-Marsh, where farmers brought their fresh produce to weekly market for the convenience and benefit of all.

He dismissed the cases and required the municipality to pay all costs. The policy of Muskoka should be generous, not mean, James believed, and enhance rather than thwart the district's important vacation economy.

———

Rich capitalists, including many drawn to Muskoka's refreshing setting from northern American states as they escaped the stench and heat of their factory-filled smoky cities, used their abundant funds to create palatial lakeside homes.

These summer palaces added depth to Muskoka's vacation economy, providing jobs for tradesmen and service providers, and business for merchants and suppliers. They were reached by luxurious wooden boats built in Muskoka, adding more income locally as skilled boat-builders worked year round to fashion craft that were among the best on the continent. The rich owners stayed all summer long, gazing down the sloping lawns to the waters' edge, getting the benefit of Muskoka lounging on their large stonework verandahs, breathing in clean air and watching the sun set while their income kept rising back in Pittsburgh and similar cities, where their workers had no such respite.

Such magnificent summer places, paced by additional resorts with gas lighting and many more humble frame cottages with coal oil lamps, were appearing around all Muskoka's main lakes. Farmers throughout the district participated in the new economy, too, learning to use their homes as resorts and their unpromising lakeside fields for tennis courts and lawn bowling greenswards.

This was not quite the New Jerusalem Thomas McMurray envisaged, mused James, but it was definitely a new sort of society.

Roads remained a challenge but the waterways offered convenience, elegance, and adventure. Boating was front and centre in this vacation economy, both transporting guests to and from resorts and offering waterborne pleasures while they were in residence.

Once railways reached Muskoka, linked to the railroads that ran into the United States, and connecting to the growing fleets of steamboats, now numbering in the many dozens, the district's unique vacation economy seemed guaranteed.

———

James mused about the "escape" made by these wealthy Americans to another country in summer from, as he remembered New York's, filth-strewn streets that were as rank as the polluted air was foul. It was easy to see what was magnetic about Muskoka — a reverse push from the opposing pole.

James captured this change, as he'd experienced it, from colonization road to railway, by writing how the early road "piercing rocky fastness of forbidding aspect, disheartened many a weary traveller who jostled over its cavities and excrescences with aching bones, but who are now able to view the rocks with half-closed eyes from the soft medium of a railway parlour car."

Even people who were not so wealthy but who happily came to Muskoka for a brief summer holiday, also had the best of both worlds, thought James — a lake and forest retreat in summer, and a nourishing cultural setting the rest of the year.

He felt torn. James was happy for Muskokans that the vacation economy was becoming vibrant, helping many people who could not succeed at farming get a new lease on life. Seeing the summer vacationers freely returning to the dynamic cities in the United States for the winter, however, made him morose.

He would be in Muskoka, year-round, for the rest of his life, a prisoner held in place by invisible strings.

In this 1890s photo at the front of the Boyers' Bracebridge home at the north end of Manitoba Street, where a medical building stands today, Hannah knits while James reads a book. Their daughters, Annie and Nellie, in white blouses, study a detail Hannah shows about stitching. Of their three sons, George stands, Fred holds "Spot," and Charles is absent.

24

Belated Exoneration

There is never a good time for a bad thing to happen. But is there a bad time for a good thing?

Mail service in Bracebridge changed for a while following January 27, 1887, when a night blaze destroyed the post office. The fire was a disaster for the town, also taking out Dr. Bridgeland's drug store, Ellison's photograph gallery, Josiah Pratt's jewellery shop, and the Independent Order of Odd Fellows meeting hall. When volunteers rushed Odd Fellows' paraphernalia out to save it from the conflagration, several men carrying a long box dropped it, and as the lid flew off a human skeleton spilled out onto the main street, causing one of the helpers to faint. He, himself, then needed to be carried away from the encroaching flames. Some onlookers were shocked, some amused, and a few took it as an omen, though of what they did not say.

Loss of a post office was serious business for any town, and in particular, busy Bracebridge, capital of Muskoka District. The *Muskoka Herald* published a report showing that Bracebridge topped all 152 Muskoka and Parry Sound post offices with 1886 stamp sales of $2,653.07, a big figure in days of penny postage, and money orders of $11,388.11. Town council swiftly accepted Clerk James Boyer's practical suggestion that the municipality rent a room in the town hall for a temporary post office. The deal was swiftly concluded. Rent would be eight dollars a month. The grateful postmaster ensured that James then got his mail delivered straight to his desk as soon as it arrived, which meant walking about ten paces.

One day mail left on his desk included a letter, postmarked from England, addressed to Isaac Boyer. Such letters were so rare it caused his heart to flutter. Over the years of his estrangement, James had only irregular correspondence with a few members of his scattered English family, mostly his brother Samuel Jelfs, clerk of the Poor Law Union in Dorset. Sam knew where to find his brother when it mattered, and understood that the name Boyer was required for a letter to reach him.

James would not have read such a letter in his town hall office. He would have taken it to a private place. Tears no doubt came to his eyes as he read it. The hushed-up financial scandal over the Stratford estate had finally broken, with a dramatic twist ending.

In an act of deathbed repentance, an aged lawyer at the Stratford firm had cleared Isaac's name. Information about the money still seemed unclear, but the one certain thing was that nineteen-year-old Jelfs had taken the fall for someone more powerful. Isaac was innocent, as he always protested he had been. At last, several careers and several countries later, forever escaping and always reinventing his life, Isaac Jelfs, or James Boyer, as he now was called, had been vindicated.

A sense of jubilation surely would have erupted if James had received this news decades earlier. Now, a confession that he'd been made a scapegoat elicited only crowning sadness. The shadow so long cast over him faded into the encroaching twilight. His intense anger was gone, dissipated by all the energy it had consumed over the years in nerve-wracking escapes, each one compounding the next, worried out of him by the unending anxiety over hiding his tracks. Instead, James's strongest emotion was an overwhelming sense of remorse about his life. The bottom fell out. His feelings drained away.

James looked about him, seeing everything with cold eyes. What, really, was he doing in this forsaken, out-of-the-way corner of the world? A crushing sense of melancholy about the way his life had turned out descended over him. He'd become, out of desperation, a British patriot in Canada. How much better if he'd never had to leave England, if only he could have remained who he really was.

For years, whenever James felt the need for balance or escape, he could find it reading a book. But now, with a diminished view of his life in light of his morose reappraisals, he just found himself staring blankly at a page, before absently setting the book aside.

He was torn apart by incompatible loyalties, and they all surfaced. He had "gone colonial" and become one of the new men opening up the Canadian frontier, working as a justice of the peace to make the British role of magistrate fit the conditions of a North American society, doing his bit to uphold the rule of law. As a homesteader he'd come right down to earth, made himself into one of the rugged men who lived with deprivation and been stoic about hardship and setbacks.

What he cherished about being an Englishman, and what he'd celebrated in the activities of the Sons of England, the Loyal Orange Lodge, and True Blue Association, was the way of life remembered from back in Britain, not the reality as it existed in Canada. Away from the homeland, he'd magnified its virtues. Now his vaunted, even excessive, patriotism revealed itself to him as a hollow sham.

His moods shifted. Days later, he'd lament his life from another angle, dwelling on the order of England that he'd missed during the best years of his life, the theatres he could have slipped into to see one of Shakespeare's plays, the presence of a cultural life that permeated all aspects of daily living, the patterns of an established society that knew assuredly what it was all about. What a contrast to life here in a small town of colonial Canada, where those touchstones of British life came only through staged events, intermittent special occasions, his little speech about the great Admiral Nelson, all just fragments of the real thing. He felt himself an exile. Now exonerated, James ached anew for what he could no longer have.

Getting the letter shocked him into a startling awareness of how the injustice he'd suffered had made him a different man, acting out a role but always fearful of being detected, living a lie that fate had forced on him. He felt hollow.

Regrets pummelled his mind the more he dwelt on how he'd ended up in Crimea, in New York, in Muskoka. He began to feel troubled about the way he now saw, with sudden clarity, a different side of British life.

In Bracebridge and around Muskoka were a number of "remittance men" who'd been dispatched to the colony by their prominent English families, to avoid embarrassment in polite British society. He'd got to know a number over the years, and found them for the most part interesting men, apart from their alcoholism, or bohemian living, or constant pursuit of loose women, or whatever other troubling attribute had caused them to be banished to Canada's backwoods.

Until now James had seen these well-bred and articulate men simply as decorations in the community, unable to do serious work, but useful since the allowance money they spent was welcome in moneyless Muskoka. Now he recognized them as discards like himself, individuals who'd become expedient so that others could get on with their comfortable lives of hypocrisy.

Muskoka was also populated by many hundreds of children shipped out to its colony of Canada from England, the so-called "home children." James at first had seen these orphans, sent to live and work on farms in the district, as youngsters getting a good opportunity in life, better than what they faced in the back alleys of East London or slums of Birmingham, or in the Homes for Indigent Children where they lived and toiled in institutional foster care.

Looking at their situation anew, from a more radical perspective, James began to see the plight of these deported children the way Hannah and Harry had understood the "home child" project from the start. Both of them had become agitated discovering the use of child orphans as farm workers. Their lives as orphans, including Harry's enslavement for more than a year of punishing work at the Boys' Farm School at Westchester, rekindled anger when they saw these relocated children indentured as labourers on district farms, getting no schooling, little food, less sleep, and supervision that mostly ranged from indifference to abuse.

James was aware of the situation, from occasional visits of the Barnardo Homes supervisor coming up from Toronto, to cases in the courts when problems arose, including an attempted murder by poisoning of one farmer by his indentured child labourer near Huntsville. He would not have known the numbers of these children, but north Muskoka would eventually receive more "home children" than any comparable part of Canada, the district's primary period of settlement and growth coinciding with the years British orphans were being relocated onto Canadian farms, from 1870 until 1930 when the program ended because unemployed Canadians in the Great Depression took the farm work.

Freed from his distorting rosy view of Britain, James now saw as Hannah and Harry did how the mighty imperial power "solved" its problems by sending them out of sight, thence out of mind — be they impoverish waifs, remittance men with alcohol on their breath, unemployed men and conscripts sent abroad to fight as expendable soldiers, or a law clerk falsely accused of theft.

He felt miserable, and had plenty of company.

<hr />

When a concerned Hannah asked what was troubling him, James showed her the letter.

As the year 1887 numbly advanced, Isaac and Hannah seemed closer than ever. They never would have met and fallen so in love had he not been in New York, and he would not have been in the United States but for escaping from the Dragoon's ranks in Crimea, and he would not have been fighting there had he not been dispatched from Stratford.

Deep into the nights, they talked about life's bizarre pattern of unexpected turnings. Hannah talked about the series of fateful episodes that had similarly redirected, many times over, the course of her own life. If her mother had not died in childbirth, her father would not have wanted to leave England. If her father had not died at sea, she would not have been stranded with seven orphans in New York. If she had not fallen in love with a married man, she would not have been heartbroken. If she had not fallen in love with another married man on the rebound, she would not have ended up in the Canadian wilderness. If she had been married, she would not have had to live her Canadian life in a shadow of pretense with the constant fear the true identity of her common-law husband would be discovered and cause their house of cards to collapse.

They saw, with more force than ever before, how coincident events in each of their lives had brought them together, woven them in love, and forced them to Muskoka when it was the most remote place imaginable.

Harry, with whom Hannah shared the "good news" that James had been vindicated at long last, responded by observing with glibness worthy of his brother Thomas, and as someone becoming more religious, that "God works in mysterious ways." But they'd never really done more than allude to the Stratford story with Harry, explaining why he did not see its gravity for James, or understand how the news oddly made him feel so bleak and that his emotions pulled Hannah down with him.

Complicating the sharing of this news with Hannah's other siblings was that it revealed "James Boyer" to be "Isaac Jelfs." They knew the two had never been married, but now realized they had been mistaken, or misinformed, about his name being "Guelphs" before he took her Boyer name for his own. Hannah and James, to preserve their dignity, and above all to maintain the ruse for the sake of their children, decided to say nothing more about the tangled web that they had woven. James would just have to suck it up and carry on, "turn his face into the wind" as the British would say.

Their son George, more interested in family matters than his two brothers, was eight years old and, overhearing some of the adult conversation, grasped the key idea that his father had got a letter from England saying that back when he'd lived there somebody had said he done something wrong, but now it was clear that this was a mistake and that his father never did anything wrong or bad at all. That's all a boy needed to know.

———

But James remained weighed down by something more besides Stratford. Even though that matter appeared resolved, a second issue seemed certain to always keep him away from England. The risk of questions concerning his departure from the Dragoons remained real, at least in his mind.

He had always been vague and deliberately misleading about his military service in accounts he prepared for publication, part of his general narrative that covered the tracks of Isaac Jelfs. But the conclusion that he'd deserted from the ranks of the Dragoons, along with many other soldiers who'd fled the mad slaughter that was the Crimean War, seems inescapable. A court martial would impose as punishment the sentence of death.

—

In the depths of that winter, James would walk a slow pace down Manitoba Street and along Dominion Street to reach the town hall, sheltering against the cold wind and feeling drained of energy, with no interest in what was around him.

It was not possible to keep the small, battered craft of his life away from the swift moving current for long. Inside, waiting faces greeted him. The town constable, clutching a thin sheaf of papers about men he'd arrested and who were in the lock-up, asked if he should bring them in for trial. Alfred Hunt would come back to see him about the twenty-one appeals he was launching against his property assessments, mostly because of wrong descriptions of ownership. Folk in fetching their mail, seeing James, wanted a word. The mayor inquired about progress on the town's current item of urgency, negotiating for the iron foundry two men named Warner and Copeland wanted to open on the west side of Manitoba Street, if a tax exemption could be included in the deal. All this activity, in prior days, would have made James jubilant.

It was no surprise, looking back, that he would subject his life to scathing review, once the mainspring of almost its entire course — the calumny in Stratford — disappeared. Everything looked different now. Each step taken since that black day he recast as one mistake compounding the next. His despair and depression were inevitable.

Hannah's love sustained him through it all. The passage of time, too, would help lift his despondency. Gradually, the new life Isaac Jelfs had created for James Boyer had enough about it to pull him inexorably forward.

25

Life Must Go On

One time-tested remedy for a battered soul is the exhilaration of an election campaign.

Political temperatures were rising in the depths of that winter of James's despair, when member of Parliament A.P. Cockburn asked his "Independent Liberal" friend Boyer to do all he could to assist him in the campaign. Both men thought the election, scheduled for February 22, 1887, would be close. The uncertain outcome added dramatic excitement, all the better to re-channel James's mind onto something other than his own lament. He was, once again, deputy returning officer for Bracebridge.

Bracebridge was in the riding of North Ontario this time, the result of electoral boundaries being redrawn, which meant a large swath of populated area south of Muskoka could determine the outcome. Cockburn's challenger, Conservative candidate Frank Madill, lived down in Cannington and was well known and highly regarded in that part of the riding.

The hard-fought campaign became even more heated than normal for Bracebridge, always a political hotbed. Upon getting word through the grapevine that the Conservatives intended to disrupt the election in this community where the Liberal MP was expected to win large support, James urged Bracebridge's reeve, William Kirk, to appoint four special constables "to preserve peace and order" around the voting stations. In the end, although Bracebridge votes were given without too much disruption, thanks to the constables' restraining presence, veteran parliamentary representative A.P. Cockburn was defeated by a majority of 158.

The election was not the only political matter to keep James busy and get his life juices flowing again. An end of the long association of sections of Muskoka with neighbouring counties Victoria to the east and Simcoe to the south appeared imminent. Early in 1887 both county councils passed resolutions calling for separation from Muskoka, on the grounds that the large distances between the locales made conduct of routine business arduous and expensive.

If handled right, Muskoka leaders realized, this could become another step forward in the district's progress. On March 28 Bracebridge council passed its own resolution, urging the Ontario government to sever Muskoka from these counties and make Muskoka District a provisional judicial district, with Bracebridge to continue as its centre.

Council directed the reeve and James, as town clerk, to go down to Toronto as a delegation to represent Bracebridge and "interview the government in the matter." In their persuasive talk with Premier and Attorney-General Oliver Mowat, they made it plain that Bracebridge would provide accommodation for a district judge, court offices in the town hall building, and that the town hall's council chambers would serve for a courtroom. James was quite specific describing these arrangements, having been holding his Magistrate's Court in this facility for nearly a decade since Mowat first appointed him.

James, in step with most other Muskokans, believed it was high time for the district to get its own judge. Because the nearest judge was in Barrie, the cost and inconvenience of holding trials for serious matters was causing deterioration of the justice system in both Muskoka District and Parry Sound District.

A variety of local and political matters similarly stirred James, each helping rekindle interest in the world around him because he was forced to look not to the past but to the future.

Reading even seemed possible again, and his involvement with the Mechanics' Institute Library resumed. It was time for action, too, because by 1887 the growing library, already relocated across the street before the big fire, again needed a bigger place. Better space for the reading room was just as important. James believed the town hall could be put to greater community service, and town council voted space for the library and reading room, free of rent, as soon as the room temporarily occupied by the post office again became available.

In 1888, the year James was elected president of the Muskoka Agricultural Society, an issue was the need to find new fairgrounds. Arrival of the Grand Trunk Railway meant its tracks, water-tower, coal bins, marshalling yards, and train station now covered much of the riverside flats where community events and the Bracebridge Fall Fair once took place.

It was fortuitous timing that James was at the helm at this time, because his position as Bracebridge municipal clerk became instrumental

This capacious agricultural hall at the Bracebridge fair grounds was one of several buildings housing the annual autumn event, when women dressed in their finery and farmers competed with produce and animals for cash prizes. James Boyer, a president of the Agricultural Society, had an abiding interest in all matters agricultural and cherished the fall fairs.

in putting through a major deal. Alfred Hunt, the banker and poultry man who served at times as councillor and mayor of Bracebridge, was also a big landowner around town. He offered the Agricultural Society a rare piece of real estate in the hilly community of bedrock outcroppings: a large section of flat fertile farmland on the southwest side of Bracebridge. In the low-lying area known as "the Hollow," the land was perfect for new fairgrounds. James Boyer, as president of the Agricultural Society, town clerk, and land conveyancer, became central in putting through the acquisition. The purchase price paid to Hunt was $2,400. Terms of payment were made easy.

That was not the end of it. By 1890, when James was immediate past-president of the Agricultural Society, its directors petitioned Bracebridge council to assume the Society's obligations and take over ownership of the fairground property bought from Hunt in 1888. The financial obligations included a $2,600 mortgage, held by Town Councillor Hunt, on the Agricultural Hall that had since been built at the grounds.

The proposal was referred to a committee of council, whose proceedings Clerk Boyer recorded and whose deliberations he helped advise. The committee recommended council secure the Agricultural Society's land as a public park. Boyer then drafted Bylaw Number 17 to authorize issuing debentures and paying off Hunt's mortgage. He next acted as returning officer for the plebiscite in which Bracebridge voters gave their approval to the deal. The debentures were issued, Hunt was paid off, and the town acquired ten acres for its new municipal park. In time the locale would be designated Jubilee Park, and for a century would boast agricultural buildings, stables, show grounds, cricket fields, baseball diamonds, and a racetrack.

—

James was definitely being lifted up by the public affairs of Bracebridge. In the late 1880s, he happily noted to council, repeating his lines from 1875 to Macaulay Township council when the place first got big enough to be a village, that the village had now grown enough to become a town.

In 1889 the private bill sponsored in Ontario's legislature by Muskoka MPP George Marter to incorporate Bracebridge as a town was passed into law. When Marter sent a telegram to the town office confirming the enactment, James relayed word to Chief Constable Robert Armstrong that the new municipal milestone had been reached. The chief constable honoured the historic moment by ringing the town bell for a full hour, proving both his fine sense of occasion and formidable physical strength, as the community celebrated.

The following week Clerk Boyer gave notice in the *Muskoka Herald* and *Bracebridge Gazette* that a meeting would be held to elect the first town council. Only fifty ratepayers attended. James described it as a "mild affair." Samuel Armstrong was elected mayor by acclamation. So was the reeve, and all councillors, the only time all political offices in Bracebridge were filled without a vote having to take place. Pragmatic townsfolk saw little need to change the composition of the village council, now that it was to become a town council, because the only real difference was a legal designation for their municipality made down in Toronto. On the ground, nothing had changed in Bracebridge from one day to the next.

As James listened to Mayor Armstrong's inaugural address, he found himself by force of long habit recording notes about how Sam "hoped the council would have an eye single to the best interests of the town during the balance of the year, and, while establishing a precedent for future years, act in a business-like and gentlemanly manner, regardless of difference of opinion, thus proving themselves worthy of the honour conferred upon them."

His minutes also record that Bracebridge's new town council "recognized that the clerk's work had been increasing and that with town incorporation he would be busier than ever," and asked the finance committee "to report on a more adequate salary," since there had been no increase in his yearly remuneration of $240 for a number of years. In the end, he got $20 more, an annual amount of $260, paid in quarterly instalments of $65.

The wee amount was generous. Bracebridge's council in this era was bec-oming notoriously tight-fisted on administrative and oper-ating expenses. Several years later, when council engaged a chartered accountant from Lindsay to audit the town's accounts, a discrepancy of $3,452.99 was found and Bracebridge's treasurer was not only discharged from office but charged with theft. At trial he was shown to have handled between thirty to forty thousand dollars a year, in small sums, entailing a great deal of clerical work. The town council had been paying the treasurer a salary of just one hundred dollars, out of which he had to provide an office and heat it. The man, 54, also had a wife and seven small children. The district judge described the amount of his salary as "a scandal on the town" then sentenced the former treasurer to a year in jail. Council took exception to the judge's "scandal" comment and complained to the minister of justice, while newspapers in Orillia and Barrie editorialized that Bracebridge had "received a sharp lesson on the necessity of giving proper remuneration to its officials."

Meanwhile, the Boyers, supported mainly by James's pay as town clerk, managed to get by with frugal living and producing as much of their own food as they could.

—

The town was, ever since arrival of the railway in 1885, busier than ever. A major advance for the municipality came with the electrification of the town, which itself was directly related to another significant step forward, the building of another leather tannery.

On October 12, 1890, James wrote Hannah, at the time visiting her sisters in the United States, "There is talk of another very large Tannery in Bracebridge. I have written to the parties to meet the council tomorrow night."

The town's success in landing this second tannery illustrated the tight interaction of government, industry, and municipal development in Bracebridge. Council negotiated with David W. Alexander of Toronto to establish the tannery, offering a two thousand dollar bonus to sweeten the deal. James drafted a bylaw for voters to approve of the incentive payment, which they did, in the plebiscite he conducted.

The new tannery would be located on the south side of the river, on land still part of Macaulay Township, although this area, which in earlier days had been a gathering place for Chippewas, was now increasingly connected to the town in social and economic ways because of its immediate proximity. The J.D. Shier lumber mills and Singleton Brown's shingle mill were in that section, as were a growing number of homes. When the residents in those houses applied to Bracebridge for this section to be annexed by the town, council promptly voted money to get the necessary private bill passed through Ontario's legislature, as well as offering $150 to Macaulay Township council if its members would lobby to get the act passed. They did. James travelled to Toronto himself, as well, and spent time at the legislature with MPPs and municipal affairs officials to ensure the measure was clearly explained and fully supported.

The town's borders, at the end of this exercise, were extended, and within that larger area appeared the sprawling new Shaw Tannery, offering more jobs to Muskokans and boosting the prosperity of Bracebridge and the central part of the district.

Although the town of Bracebridge had been looking into the matter of electric lighting before this, it was the Shaw tannery's construction in 1892 of the first hydroelectric plant at the falls that really got things moving. Because the electricity was generated by a private company, the town initially contracted with the tannery to buy a flow of its power for street lighting. The next step came when the town purchased the tannery's generating station outright, in 1894.

As town clerk, James, among other duties in Bracebridge's hydroelectric initiative, conducted the plebiscite by which ratepayers voted to raise funds for the municipal hydroelectric system. Voters approved. Although steam-powered electric plants had been built or acquired by other towns and cities before this date, acquisition of the tannery's plant made Bracebridge the first owner of a municipal hydroelectric system in Ontario.

For the next eight years, electric service was confined almost entirely to lighting, rather than to power motors, due to the modest capacity of the original generating station. Still, it was a major improvement over what had existed. The electric works soon benefited townsfolk and existing business operations, as installation of thirteen streetlights transformed several main streets downtown, allowing businesses to extend their hours of operation, and increasing safety in the roads at night. Also, as stores and workplaces acquired electric lighting, Bracebridge surged toward the twentieth century and a new age of modernity, ease, and convenience.

With Bracebridge already in the hydroelectric field, and with a desire to expand the amount of electricity serving the community, council took the decision to build a new, larger generating station at the foot of the Bracebridge falls. When it was completed in 1902, giving the town enough generating capacity to supply power needs of industry, Bracebridge moved fully into a new era.

Besides unleashing an exhilarating mood of progress in the community, Bracebridge gained a new competitive advantage. With the town's ownership of the electricity supply, council began offering power at low cost to the new industries and businesses Bracebridge was competing against other Ontario municipalities to attract. It was a great incentive.

Within the three decades since the first squatter arrived by canoe, Bracebridge had grown to become a vibrant economic centre, despite the number of marginal free grant farms in its surrounding townships. In 1890 the building of the Shaw leather tannery, coupled with creation of a major park in the town that year, exemplified how the community embraced economic development that was strong and cultural life that was vital. Townsfolk had a robust sense of Bracebridge as a go-ahead community.

For originals like James and Hannah who had seen the primitive settlement in the late 1860s, it was close to a miracle.

26

—

The View from Magistrate's Bench

James's inescapable work at the town office had helped pull him out of his doldrums. At the same time, his role as magistrate demanded that he preside in court, regardless of his depressed feelings. The turmoil in other people's lives, as dramatized in the cases before him, helped James place his own lament in perspective.

Quite apart from how they assisted in him regaining some balance, the cases took on a bigger role, too, beyond merely meting out justice in the courtroom. They were morality plays sending signals about proper conduct, through the gossip grapevine and district newspapers when editors felt a case had "news value," to folk around town and across Muskoka. Preachers picked up on them as illustrations for Sunday's sermon. Elected representatives might mention a trial's outcome at a public meeting to make a point. Each case James decided broadcast to the full community news about the rule of law in Canada.

The courtroom dramas and brief appearances by bit actors showed behaviours that would not be tolerated. They portrayed the shame of pitiable souls who had run afoul of the law. They made sharp examples of crime being answered by severe punishment. A devotee of Shakespeare, James felt he was in a kind of theatre, having the best seat in the house to experience the smells and sounds, the squirming and sweating, the bravado or contrition of the raw characters acting out their cameo performances as he looked on. But he was also an actor in these plays himself, scripting their outcome and delivering the final lines, his sentence, at the end of each brief performance.

His Magistrate's Court, sometimes called "police court" in the newspapers because the constabulary generated most of its cases, was the place where James dealt with not high crimes, but low-life enjoyment of a Bracebridge brothel; not capital murder, but someone caught running a knife across the guy-wire of a tent at an evangelical prayer meeting, or threatening to slash his wife's throat "from ear to ear"; not defrauding the government of thousands of dollars, but lifting a silk scarf or stealing a dog.

Yet James knew the cases loomed large in the lives of the troubled individuals before him. He believed, as he looked upon wretches from his bench, that the manner in which small people on the margins get treated reveals a big truth about a society. Never before had he understood this so viscerally.

—

A number of cases brought before Magistrate Boyer by unpaid labourers suggest his sympathies lay with the workingman, but nothing was black-and-white. Because he also lived in the community that produced these cases, James knew the difference between a malingering worker and a struggling contractor trying to make ends meet while providing local employment.

His verdicts concerning the plight of down-and-out men brought into court by the town constable for being unemployed vagrants with no visible means of support and found loitering about town or sleeping in a church or the fire hall, suggest that, in the department of "hard love," James was generous to a fault. Vagrant James Ferguson, charged with "having no visible means of subsistence" one December in Bracebridge, was sent to jail for ten weeks. Alexander Bolton, charged one November by District Constable Robert E. Armstrong for "not having any visible means of maintaining himself and living without employment," got six months hard labour in the common jail. William Kirby, on the same charge, got twenty-one days. James Harvie, likewise without support or employment, spent thirty days locked up. Henry Alexander Evans: hard labour for three months. William Inman: thirty days. William Elliott: three months. Elizabeth Jackson: a two dollar fine.

Of all the vagrancy cases, Jackson's was the only one where James gave the choice of serving time or paying a fine, understanding that a female "not having any visible means of maintaining herself" had options generally unavailable to male vagrants in that era. Besides, there was no separate jail facility for females.

No public support program for indigent or "homeless" people existed, either. Canada's small towns like Bracebridge lacked institutions to house vagrants in wintertime. Being ordered into jail was a crude form of social welfare for the homeless. A cold and hungry man might get a place to stay that was safe, heated, dry, and clean, with a couple of meals a day in the bargain. The constables and the magistrate, running what seemed like a heartless operation, were providing just about the only social welfare available to the homeless. Usually the cells and jail door were not even locked when these wretches were the only ones serving time.

When Jeremiah Crowder appeared before James, charged by the Township of Cardwell's Local Board of Health for "neglect" in notifying the board "of diphtheria in his house at Cardwell," he listened intently to the hardship case of the underfed Crowder family. He learned that a sign warning people to keep away had been posted near the Crowder place. He heard how both Jeremiah's son and daughter died in the house. He knew that sombre experience. Whether James had tears in his eyes was not recorded. That he dismissed the charge was.

When James heard the case of William E. Fleming, brought to court by Constable Alfred Stunden on the charge that "at the Village of Huntsville he did threaten to kill one Blanche Royal," a story unfolded that might have come right off the pages of one of the tragic novels he enjoyed reading. Fleming had developed an obsessive attraction to Blanche Royal in Washington, D.C. When she moved to Toronto, seeking to distance herself from the unwanted but ardent man, he followed her there. When she came north to Huntsville, with the idea that remote Muskoka could offer a safe haven for someone seeking to escape the complications of unwanted love, he stalked her, both in the village and out in Stisted Township.

Will followed Blanche about, wherever she went. He had boys carry his letters of proposal to her, then wait for an answer. Sometimes he handed his written appeal to her himself, but then snatched the letter back before she'd read more than a page or two. His offer was straightforward: Blanche should marry him, or else he would kill her. "It's no use you running away from me," he said on one occasion, "for a pistol shot will reach a long way." One of his letters, Blanche Royal testified, "said that he intended to kill me that night at eight o'clock so I'd better say my prayers." Another time, "when going out the door, he threatened to cut my throat from ear to ear with a razor. I am in fear that he will take my life."

James Boyer ordered William Fleming to enter into a peace bond for two hundred dollars and a surety for two hundred dollars and pay all costs in the case. When he failed to do so, James put him in jail for a year.

In some of the civil actions, when one person sued another over a fight they'd had, the plaintiff and defendant reached a compromise without the court having to make a finding. Then, James added a simple note beneath his brief record of the case, "Settled between the parties." This was not a pre-trial settlement. The case had already begun to be heard in court when some resolution of the issue, helped by means of an apology, perhaps, or maybe a payment, was achieved. James Boyer was a man who could remain calm in the midst of hot feelings and anger, and gave off a formidable impression when he wanted to look sternly upon, say, a clutch of inebriated street brawlers appearing before him. A pointed question from him, in that context, proved conducive on more than one occasion to avoiding a public trial for a private dispute.

Some characters having run-ins with the law were tough. In a couple of cases, the defendant absconded, taking off rather than submitting to the jurisdiction of the court or hanging around to serve jail time. In such cases, if James felt the matter warranted, he would order the sheriff to find him and bring him back. Sometimes those who stayed to face him in court were wild men. In the 1895 case of Frederick Donald, a very violent person, James ordered "the defendant to be constricted" and he was placed in manacles and chains.

—

Because he wore many hats for his various community responsibilities, some of James's duties overlapped and guided his decision-making. As clerk of the municipality, he knew all about council's desire to get a better jail, its need to cover the costs of policing, and some councillors' anxiety over public complaints about derelicts around town and prostitutes in Bracebridge brothels.

As both JP and clerk, his first-hand knowledge helped the community find its balance point in such matters of public order and community morals, as well as in common problems such as livestock being at large in the streets and grazing in peoples' gardens. James's overlapping roles even came into play when council contemplated issuing a revolver to the town's night constable but was concerned about its cost. Boyer as clerk pointed out that, as justice of the peace, he had recently confiscated a handgun that could either be sold to raise five or ten dollars for the court, or acquired with next to no payment by the municipality.

In his pivotal position, dealing with matters small and large, James was again hitting his stride by being back in the action. Also, the more he saw of other people's problems with money, marriage, and betrayal, the more it diminished his own miseries and regrets.

—

Whenever Hannah was visiting her sisters in the United States, the two wrote regularly to each other. In one letter, James included a summary of his JP's work, his accounts hinting at the kind of supper-table conversation they'd otherwise enjoy as he'd report to her on the day's doings.

"I had two magistrate cases on Friday and two on Saturday. We have the notorious Rooney in Jail again. He broke Jail here in March 1889. He is not likely to break out again, as I see he has a pair of bracelets on his legs, built more for strength than ornament." Another tale was of a police chase, circa 1891. "One man robbed Frank Noble of a pocket book with eighty-two dollars in it on Friday afternoon. Our big Policeman followed him to Gravenhurst and captured him with the pocket book and eighty dollars of the money."

Other days were more lacklustre. "John A. Palmer was up before me yesterday on a charge of obtaining money under false pretences. After a long and tedious hearing, the case was dismissed." In another letter, James reported, "The two Montgomerys were up before Spencer & myself yesterday for selling whiskey. One was fined one hundred dollars and the other fifty dollars. I was sitting with Judge Mahaffy in Court on Friday last."

Judging from his letters to Hannah, James was keeping close watch on judicial matters beyond his own court. Once he recounted for her details of "considerable excitement" in Bracebridge because eleven or twelve firms were being sued for one hundred dollars each over failing to register their business partnerships as required by law. This litigation had been "initiated by the notorious Montgomery brothers," who kept the Albion Hotel by the train station, "no doubt to make money, as the party suing gets half the amount, but it's possible they may be disappointed as the Judge has power to remit the fines."

As for judicial matters beyond Muskoka, which he also followed, James informed Hannah, "There has been a terrible murder of two School children in the County of Russell which puts the Birchall case in the shade, but they have arrested the wretch. I think Ontario is getting a not very enviable reputation for crimes of that kind."

———

James relished his role as Muskoka magistrate, which allowed him to be central to the action while remaining a dispassionate observer. No other position could have given him a broader, deeper, or more emotional link to what was happening at ground level in Muskoka.

Constables and game wardens encountered one slice of rawness, when it involved a breach of the Criminal Code or the game laws. James learned about that, when such cases came to court, but he saw much more than the constables or game wardens when private litigation came before him involving unpaid employees and employers, fighting neighbours, or a husband and his battered wife. This was not yet an era of social workers who would be privy to such highly personal matters, nor of labour relations boards whose members confronted such workplace disputes, nor of workers' compensation programs that dealt with the plight of a labourer injured on the job. These matters of daily life in Muskoka, in an age of government's minimal role in social or economic life, fetched up only before the court.

Municipal clerks, including James, played a role in running villages and townships, but not in determining the individual fates of people living in them the way the JP did. The clergy, in particular those with the Salvation Army, saw hardship cases; they did not, however, see the situations arising with fighting farmers, or unlicensed operators of boats, or neighbours battling one another over the location of a line fence or the right to draw water from a well. Newspaper editors might opine on public meetings, local issues, and the good or bad fortunes of particular citizens, but were interested in what would stir up his paper's readers or could be used to advance a pet policy idea, and did not need, the way the JP did, to also deal with petty or mundane cases of people at the margins of Muskoka's society. James Boyer faced it all, and heard everything, and not just cases from around Bracebridge but across the entire district.

—

As his letters to Hannah make clear, James also followed trials much further afield than Muskoka, including cases in the rest of Ontario and beyond. In the reading room of the Mechanics' Institute Library, he indulged his particular interest in reading New York publications, many of which reported trials of those accused in the city's horrific thefts. It was in one of those that he learned of the role of Oakey Hall in a number of scandals, something that his intuition — and his stinging memory of being falsely blamed for fraud in Stratford — had warned him to steer well clear of.

Hall had by 1871 been accused, along with William "Boss" Tweed of Tammany Hall and other city officials who were also members of

"The Ring," of stealing staggering amounts of money from the public coffers by skimming city funds through kick-back and rake-off schemes. James had, month by month over the years, kept up with the news of Oakey Hall's three criminal trials, and how he'd been acquitted.

But news of the flamboyant Hall continued to make the papers, and James became mesmerized by accounts of how he "simply vanished." It later emerged that Oakey Hall had gone to England, under an assumed name and with a new identity in theatre as an actor. Still later, James was stunned to read, Hall had reappeared in the United States with a new "wife" in the person of Lydia Noakes Clifton, although no journalist could find any marriage record that made it official. Meanwhile, Oakey Hall's existing, legally married wife, Katherine Hall, continued to live, in a state of perplexity and shame, at their former home over in Milburn, New Jersey.

—

From 1878 to 1900, James adjudicated hundreds of cases. A few provided eyebrow-raising amusement, such as the night more than a dozen young men of the village were arrested for conducting an old-fashioned charivari outside the house of a couple of newlyweds, demanding the bride be sent out to them as the price for stopping the noise they were making with tin pots and loud shouts. Most cases, though, left him in awe of life's enduring rawness.

Sometimes he would reflect on how, one-by-one, the cases before him revealed the rough-and-ready life that people, come to Muskoka with soaring hopes, now found themselves living. James was privy to things most others were not. His courtroom sessions illuminated the true social conditions and hard culture of Muskoka, and dramatized the terrible predicaments people could get into. He understood.

Once his courtroom cleared, silence and calm descended. The Muskoka magistrate would wait for the ink to dry on the page of his bench book. It was a brief moment to organize papers and gather his thoughts.

Then he'd close his bench book, ready for the next case.

27

James Boyer's Last Escapes

In 1899 James Boyer retired as Bracebridge municipal clerk, fulfilling a quarter century in his role administering, recording, guiding, thwarting, reporting, conducting elections, holding plebiscites, keeping some information secret, and publishing other information as widely as possible. He had participated in over four thousand meetings, and travelled hundreds of times, to advance the interests of his municipality, the agriculturalists of Muskoka, and the fraternal organizations and church to which he belonged. It had been a good run, by any standard.

The next year James retired as magistrate for Muskoka, a position he'd held since 1878, having decided more than a thousand cases. He wished his friend and fellow municipal clerk from Monck Township, William Spencer, whom the government appointed to take his place, the very best. He hoped Spencer would enjoy the new court house facilities James had worked to get but would never occupy himself.

On June 1, 1900, James and Hannah attended the opening of the imposing two-storey brick court house on Dominion Street, a milestone event in Muskoka's history. It signalled a new era beginning, appropriate at the end of one century and the start of another. The year 1900 was also a neat point of transition for James to be closing his own career. It had been three decades since he'd heard Thomas McMurray's uplifting speech in this same community, much more primitive then, about the bright future that awaited Muskoka. James Boyer had succeeded in fashioning his Canadian life by working hard with others to create that new Muskoka community. His career and the district's evolution had become entwined, as was the case for all the pioneers who'd understood Muskoka would be what they made of it.

Inaugurating the court house, Mayor John Thomson presented Judge W.C. Mahaffy with one of James's illuminated addresses. It looked splendid, signed by the mayor himself, each town councillor, and all nine members of the Muskoka bar. Twelve years before, in 1888, Muskoka and Parry Sound had been put together for municipal and judicial purposes. Then, four years before, in 1896, Muskoka was separated from Parry Sound, becoming a compact and united district. "For twelve years," said Mayor Thomson, "Bracebridge had gratuitously supplied a courtroom, judge's chamber, and other conveniences for the administration of justice," but now that a new and more suitable building with modern conveniences had been erected by the government, "the town could lay down the burden it had then assumed." He celebrated the fact Muskoka now formed "a compact and united district."

The much-needed courthouse for Muskoka District, built of red brick at the corner of Dominion and Ontario streets in Bracebridge, was ready for occupancy in 1900, its improved facilities for the magistrate's court ready just after James Boyer retired. It is now officially designated an Ontario Historic Site.

Once the proceedings adjourned, the Boyers shook hands with many in attendance, chatted amiably, then walked the half-dozen blocks home, arm in arm. If the town could lay down a burden it had earlier assumed, so might James Boyer. He was sixty-six, she fifty-nine. The pair looked ahead to easy, gentle days together.

———

As the "Gay Nineties" ended and one century folded into the next, however, life for the Boyers turned for the worse.

The following year, 1901, James suffered a stroke that left him paralyzed and bedridden at home. He would remain completely secluded in the family's small house at the north end of Manitoba Street for the next three and a half years. There was little money. His beard grew very full, and began to turn white.

Their daughters, become grown women, had left home and were not even in town to help out. In 1893, when Brooklyn-born Annie turned twenty-five, she married John Hanson of Toronto, and left Bracebridge to live with him, 125 miles away. Their second daughter, Nellie, born in a drafty cabin during their first Muskoka winter, had married John W. Perkins and was living with him in Toronto, also.

Hannah Boyer fetches wind-dried washing from her clothesline behind the family's Manitoba Street home, while a chicken strolls the straw-littered yard. Hannah also had a nearby lot with a large vegetable garden. With little money the Boyers were back where they started: self-reliant, scrimping, trying to survive.

Fred, their youngest, who'd been born in 1883 at the Manitoba Street house, had finished school and gone north for farm work, living in Parry Sound District near Powassan. Fred liked rural life and farming so much that in his twenties he would leave the rocky Canadian Shield to farm southwestern Ontario's more fertile and flatter fields, living at Comber. That is where he would remain, with his wife and their daughter Helen, until his death in 1952.

In these days of his father's confinement, Fred, too, was away, even further from Bracebridge than his sisters in Toronto. Son George Boyer had taken off for sales work on the road, travelling around Ontario and beyond. Only Charles remained in the Manitoba Street house. Compared to times past, the place was quiet, and because of its languishing patient, forlorn.

With his retirement, James's income ended. Despite the fact he'd spent thirty years handling real estate deals for others, and even though he and Hannah had dabbled in land deals during their early Muskoka days, they now owned no property, except the Manitoba Street house and the lot on which it sat. Neither James nor Hannah had investments, or much in the way of savings, either. Unable because of his stroke to practise calligraphy, he could no longer earn even small money creating illuminated addresses.

Nor could James write notes or articles, as he'd habitually done all his life. The quill driver's hand had been stilled. A lifelong journey made in close company with his pen was at its end. James attempted to read his books, but doing so while bedridden and paralyzed was such a chore it left him more irritable than inspired.

These limitations, both financial and physical, became a source of abiding frustration. To get by Hannah relied on what money their sons earned and shared, her homegrown vegetables and apples, and prayer. She was in helpless despair, seeing the man she loved so vulnerable, the one who'd always been so active and self-reliant now quiet and dependent.

—

George was twenty-two and advancing into a promising career when his father was stricken with paralysis.

He'd already worked six years, starting out, after passing the teacher's examination in July 1893, like his father, teaching barefoot children in a one-room Macaulay Township school. Next, he joined the Shaw-Cassels Tanning Company in Bracebridge, working in the front office handling payroll and administration. From there, George landed a job travelling as a sales representative for the International Business School of Chicago.

It was at this time George, kind and gentle by nature with a peace-loving idealism about him, learned to speak Esperanto. He and several million other people around the world believed that if people everywhere would acquire this easily learned and politically neutral language, as an auxiliary tongue, they could transcend nationality and understand one another better. Esperanto — "one who hopes" — illuminated for George an important pathway to a better future, which is why he learned, spoke, and advocated Esperanto as a path to international harmony. He had acquired from his father a strong antipathy to war.

He was a young man developing an interesting life in the wider world beyond Bracebridge. But George became distressed about his parents' plight. He learned of the doctor's prognosis that his father would not recover. He knew the strain on his mother had become unbearable. In 1903 dutiful son George returned to the family home he thought he'd left behind.

Back in Bracebridge he got work at the *Muskoka Herald*. One of Muskoka's pioneer publishers, Edgar Bastedo, owner of the business, began teaching George the trade, setting type, proofreading, and operating the printing press, as well as getting ads and writing news.

James seemed proud when told about this continuity, a second Boyer generation in newspaper work. He indicated he thought George was on a good course for his future. The production of a weekly newspaper brought memories of his time at the *Northern Advocate*. George's work in printing and publishing gave James a vicarious sense of what might have been his career if only E.F. Stephenson hadn't come to town with the competitor *Gazette*, if only Thomas McMurray's businesses hadn't collapsed in the depression, if only his own newspaper hadn't folded. Because the *Herald* was using some of the *Advocate*'s foundry type and printing equipment, both James and George believed there was genuine continuity, especially now that another Boyer was writing and editing for the Bracebridge paper. George began to see his role in Muskoka's newspaper work as an engaging vocation on its own, but also a way to honour his father, giving the man pride when he had little else to feel good about.

James was just as pleased that George shared his keenness about all matters agricultural. His son had taken on the secretary's role for the South Muskoka Agricultural Society, and not as a duty but a pleasure. George delighted to be among farm animals as much as he relished being in the print shop — there were great smells and sounds and activity in both places, though each was a world apart. George was also following James's footsteps in choir work at the Bracebridge Methodist Church, and by age nineteen was choir director.

—

Charles, now twenty-five, was living at home on Manitoba Street.

He occupied a special place within the family. For Hannah and James, Charles was their oldest living son. For George and Fred, as well as the girls, he was the "older brother," with all the prince-like qualities that entailed. George followed him at school, and played on his teams, and the two brothers enjoyed music and played various instruments, but when it came to dancing, Charles outshone George and just about everyone else.

Charles had been happily following his father's patterns, living the example of a dad to whom he felt very close. Like James he was an avid reader, especially enjoying the articles in *Chambers's Journal of Popular Literature, Science, and Arts*. Whenever he bought a series of the *Journals*, bound in a hardcover volume, which could run to more than four hundred pages of small print, he'd inscribe his name inside the front cover, "*Charles Boyer, Bracebridge*," displaying an open, artful flourish. He had an easy, fun-loving way, and would go to Toronto by train whenever he could, staying with his sisters, exploring the city, and spending holidays. In Bracebridge Charles was regularly engaged with athletics, never missing a game of the cricket, lacrosse, and baseball junior teams.

After completing his education at the Bracebridge schools, Charles turned around and began teaching school himself, a starting position for all Boyer men it seemed. Not finding a Macaulay school opening, Charles left Bracebridge in 1895 to teach in north Muskoka, west of Huntsville, at the frame Ashworth School beside Douglas Lake in Stisted Township's Number 7 school section. He was nineteen years old. The one-room school was open only six months a year, from May to November. During the hot summer days of 1895, Charles happily "spent more time," according to his pupil Will Hall, "fooling around Douglas Lake on a raft than teaching." Had the parents "come to see what was going on," Hall believed, Charles Boyer "would have been fired in a hurry."

That winter, with the lake frozen and school closed, Charles returned to Bracebridge and, becoming more ambitious, took up another of his father's careers by starting as a law clerk in Bracebridge lawyer Orville Arnold's office. This included copyist work, just as his father had begun his career. It was no stretch for artful Charles to also learn calligraphy, which he did, hoping to pick up his father's sideline of crafting illuminated addresses.

Each son brought money into the home, which helped reduce some anxiety. George, more than his older brother, imparted a calm steadiness to the place that was a boon to both parents. Now and then Annie would come north from Toronto by train to help with housework and support her mother in the manner unique to women of shared blood. Other times, it was daughter Nell's turn.

Then, against all odds, James pulled off another escape. This time, he did not even have to relocate. He emerged from the straitjacket of paralysis that had imprisoned him for more than forty months. His body had done its healing work. He first recovered use of his right arm, and then he was able to be up and walk about.

Using a pencil and lined sheets, he began writing down all the things that had been cycling through his mind during the years of incapacity. Most important was his account of Muskoka's early decades of settlement, for which he drew on personal experiences and first-hand knowledge gained through more than thirty years as recording secretary and clerk of most organizations in the community. George set the articles into type and published them through the *Muskoka Herald*'s columns, most of them appearing throughout 1905.

More than three decades after his newspaper career in Muskoka ended, James Boyer had found a small way to resurrect it.

—

Three more years passed. The seasons changed slowly as James remained isolated in his Manitoba Street home. His large beard was now quite white.

For a while he appeared to be improving from his long paralytic affliction. In addition to being able to write, as he had been doing again since 1905, he was now also "able to move about, read, and do light work occasionally as a pastime." Through the winter of 1907–1908, however, "he became gradually weaker." By mid-April he was obliged to remain in bed, suffering painful intestinal trouble. There was a slight rally at the start of May, George Boyer informed the public, but not enough to offset James's ineluctable decline.

On the morning of Friday, May 8, Dr. Francis Williams, a friend as well as family physician, come up from his downtown medical office by Chancery Lane to the Manitoba Street home, examined his patient, and advised the family that James's recovery was impossible. "The end," he quietly told Hannah as they stood apart, "is near."

That morning, James slipped into a state of semi-consciousness. On the morning of Monday, May 11, he again became conscious. He looked around at those circling his bed, recognizing the members of his family who had come from all directions to be present. He bade them goodbye. Hannah held his hand, stroked his head. He asked to have the Lord's Prayer repeated. Hannah, Charles, George, Fred, Annie, and Nellie then enwrapped him with their voices, little more than whispers:

> *Our Father, which art in heaven,*
> *hallowed be thy name;*
> *thy kingdom come;*
> *thy will be done,*
> *in earth as it is in heaven.*

Give us this day our daily bread.
And forgive us our trespasses,
as we forgive them that trespass against us.
And lead us not into temptation;
but deliver us from evil.
Amen.

Several could not complete it all, their voices breaking. Tears welled up in all eyes. James slipped again into the murky twilight of half-life.

At last, in the quiet darkness of a spring night, Tuesday, May 12, 1908, just after 1 a.m., "death terminated the long illness of our old townsman," his son George informed readers of that week's *Muskoka Herald*.

Townsman James Isaac Boyer had lived seventy-two years, the lives of two men, and was confident he was taking the secret of his double life to the grave. When James died, Dr. Williams reappeared, conducted his examination, and would the following day attribute James Boyer's death to a serious intestinal problem of some month's duration, known as ileitis, an inflammation of the small intestines that is nasty, lingering and, in that

Image of a man who drew from Shakespeare to call himself "a shadow of the substance."

era, potentially fatal. In James's case, so it proved to be. His vigorous and eventful life had ended. He had made his final escape.

That Thursday afternoon Reverend W.R. Barker, the Methodist minister, conducted a short private service with the Boyer family in the Manitoba Street house. He had only come to Bracebridge from Uxbridge in 1905, after James was house-bound and unable to attend church, so he made pastoral visits to his incapacitated parishioner. Now, he returned for the funeral, which began at 3 p.m. and was concluded in brisk order.

The pallbearers to the Anglican Cemetery, further north on Manitoba Street, were his three sons Charles, George, and Fred, paired on the other side of the casket by his erstwhile brother-in-law, Harry Boyer, and two of Harry's sons, Thomas and Sam. At graveside, Reverend Canon William Burt, of the Church of England, conducted a service of committal.

Every member of Bracebridge Town Council was in attendance. Members of his Loyal Orange Lodge showed up in strength. So did James's fellow friends from the Independent Order of Foresters. Members of the Odd Fellows came in ranks. The entire executive of the Muskoka Agricultural Society stood solemnly in the large assembly gathered at the cemetery outside town, beside a field with grazing milk cows.

With information of the Thursday burial publicized in that morning's *Muskoka Herald*, a great many townsfolk came to St. Thomas's Cemetery that afternoon as well, to witness the final passage of "respected pioneer citizen James Boyer." In his four decades among them, he had made the most of his new Canadian life, and each person present had a story to tell. He had touched their lives and affairs in a great many ways.

———

Harry Boyer worked solemnly, downtown in his Bracebridge "tombstone factory," chiseling his brother-in-law's large granite grave marker with the words of an epitaph James had written out for him several years earlier.

The stone was large, big enough to accommodate the names of other Boyers whose remains would be added to the family plot, at the very front of the cemetery, in years to come.

The words Harry cut into the grey stone can still be made out, although the lettering is now weather-worn and lichen-covered.

What can be discerned is James Boyer's new Canadian name, the intentionally wrong date of his birth, and four cryptic words ...

MY HEAVENLY FATHER KNOWS

—

After coming to Muskoka, James never returned to England or the United States, would never see his wife Eliza or their daughter Annie again. After that last summer of 1869, Isaac Jelfs dropped from sight in New York. Neither Eliza nor Annie ever managed to get any news of his whereabouts, or his fate. No American census takers, compilers of law firm registries and city directories, newspaper reporters, or secretaries of patriotic societies, ever recorded his name after that date.

In the period following Isaac Jelfs's departure from Brooklyn, James Boyer, a man never before known to exist and for whom no historical records can be traced in the United States or Great Britain, began to make his many appearances in the public records and community organizations, newspaper accounts, and civic proceedings in the remote Canadian village of Bracebridge.

Back in Brooklyn Eliza struggled in a state of personal uncertainty and social limbo. She supported her daughter and herself by taking in tenants for rent and by sewing for wages. She became, in a pattern familiar to many women faced with a crisis in life, more devoted in her church attendance and more immersed in the distraction of good causes in her community, perhaps even seeking thereby to expiate some misplaced sense of guilt. When census takers or others asked about her marital status, uncertain Eliza revealed her conundrum by sometimes describing herself as a "widow," other times as "married, but solo."

Did she think her husband had died somewhere, his body unfound or unreported? In March 1871 the *Lain Brooklyn City Directory* listed Eliza Jelfs as "widow," a description appearing for her in these directories up to 1880. Or, did she think Isaac had simply abandoned her? She was uncertain, for in the very same period she described herself to an 1875

New York State census taker as "married, but no spouse in the house."

The *Lain Directory* for 1871 shows Eliza still living in the Jelfs home at 166 9th Street, indicating that at this time she was renting the entire house at 259 18th Street. Three years later she had made 259 18th Street her principal residence. Isaac's contingency plan to provide for Eliza and Annie by putting the property in her sole name seemed to have worked, to a degree, following his disappearance. Census reports in subsequent years show other families living at the large house she owned, with a number of renters paying her income. She kept the house Isaac bought her at 259 18th Street for a decade, and then sold it in September 1878 to buy a different residence nearby at 208 18th Street, in all probability making a good profit judging from the way house prices rose in that period.

Apart from such financial considerations, Eliza had to deal with the emotional fallout of her husband's disappearance. Doubtless she was mystified, or livid, depending on what she believed had been the fate of the husband who'd utterly vanished. In that 1878 real estate transaction, a decade after being deserted, she still identified herself as "Eliza Jelfs, wife of Isaac Jelfs." A couple of years later, she revised her announced status, again describing herself to the 1880 U.S. census takers, with somewhat more precision, as "married, but no spouse in household."

When Eliza died on October 18, 1881, a victim of tuberculosis, she was just fifty years old. She was buried alongside the Jelfs's children Thomas, Caroline, and William in Green-Wood Cemetery. The records prepared by Moses Genung, a Brooklyn funeral director, suggest that by then Eliza had accepted that her husband had died, or at least was dead to her, with her marital status stated unambiguously as widow.

The *Brooklyn Daily Eagle*, referring to her as "wife of Isaac Jelfs, a former resident of this city," spoke in glowing terms of Eliza as someone who had continued to play a role in her community, "a worthy woman who had many friends in Brooklyn."

Their daughter, Annie Elizabeth Jelfs, was two years old when her father vanished, fourteen when her mother died. She had no other family. Left on her own, Annie Jelfs disappeared from all records after 1881. The happiest possibility is that she married and, thus acquiring a different surname, could just no longer be traced.

Her father, to be sure, had remained beyond all trace.

———

James's life was a tragic story. He lived all his life with the consequences of being made a scapegoat in Stratford. He knew he was innocent but was unable to fight the system because he did not know how. Wrongly blamed he could do nothing about it but escape. When he received word of his vindication, years later, it was too late. He was embedded in a new life, as a different man, rooted in another country.

In the days following his burial, Hannah returned often to James's grave. She sobbed. She said a prayer. She looked at the family plot and its long rectangle of fresh earth, and knew that one day another would be dug for her, right there, beside the man she unfailingly loved.

It was only a matter of time.

28

Unrequited Love

After James's death, things began to unravel.

The Boyers appeared close because family members shared avid interest in music, church, farming, and community affairs. Yet there was a large realm of unspoken thought; few confidences were shared, and the real depths of family doings often went unplumbed. Each of the family's members displayed amicable independence. "My brothers did not confide in me," George observed. The Boyers stayed a close-knit family by remaining apart.

This regime of discreet secrecy under the Boyer roof arose from the stubborn resolve of James and Hannah to never talk about their past, except in innocuous details. They had begun a bold new chapter for their lives when entering Muskoka in 1869, and their personal narrative required there be no looking back at earlier chapters. If they shared a watchword, it was "Forward!"

This "eyes only to the future" stance expressed an outlook that resilient Hannah and stoic James had each acquired as their buffer against self-pity. Over the years, apart from the unbreakable love between the two of them, the Boyer family's emotional restraint became a hallmark trait, giving its members the comfort of privacy, yet denying them closeness that comes by sharing life's adventures. In this detached family, with the exception of the strong love between Hannah and James, the closest emotional link to be forged was the one between James and his son Charles.

Charles had been born just before the Boyers moved into Bracebridge from the homestead, their second son, but the first to live into adulthood. As Charles was growing up, James saw qualities in the boy that, to his unexpected delight, reminded him of himself as a youth. Though now far removed from Moreton-in-Marsh, he sometimes would build bridges to the place of his youth in his mind, savouring small comforts in pleasant memories, and inexplicably Charles became a part of his reconnections to those lost, happy days. This no doubt contributed to the strong bond between them.

Known by most everybody in the small town, Charles was amiable and intelligent, musical and creative, an imaginative and even romantic man. Although appearing to be outgoing and social in a classroom with his pupils or on a dance floor with the ladies, Charles — again like his father — had another side, one that he fulfilled by pursuing his own interests in solitude.

He liked keeping to himself, a trait captured in a small way by the 1890s photograph of the Boyer family at the Manitoba Street house from which Charles Boyer is the only one absent, and not missing on account of being the photographer.

"A clever student at school," reported the *Muskoka Herald* of Charles Boyer. The community could see that James Boyer's oldest son had become his protégée. Noted the *Herald*, "an excellent pensman, Charlie, under the direction of his father, became one of the best office clerks any lawyer in Bracebridge ever had." The *Gazette* added that he was "most accurate and systematic in his work." Just like his dad.

James was also keen to teach Charles about patents, once he saw how his son became fascinated listening to his uncle Harry Boyer, who was never reticent about *his* past, describe his adventures in New York as a runner at the U.S. Patent Office. Charles became curious, keen to learn more about patents. In New York patent work had been an important part of Isaac Jelfs's law practice, with news reports on some of his patent cases even appearing in the city's newspapers. In Bracebridge he took pleasure in explaining to his inquisitive son how inventors discover better ways of making things work, through close observation and applied ingenuity.

Charles soon wanted to invent something himself. Drawing on his observations at Orville Arnold's law office, where the newly invented typewriter was just starting to displace his craft as a copyist and where after-hours mail was left at the office without secure delivery, Charles sought to devise equipment that would improve both so that he could patent the plans and become rich.

———

The extent to which father and son were connected did not take long to reveal itself after James's death in May 1908. Charles had lost his anchor.

"Since his father's death, about a year ago, he had not been himself," explained the *Herald* in April 1909, "but acted strangely, though without creating the impression that his mind was rapidly weakening."

At first, following his father's death, Charles, now in his early thirties, resolved to establish himself as his own man and to rise above the poverty of his family. He vowed to do three things: make lots of money as an inventor, buy his own home, and find a wife.

His best prospect for marriage, Charles believed, was Viola Cripps, an attractive and intelligent woman who taught school at Hillsdale west of Huntsville. Charles first met her at a dance in Huntsville and felt love's spark.

Could family history repeat itself? His father and mother had met at a dance, fell in love, and soon married.

Charles became convinced destiny was at work for him, once Viola came to Bracebridge, moving into a home on James Street with her parents and brother, William, just a block away. In July 1908 Charles began calling on her residence every week, and started, at least in his own mind, "going with her." When not arriving in person at the Cripps's front door, Charles substituted boxes of expensive flowers, shipped up from Toronto and bearing messages from him. Viola discouraged his intentions. As a consequence the flowers from Charles began arriving with greater frequency.

During their times together, Charles told Viola he was worried about business matters, his work at the law office, and was very concerned about a patent he was working on. Several times he proposed marriage.

In January 1909 he said that, if she did not marry him and if his invention failed, he would shoot himself. Viola never consented to marry him, nor, in her mind, ever led him to believe she would.

Yet, on February 23, Charles read her letter in which she quoted these poetic lines:

> *The eagle may forget the rock,*
> *The ocean bird the sea;*
> *The flowers may forget to bloom,*
> *But I'll remember thee.*

A woman trying to break off with a man may have thought this poetic turn a gentle way to indicate that he was still special to her all the same. Charles took it as encouragement. He read and re-read the poetic message, a clear sign that precious Viola would still hold him, at least in her memory, when all else in nature fell away. So he persisted, for the next seven weeks, visiting her home and sending her flowers, doing everything he could to impress her, in the timeless fashion of those wracked by unrequited love.

Charles had earlier told Orville Arnold about his invention for an automatic letterbox. Now, he informed the lawyer that it had been perfected. Arnold gave his law clerk money to go to Toronto to get the model made for the letterbox prototype. Sometime after that Charles asked Arnold "to go to Toronto and close the bargain with Morgan, Hunter & Co." Meanwhile, Elizabeth Weis, stenographer in the Orville M. Arnold Law Office where Charles clerked, knew he had written out an agreement regarding the patent for the letterbox, which he kept under the blotter on his desk in the law office. She knew nothing about the signature of Morgan, Hunter & Co., which appeared on the agreement, but at Charles's request Elizabeth witnessed the document, signing her name at Charles's request as "Etta Kinton," something she agreed to when he assured her he was "just having a joke on someone."

On Sunday evening, April 18, visiting the Cripps's home, Charles told Viola that his invention was alright, that he had an agreement with a New York firm, and that this was all evidence of his bright future. "I'm going to get one hundred thousand dollars for the patent," he proudly announced, adding that he'd already received an advance of five hundred dollars on it. He then showed his intended fiancée his plan for the patent, an automatic letterbox. Next, he told her he would be following up this success with an improvement for the typewriter he was working on and would patent, too. To top off his good news, Charles announced that he had bought a home where they could live as husband and wife.

When Viola inquired about the house, because that seemed a concrete development she might better evaluate, he told her it was James Hall's residence and he'd paid $1,100 for it. With a grand flourish, Charles left the agreement and patent plan with her when he left. Viola looked it over and suspected he had drawn up the agreement himself.

When Charles returned to the Cripps's home two days later, on Tuesday evening, April 20, Viola told him again, as she had three or four times before, that she did not accept his offer of marriage. She asked him never to come back, and closed the door.

Obscured in the shadows, waiting for the southbound train at Bracebridge station, Hannah Boyer is being helped with her trunk and suitcase by son George. She will depart for Toronto, leaving Bracebridge after the loss of her beloved companion, James.

His deteriorating health and desperate frame of mind measured accurately the depth of Charles's deep wound from this one-sided love affair. The worse his appearance got and the more frenetic his mind grew, the harder he pressed her to marry him. The more bizarre his claims of patents and big income became, the more anxious Viola was to have nothing more to do with Charles. She was in a perverse dilemma, because she had to be firm with him that she did not want him, but her firmer rejections seemed the primary cause of his downward spiral.

George saw his brother Charles when he slept at the Boyer home on Manitoba Street on Tuesday night. It was a place with a different feel now that his father was gone. Their mother Hannah had gone away, missing the man she'd loved with such intensity that she wanted to stay indefinitely with her daughter Annie in Toronto, away from the house on Manitoba Street where James had died, out of Muskoka and all its memories of hard times.

After their mother departed, George had noticed that Charles seemed even more rudderless. For several weeks George had observed his brother "acting strangely," but Charles "did not talk much" and had certainly not told him of any difficulties, nor anything about his invention or patent agreement.

Late the following morning, hardware merchant James Whitten sold Charles a revolver. To go with it, Charles also specified he wanted long cartridges. Raising his eyes to fix a gaze on Boyer across the store counter, Whitten asked, "What do you want a revolver for?"

"Nothing serious," replied Charles.

Whitten did not notice anything peculiar in Boyer's manner, but turned to a clerk in the store after he left and said, "I wonder what he wants a revolver for."

George saw his brother midday, but Charles was rushing and did not stop to speak. Elizabeth Weis of the law office encountered him complaining of headaches. She found him unintelligible in what he said, as he headed to the train station. That same Wednesday Viola got a message from Charles, in the form of a telegram sent from Atherley down in Simcoe County, to expect something. The day after that, a box of flowers arrived for her.

The flowers were not the only arrival at the Cripps's James Street house that Thursday, April 22. Another suitor for Viola, William Conlon from Hillsdale, had come down from the north and shown up at her Bracebridge home. He'd arrived by train in the morning and was still with Viola in the front room of the Cripps's home when her mother and brother William went to bed for the night. Her father was not at home.

Around five minutes past ten that evening, Viola and Bill Conlon heard a noise they thought was the stove. To the ears of her brother, William, upstairs but not yet asleep, it was "a curious noise, like one stone striking another." A few minutes afterwards, the couple in the front room heard the back door rattle. Viola took a lantern to investigate, and on reaching the kitchen found Charles lying on the step of the door, his head and shoulders inside the kitchen where he'd fallen, the first she was aware of his presence at her home that evening.

"Charlie Boyer has shot himself in our back kitchen!" she screamed.

Tears streamed down her cheeks. William, hearing his sister's screams, dressed and ran out of the house at once to look for Constable McConnell. Ten frantic minutes later, he found him by the alleyway in the centre of town. The police chief immediately returned with Cripps and found Charles Boyer lying on his right side where he had fallen, a wound in his breast like a small bullet hole. A .22 revolver, apparently new, near the body, contained six shells, five full and one empty.

Perhaps his plan, to the extent Charles could form one, was to take his new revolver and threaten to kill himself in Viola's presence in a desperate final attempt to get her to agree to marriage. But on coming to the front of the house he found a different scene than the one he'd imagined, seeing his cherished Viola through the window with another man. What is certain is that he then went around to the rear of the Cripps's house, shot himself at the back door, then entered.

Pools of blood followed him as far as he got before collapsing. Chief McConnell summoned the coroner, who pronounced Charles Boyer dead. He ordered the body removed to the Boyer home on Manitoba Street.

The *Bracebridge Gazette* reported that "the deceased was madly in love with Miss Cripps." Orville Arnold, who found Charles "always nice and amiable," had become "alarmed at his failing appearance," heard him "frequently complain of being unwell," and, when Charles "appeared unable to concentrate his mind on any work for the last two weeks," had privately confided to his wife he "feared Charlie was failing mentally."

Dr. Peter McGibbon conducted a coroner's inquest at the spacious new Bracebridge courthouse, with a large jury of seventeen prominent townsmen listening intently to evidence. People turned out *en masse* that Friday night to learn first-hand details of Charles's dramatic and heart-wrenching death. The large place was so overcrowded it became "stifling."

The jury's verdict was that Charles Boyer "came to his death by a shot from his own hand whilst temporarily insane." George Boyer, deeply saddened by the tragedy of his older brother, said he had seen with his own eyes Charles's "rapidly deteriorating health, ever since our father died."

Charles's remains were interred at the Anglican Cemetery in a burial service that Sunday afternoon, April 25, a fresh grave beside the one of James Isaac Boyer, who had been dead less than a year. Father and son, alike in more ways than they'd ever know.

Harry Boyer returned later in the week to chisel another of his family's names and dates into the hulking granite monument:

CHARLES ERNEST BOYER

MARCH 28, 1876 ~ APRIL 22, 1909

29

—

The Dutiful Son

James Boyer had a double life. He also had a second life, through his son George. In Charles he'd seen a younger version of his Isaac Jelfs self, but George was the one who struggled to embody the reality of the Canadian persona James had created.

Back in Bracebridge, with things still raw in the wake of Charles's bitter suicide, George Boyer was now the only descendent of Hannah and James still in the Manitoba Street house.

Each day he rose, dressed, cooked some porridge, ate alone, closed the door on eerie silence, and walked to the Muskoka Herald building on Dominion Street where he could immerse himself in the work of getting out another week's newspaper. Wherever George went he felt conscious of a community watching him, murmuring after he'd passed about his dead brother and the tragedy that had befallen the Boyers. He felt fragile. He put on as strong a face as he could.

On Sundays George's walk was again to Dominion Street, but his destination was a couple of buildings before the newspaper office, the cavernous redbrick Methodist church. For some weeks after his brother's death, George found it easier to just move his lips when singing with his choir, staying silent in order to keep his voice from breaking with emotion. He felt self-conscious. The music moved him to tears he dared not shed.

Nobody ever really talked about Charles Boyer again. Silence swallowed guilt, time softened shame, and new interests filled the hollow he'd left behind.

George resolved to be a force for good in Bracebridge, a person to look up to, as a way of proving that he was not his brother. He was gentle by nature, but his determination was of steel.

George Boyer had many things to engage him in his anxious resolve to do good works in the community. When Edgar Bastedo was appointed sheriff of Muskoka in 1906, printer George had stepped into his place as editor of the *Muskoka Herald*. In addition to editing a district newspaper, he was also active in Methodist church work, was secretary of the Muskoka Conservative Association, and secretary of the South Muskoka Agricultural Society. Like his father, George could never stop taking on more roles. He trained and coached several of the town lacrosse teams, including the Bracebridge Juniors, who, in 1906, went all the way to win the Canadian championship.

But by 1909 George's main new interest was church music — not so much his choir as the vivacious young woman he'd invited to become organist. Victoria Archer, eight years younger than he, was an accomplished pianist, among her many attributes. Of the Browning Island Archer family, she was also of pioneer Muskoka stock, her parents' families both having come to Muskoka before Confederation.

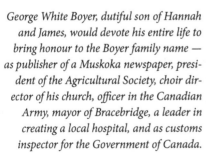

George White Boyer, dutiful son of Hannah and James, would devote his entire life to bring honour to the Boyer family name — as publisher of a Muskoka newspaper, president of the Agricultural Society, choir director of his church, officer in the Canadian Army, mayor of Bracebridge, a leader in creating a local hospital, and as customs inspector for the Government of Canada.

Known to all as "Vic," she liked people, was quick-thinking, and had an aptitude for business. She'd taken bookkeeping in high school, and after graduating first landed a job as bookkeeper at James Fenn's Bracebridge hardware store, then headed west to join the T. Eaton Company's office staff at its department store in Winnipeg. Upon her return to Bracebridge a year later, George elevated Victoria Archer from piano player for children in the Sunday school to organist for adults in the church.

On October 4, 1911, George and Victoria became husband and wife. He was thirty-three, she twenty-five. Their marriage service in the Bracebridge Methodist church was the first church wedding since the building had been built back in 1889. Weddings took place in houses, usually the bride's, but a church wedding was appropriate for George and Vic. Since they fell in love making music in the house of the Lord, where better to marry than at His place?

Vic's mother, Jane Bryers, had come to Muskoka from Hamilton around 1870, and after marrying William Archer in 1873 took the Archer family name. Among those attending this 1911 wedding of her daughter were Bryers family members who, observing a "Boyer" marrying a "Bryers," quipped that it was *almost* as odd as the groom's mother and father having had the identical surname. Hannah and James's story was just so strange that people could not let it go.

George was joined by his bride in the Manitoba Street house, where Vic quickly took charge setting up housekeeping. She had the freedom to do so because her mother-in-law, Hannah, had more or less vacated the family home, staying down in Toronto with her daughter Annie Hanson for long periods, and making extended tours to the United States to stay with various sisters.

Hannah had found her Bracebridge house heavy with the sombre memories of funerals, first for her beloved James, then for her lost Charles, whose death she blamed on her own absence in the times that love drove him mad. Funerals, like weddings, were conducted from a family's home in those days. Hannah could hardly stand to be in the place anymore.

—

But the newlyweds knew only joy.

In quick order Vic transformed the Manitoba Street house into a welcoming home with her take-charge manner and attentive touches, including fresh flowers on the table. She even made those darkest days of the year before Christmas brighter, by giving birth to a son, Robert James Boyer, on December 14, 1913.

George liked the idea that, in this house where he'd been born, his son had also drawn his first breath. When summer came, on evenings after supper, they would put baby Bob in a canoe and paddle down the river and across Lake Muskoka to Browning Island for a visit with Vic's parents, then paddle back upstream in the dark to Bracebridge.

When the First World War began in 1914, Muskoka reservists were called up and a number of young men enlisted. Two years later, in 1916, when the sickening slaughter in Europe drove the British to demand still more men from its colonies, an entire battalion of soldiers was recruited from across the district. George Boyer obtained an officer's commission as paymaster with Muskoka's own 122nd Battalion, and left the newspaper for army service. George still did not believe in war, but felt a higher duty.

The 122nd was moved to Camp Borden, but became unpopular there with other soldiers, first by assisting high command in putting down an insurrection among some of the troops, and next by defeating all other battalions in lacrosse — Captain George Boyer coached the team, which included many of his 1906 Canadian championship players, who'd now switched uniforms from those of the Bracebridge Juniors to those of the Canadian Army.

For its own safety, the 122nd was transported from Camp Borden to Galt, Ontario, where they camped and trained through the winter of 1916–17. Vic took baby Bob to live in a Galt apartment so she could be with the man she loved. Once George went overseas, they both understood this could be the last time they'd ever see one another.

In mid-September 1916, the exchange called the Battle of the Somme was into its fifth month. In this fighting more than 24,000 Canadian and

Newfoundland soldiers had already died. Distraught young German soldiers, having no other choice except to keep firing belt after belt of shells into the folding ranks of Canadian soldiers charging directly at them, spewed vomit over their scorching machine guns and felt hot tears streaming down their grimy cheeks. Wave after wave attacked across cratered open stretches and through barbed-wire, bodies piling upon bodies.

Muskoka's newspapers reported the deaths of local soldiers, mounting week by week. Details were sparse. The costs seemed beyond ability to pay. By the spring of 1917, the 122nd was ordered overseas. Vic returned with Bob to Bracebridge and lived at her parent's home. It was there her second son, George Wilson, was born May 21, 1917.

George survived, but during the fighting in France, suffered severe burns to his legs in a German attack, escaping with his life from the flaming wooden officers' building that had been shelled. His wounds would afflict George the rest of his life, and he'd sweat through hot Muskoka summers in long underwear worn to prevent his pants fabric rubbing his scarred and sensitive legs. Walking was, for the rest of his days, a painful chore. He never let on.

In June 1918 Victoria Boyer and her son Bob both miss husband and dad, Captain George Boyer, overseas with the embattled Canadian Expeditionary Force in France. Just as sensitive would be his second son Wilson, who would weep in silence upon hearing classical music in a minor key. George would return months after the war ended, delayed by officer's work and recovering from war wounds of badly burned legs.

Getting home at last in the summer of 1919, Captain George Boyer beamed with joy to see his second son, Wilson, now two years old, for the first time.

—

In 1919, George Boyer formed the Muskoka Publishing Company Limited and bought the *Muskoka Herald* business, setting a course for printing, publishing, and journalism over the rest of his ninety years on earth.

Vic and George remained the closest companions, sharing their love through community life and political activity. She was active in the Ladies' Aid Society, which assisted women in need, and became its president. In the 1920s Vic became a member of the Clef Club, a ladies' music organization that would continue for six decades. Through the 1920s she was active also in the Bracebridge Ladies' Snowshoeing and Skating Club, whose members got together every week through the winter. She became president of it, too. With the change of seasons, Vic and George enjoyed sport together in the Lawn Bowling Club, about the most strenuous sport he could play because of his legs. Going to community events, he often took a taxi, which seemed a bit much to some who did not know that only by being delivered directly to an event was it possible for him to attend at all.

On the political front, George was Muskoka's returning officer for a provincial by-election, was elected a Bracebridge councillor after the war, and became increasingly active supporting the Conservative Party, with Vic's enthusiastic support. When it came to get voters to the polls on election day, she was most effective. She then deployed her campaign skill with great effect in 1925, helping get George elected mayor of Bracebridge.

That same year the decision had been reached by three of Canada's Protestant churches, the Methodists, Congregationalists, and Presbyterians, to unite as a single entity. The idea had been much debated at national and local levels. In Bracebridge the Presbyterian minister led half his congregation, on the Sunday morning of union, in a procession from their church, walking together the two and a-half blocks to the Methodist church on Dominion Street. The Boyers were among the large congregation to welcome their fellow Christians. The other half of the divided Presbyterian congregation, who'd opted to stay out of church union, remained stubborn in their building at the corner of McMurray and Quebec streets, as "continuing Presbyterians," with the result that, despite union, Bracebridge still had a Presbyterian church.

Such a split between members of the same congregation showed how contentious religious life could be, but the Boyers had discussed the proposal and were all in favour. They understood church union. Vic's grandfather, Reverend Marmaduke D. Archer, had come to Muskoka in 1866 as a missionary of the Methodist *Episcopal* Church, one of several branches of Methodism in Canada at the time. Her own parents, William and Jane Archer, had joined the *Wesleyan* Methodist congregation. James and Hannah Boyer had become members of the *Primitive* Methodists. In 1889 all these Methodist bodies united and erected the large church building on Dominion Street where, more than two decades later, George and Vic had been the first have a church wedding. To Vic, church union seemed natural, inevitable. To George, getting together had the same goal for Canadian Christians as speaking Esperanto did for the world: one channel of communication, less misunderstanding.

Besides, those coming to join included the best members of the Presbyterian choir. George had resumed being choir master after the war, and would keep leading the choristers until 1949, at which point he had reached the half-century mark in this role, although Vic would continue as organist only until 1923. George was happy with his more robust choir. Soon, the Sunday morning anthems alone made it worth going to church.

The Methodist Boyers were now members of the United Church of Canada. They worshipped in the same building where James Boyer had been secretary and sang in the choir. George had followed his father, both in church music and in becoming the congregation's recording steward in 1898, when he was twenty. That position he would continue to hold for sixty years. As if being choir director and recording steward were not enough, George was elected, by the members of Bracebridge United Church at the first meeting in 1925, to be clerk of session, a position akin to chairman, in which role he would continuously serve until 1966, while also remaining in his other roles.

There was large work to be done building Muskoka and its towns, for the district was still young in the 1920s. To promote agriculture, he went on from president of the local agricultural society to become president of the Association of Agricultural Societies of Ontario. George became an ardent proponent for creation of a general hospital to serve the people of Muskoka, and after his term as mayor took up the cause with true focus. In 1928 he convened a local group in his editor's office to advance the plan, and then headed the fund-raising campaign. Named Bracebridge Memorial Hospital to honour soldiers who'd died in the First World War, including thirty-four from the town of Bracebridge itself, it was opened that same year, on November 11, Armistice Day. George, a fine public speaker who paid close attention to the mood of his audiences, addressed the hundreds of his fellow citizens present. He would then go on to serve as a member of the hospital board for many years.

George, with his loving companion Vic, had redeemed the Boyer name in Bracebridge. His brother's fate had long been forgotten. Perhaps he could next represent all Muskoka in the Ontario legislature, or the House of Commons in Ottawa.

For the dutiful son, the future loomed bright.

30

—

Free and Unshackled

If Charles Boyer lost his rudder when his father died in 1908, Hannah Boyer felt herself cast adrift and sinking without the man she'd given her life to.

She and James had been warm, attentive, supportive, courageous, and steadfast. They were generous to each other, and humorous with one another. From the night they met at a dance hall in Brooklyn to the time of his death in Bracebridge, a bond of secrecy and a band of love united them as one.

Every treasured letter James wrote, when she was away from him with her sisters in the United States, or he away from her on official duties, she kept.

"My dear Wife, Another week gone, the time is getting shorter when I hope to see you. I am very pleased to hear you are enjoying yourself .... the kindest love, your affectionate husband, James."

He took effort in such letters, between such words of salutation and benediction, to reassure her about the children, send news from the town, and report on his busy life. Meticulous letters, they were artifacts of love. James always had time for Hannah, whether she was near or far.

But with him gone, staying in Bracebridge had become a taunting trial for Hannah. Every person she met and spoke with mentioned her sad loss. Every place she went reminded Hannah of her full life, now empty.

She would have to do her best to make another life, without him. As she boarded the southbound train, George helped his mother with all her luggage. She travelled often, but never before with so many belongings. She was going, she said, for an "indefinite stay" with her daughter Annie, Mrs. John Hanson.

Indefinite became extended. The years passed and Hannah remained more or less in residence with her first-born daughter in Toronto, a city the two of them first saw together on the "honeymoon" trip on their way to Muskoka in 1869. Annie's husband, John Hanson, was doing well enough to own a spacious house, and was an agreeable sort of son-in-law. Hannah began to discover opportunities for entertainment and a life of ease in Ontario's capital, attending some concerts and joining a church group populated mostly by other widows, and some spinsters. For the first time in her life, she began to feel free of responsibility.

Even the fate of Hannah's siblings was now in the hands of others, she accepted. Missing sister Emma, who had eventually turned up, had married an American named Andrew Marsh, and after his death, she moved in with her daughter, Bessie, remaining with her until she herself died in her seventies. Sister Lydia left the orphanage the minute she was old enough and moved in with Emma and her husband until, as a young woman, she married Walter C. Tower. In the 1920s the Towers moved to Canada with their daughter, Florence, and settled in Barrie, not too far from Hannah, Harry, and Lizzy up in Muskoka.

While many were converging on Muskoka, that was not the case of all. Hannah's brother Thomas had stayed in the United States, become a member of the Massachusetts bar, clerked for a judge, got married, and become the father of four children. He not only became an American lawyer, but even followed his brother-in-law's example by taking up the practice of law on Broadway Avenue in New York. The parallel did not end there. One day Thomas Boyer pulled off a disappearing act of his own. Overnight he vanished from the life of his wife and children, leaving his home and law practice behind, never to be heard from again.

———

In summertime Muskoka beckoned in its usual way. Hannah would return to the district, but rather than intrude long at the Manitoba Street house, now the home of Vic and George and their two boys, she would have a good visit, then go over to see Harry and his tribe, and next progress aboard the *Segwun* from Bracebridge up to Windermere where she'd spend July and August enjoying the good life at ease with Lizzy in her sister's prestigious resort.

But in 1929 Hannah did not make her annual summer trip back to Muskoka, at least not alive. Her remains were brought to "her home" on Manitoba Street by train from Toronto on Friday night, July 5. Death had come suddenly the morning before. "She had not been in her usual health for several weeks," son George informed readers of his newspaper, "but it was hoped she might recover sufficiently to come to Muskoka and benefit from the change. Yet the weight of years was too great and she gradually became weaker, and passed away in her sleep."

Reverend William Farmer of Bracebridge United Church conducted the funeral service on Saturday afternoon in the Manitoba Street house, the first and only place she ever lived in Bracebridge after leaving the homestead she and James had made in Macaulay's forest. The small house was filled with floral tributes and crowded with family members. Lizzy came in from Windermere. Lydia arrived, with her husband, Walter Tower, from Barrie. Harry Boyer and Flora were present with their children. Hannah's daughters Annie Hanson and Nellie Perkins had come together on the train from Toronto. Son Fred Boyer had travelled at once from his farm at Comber, bringing his daughter. A number of Hannah's grandchildren, cousins from Comber, Toronto, and Bracebridge, some meeting for the first time, shyly greeted one another in the sombre setting. George, Vic, Robert, and Wilson Boyer attended Hannah's funeral service by staying home.

After Reverend Mr. Farmer's commendation to complete the ritual, they walked behind the casket up Manitoba Street to the Anglican Cemetery.

Hannah was again, forever, with James. Their secret had gone with them to their graves. Some of those present puzzled as they looked at the hulking family tombstone which proclaimed, as if in some ominous, off-stage clue from James:

J. Patrick Boyer

MY HEAVENLY FATHER KNOWS

That fall, on October 29, the stock market crashed. Share values plummeted, making paupers out of plutocrats overnight. The economy slowed, and then sputtered to a halt, ushering in what would become the Great Depression that dragged on through a decade which would rightly be dubbed the "Dirty Thirties."

George Boyer had to save his newspaper and printing business. The *Muskoka Herald* was an important part of the Muskoka community. It also provided his family's limited livelihood.

By this time Robert had learned printing from his father, and twelve-year-old Wilson was also helping in the print shop, marking the start of a third generation of Boyers in Muskoka's newspaper business.

As the Muskoka economy collapsed along with that of the rest of the world, the bottom fell out for the Boyers. Robert had to leave high school part way through Grade 12, bidding bleak farewell to his hopes for university. At age nineteen he became editor of the *Muskoka Herald*. He worked without pay, doing all he could to help save the newspaper.

Vic took over as the Muskoka Publishing Company's bookkeeper, and tried drumming up small accounts through classified ads. Many people were trying to sell off possessions, a piece of furniture or some farm equipment, to gain money for the coming week or two. Wilson learned more about printing and helped get the paper out, showing real aptitude for running machinery.

George, thanks to his Conservative Party connections, got an appointment from the government of R.B. Bennett in Ottawa, as inland customs agent at Bracebridge. He used his salary to subsidize the print shop, and pay for the few groceries Vic needed. She was getting all she could from the gardens at the Manitoba Street house, and from the Archer's farm on Browning Island.

The Boyer family business was in stiff competition with the *Bracebridge Gazette*, whose proprietor and editor, George Thomas, was a magnet for printing orders. A remarkable and interesting man, he was prominent in town as teacher, businessman, councillor, and mayor. He was also an ardent Liberal, and had run for Parliament in the 1917 general election. Thomas had strong opinions and could be somewhat imperious in his front-page "Comment" column, which he used to uphold the Grit cause and deride the rival Conservative *Muskoka Herald*, and, on occasion, in back-of-the-hand ways, its Boyer publishers. Although the rival papers were produced in printing shops just yards apart, the icy distance between their publishers was too great to measure.

Late one spring afternoon, Aunt Lizzy from Windermere, now grandmotherly and grey-haired, pulled up at the Boyer home in a car driven by her daughter, Gertrude Aitkin, who, along with Lizzy's son, Leslie Aitkin, had been helping her run Windermere House after Thomas Aitkin's death in 1919. These days Lizzy mostly spent her time mingling with prestigious hotel guests at Windermere House and sitting for long periods in her wicker chair on the front verandah gazing over the lake. It was clear that the imperious Lizzy still pretty much considered the Manitoba Street place, where she'd lived freely off her sister Hannah and James for years, to be her own precinct in Bracebridge. She took it for granted she and her daughter would be served supper.

The two Windermere in-laws ate heartily from the little food on her nephew's table. She chattered on to George and Vic and their boys about "what a splendid man that Mr. Thomas is." Just as at Windermere House, Lizzy liked associating with prestigious folk, and George Thomas was a man of prestige. She prattled on about how he'd given her a tour of the *Gazette*'s printing plant, "such a fascinating operation to see." The silent Boyers already knew; it was only thirty paces from their own plant, and they knew very well what printing equipment looked like. "Oh, I suppose I shouldn't keep going on about another printing business, should I?" she finally said, in a smaller voice. She fell quiet, and just ate.

When Bob escorted his Aunt Lizzy and Gertrude to their car after supper, he gasped to see the back seat crammed with production from the *Gazette*'s print shop — Windermere House menu forms, guest cards, posters, price lists, excursion timetables, letterheads, envelopes, notepads, invoice forms, and golfers' cards — Lizzy's entire printing order for the coming tourist season.

George was livid when his son came back inside and reported what he had seen. Any relative who took a lucrative printing job to his arch rival but came to eat off his table, when there was no money for food, ended everything. In one angry flash, any remaining sentiment George W. Boyer may have had about "family" vanished.

Not long after, George was forced, with Vic and their boys, to accept the bitter truth that the Dirty Thirties had reached their own front door and entered. They had lost the family home on Manitoba Street to unpaid municipal taxes. A number of Bracebridge homes were being separated from the families who lived in them, because that's what arrears of property taxes led to when people put the only money they could get toward food. The stranglehold of the Great Depression had grown even tighter.

Forced to move out, the Boyers found rental space on Dominion Street, just across from the Herald Building. In an ironic twist, the place had been the original structure for the *Northern Advocate*. The frame building had since been turned sideways to face Dominion Street, covered with redbrick veneer, given a front verandah, and became the home of Samuel H. Armstrong, Bracebridge businessman, mayor, and Muskoka's member in the Ontario legislature. After that highpoint, it had been converted to a triplex; the Boyers would rent a section of the house. They'd be in the same building where James Boyer once edited the *Advocate*. From this same place, James's embattled son George and his family would now cross Dominion Street to the Herald and do their best to keep this newspaper from failing, too.

First they had to move their belongings from Manitoba Street. With every step of this work, George felt more and more incensed. Thousands of others were losing jobs, homes, and even their desperate lives. But that bleak reality did nothing to lighten George's own despair. He had lost the house occupied by the Boyers for six decades, and over three generations. He overflowed with resentment, dwelling on how money from that huge Windermere House printing job might have helped pay the overdue taxes and save the home. Lizzy had done nothing to help him save this house she'd shared with his family for years. If anything, she'd contributed in her unthinking way to its forfeiture.

Bob, in moving furniture out of the house, took away the kitchen table. The family trunks stowed beneath came into view. George saw them and, still inflamed, was adamant that no trunks of family records would go to their new place. He knew the record of family turmoil their contents held. If Boyers like Lizzy caused moneyless George to lose the family foothold in Muskoka — the house purchased from the sale of the original homestead, maybe even his prized *Muskoka Herald* — then he would wash his hands of all the past Boyer family turmoil and stand or fall on his own, with just Vic and his boys.

A former mayor of the town, a captain in the army, a founder of the local hospital, publisher of a district newspaper, a pillar of the community's largest church, the Canadian government's customs inspector, George Boyer was humiliated. He'd tried so hard to build things up, to focus on positive accomplishment, to honour his father, to create brightness that could cast away the shadow of Charles's tragic death. Again he walked through the streets of Bracebridge, awkward and embarrassed, people murmuring after he'd passed about the curse that seemed to be over the Boyers.

The Boyer family trunks were destroyed at the town dump.

That is why the letter James Boyer received from England, which exculpated him in the Stratford swindle, cannot be identified either as to exact date or who in fact wrote it. Also in the trunks of family records and memorabilia destroyed during that Depression low point, according to Robert Boyer, were James's well-used copy of Handel's *Messiah*, his clarinet, letterhead from millinery shops in New York where Hannah worked, and bundles of letters.

―

All that remained of the closely guarded letter from England that had vindicated James was now the memory of it.

As a curious youth, Robert had spent hours looking through the trunks, kept under the kitchen table at the cramped Manitoba Street house. He marvelled at their contents, looked over documents, and read many of the letters. But his discovery of buried treasures ended when his father came through the door one day and saw the scene. His admonition was unequivocal: "Don't you *ever* look in there again!"

George was aware of the trunks' contents. So too now, in some particulars, was Robert. Before the trunk was put off-limits, he saw and read "*the* letter." On October 17, 2004, Robert Boyer told me, a dozen weeks before he died and knowing he would soon be gone, "I saw the exact document. My father did not want it around."

Robert's was not the only memory. Because of the letter's high importance for its exoneration of James, Hannah had shown it at opportune times to selected family members. When she handed it to her niece Caroline, one of Harry Boyer's daughters, she read it in disbelief. Years later Caroline would tell her daughter-in-law Keitha Boyer, "It was such a tragedy that this shadow was over James unnecessarily."

———

Sometimes travel and duty had kept James and Hannah apart. When they could not be together, they wrote each other. Almost all the letters they exchanged were among the family records destroyed in the 1930s, but a few, tucked into books or lodged at the back of desk drawers, survived.

James's letters often began "My dear wife," a formal salutation which could mislead someone to think him an austere man whose Victorian remoteness precluded him from even employing her name, Hannah.

But between the two of them the word "wife," like a code, reinforced their deep love, and equally deep secret.

The bond they shared began in love, and remained strong as it matured through a procession of hardships and setbacks. What kept their love resilient was their need to protect one another, with fortitude and resolve, in the new life fate forced them to create in a different country. Never exchanging wedding rings in a witnessed ceremony, Hannah was bound to James by something stronger than any band of gold.

———

Before her death, Hannah's granddaughter Ruth Hanson, just a young girl, was curious to know from her grandma about her life.

"What it was like," asked Ruth, "when you were my age?"

"I don't want to talk about it!" Hannah snapped.

It was a brusque way for a woman, who cared to the ends of the earth about her family, to cut off inquiry about her past from her own cherished granddaughter.

Indeed, where to start?

James and Hannah had held secure in their unbroken love. They had kept their bond of secrecy. They had remained silent; and in their immediate family, with sons Charles, George, and Fred, and with daughters Annie and Nellie, they had kept the gulf of mystery cloaked in fictions about their lives.

It was no time to begin recounting the facts for a granddaughter. Another generation or two would be required for the truth of Hannah's story to be learned, and even then, it would be discovered only by patient peeling back of layers of secrecy and dispersing the fog of misinformation Isaac Jelfs had spread in their wake.

Only then would their love and secrets be free at last.

At the end of it all, the greatest lesson Hannah and James imparted was that we do not keep our secrets, our secrets keep us.

———

The proud and defiant claim of the *Muskoka Herald*, printed boldly in its masthead atop the front page, was

"FREE AND UNSHACKLED"

This credo was an assertion of the paper's fearless independence in politics, religion, and every other important subject where hidden interests might otherwise constrain what gets published.

However, to James Boyer, who saw the newspaper every week, those words "free and unshackled" were a constant taunt.

The very last thing James Isaac Boyer ever wanted was to have his double life known.

But now that it is, he, too, is "free and unshackled."

EXEUNT

All the world's a stage, and all the men and women merely players.
They have their exits and their entrances.
And one man in his time plays many parts.
— WILLIAM SHAKESPEARE

Acknowledgements

Keitha Boyer, wife of the late Edward Boyer, who was a grandson of Hannah's brother Harry, is custodian of the diary Harry kept, recovered miraculously at the last moment from a truckload of discarded household items going to the Bracebridge town dump. The diary contains family clues that Keitha first shared with my younger sister Alison Joan Boyer.

Alison broached the subject of James Boyer's true identity with his grandson, our father, Robert James Boyer. This provided a clue for others of us in the family to follow, which was good, because my elder sister Victoria and her husband, Dr. Douglas Billingsley, their son Johnson Billingsley and his wife, Barbara, and my own wife, Corinne Boyer, and I had all, at different intervals, made futile pilgrimages to Moreton-in-Marsh to find records of "James Boyer."

Challenged by this new idea that his great-great-grandfather had lived a dramatic life under a different identity, my nephew Johnson Billingsley launched a tireless search of deeds, ship manifests, census reports, birth and death records, military and law registries, and newspaper accounts. He hired archivists and historians to scour far-flung documents, while he himself drilled down through cyberspace into many other sources. It was Johnson who determined so many key facts recorded in this book.

His sister, my niece, Dr. Martha Savage, herself a chronicler of family genealogy, reviewed the research and suggested clarifying ideas. Other Boyer family descendants I thank for information are Ruth Rimmer (daughter of Hannah and James Boyer's eldest daughter, Annie), and

Ruth's own daughter Beth Manson in Ontario; and Penny Richards in California, a descendant of Hannah Boyer's sister Emma.

Ruth Holtz, research librarian at Bracebridge Public Library, ferreted out nuggets of Muskoka information. Bracebridge Public Library itself deserves special acknowledgement for maintaining a "Muskoka Collection," serving a municipality that otherwise lacks any public archive at all.

Elsa Franklin's unerring instinct for a good story led to her suggestion this saga of Hannah and James Boyer be told separately from the book *Raw Life* in which it would have been lost. For such guidance, and so much more, I remain fondly grateful.

Another contributor to this book is Bracebridge surveyor Douglas W. Jemmett, OLS, who identified the Boyer homestead properties in Macaulay Township, which Elise Bélanger and I explored, along with many other Muskoka pioneer sites. Elise, gifted with intuitive energy, further helped me explore many other facets of the pioneering experience.

Kirk Howard, a friend and a successful book publisher, now entering his fifth decade "defining Canada for Canadians" at the helm of Dundurn, possesses the necessary surf-rider's balance to publish books and stay afloat in today's surging sea changes sweeping over books and reading. I thank Kirk for publishing *Another Country, Another Life.* I am equally grateful to his adept Dundurn team connected with this book, including Beth Bruder, Sheila Douglas, Margaret Bryant, Synora van Drine, Caitlyn Stewart, Duncan MacDonell, Shannon Whibbs, Jennifer Gallinger, Courtney Horner, Karen McMullin, and James Hatch. Dominic Farrell, a superb editor, has been an engaging colleague. Creative Jennifer Scott was truly inspired in designing the front cover "double" of two men in one.

Careful reading and informed suggestions about the manuscript by Muskoka historian Gary Long, and by Alison Boyer and Johnson Billingsley, have clarified a number of points.

Finally, to members of my immediate and extended family, and also to many others prompted by reading *Raw Life* to tell me about secrets of their own colourful ancestors, I express appreciation for understanding. In satisfying our curiosity about history — not only of the world, or our country, or the place we grew up, but even of one's own family — it is important, as I ever urged my students, to "keep asking the next question."

Truth is always stranger than fiction. We should not flinch from it. For truth, like a mirror, can set us free by what it reveals. In the case of Isaac Jelfs and Hannah Boyer, the truth at last has set them, or at least their legacy, free. No longer does my great-grandfather's pitiful lament, "My Heavenly Father Knows," need to be directed to heaven alone.

Bibliography

Armstrong, F.H., H.A. Stevenson, J.D. Wilson, and J.J. Talman, eds. *Aspects of Nineteenth-Century Ontario*. Toronto: University of Toronto Press, 1974.

Banks, Margaret A. "Evolution of the Ontario Courts 1788–1981." In *Essays in the History of Canadian Law*. Vol. II. Edited by David H. Flaherty. Toronto: The Osgoode Society, 1983.

Barnard, Anne, chief organizer. *These Our Ancestors Were: Cemetery and Burial Records of Parry Sound and Muskoka Districts*. Bracebridge, ON: Herald-Gazette Press, 1976.

Bernstein, Iver. *The New York City Draft Riots: Their Significance for American Society and Politics in the Age of the Civil War*. New York: Oxford University Press, 1990.

Bettmann, Otto L. *The Good Old Days — They Were Terrible!* New York: Random House, 1974.

Billingsley, R. Johnson. Compendium of James and Hannah Boyer Ancestral Records. Boyer Family Archives, Bracebridge, ON.

Boyer, George W. *Early Days in Muskoka*. Bracebridge, ON: Herald-Gazette Press, 1970.

Boyer, Henry. Diary: 1868–1933. Boyer Family Archives, Bracebridge, ON.

Boyer, J. Patrick. *Raw Life: Cameos of 1890s Justice from a Magistrate's Bench Book*. Toronto: Dundurn, 2012.

_____. *Local Library, Global Passport: The Evolution of a Carnegie Library*. Toronto: Blue Butterfly Books, 2008.

Boyer, Robert J. *Early Exploration and Surveying of Muskoka District.* Bracebridge, ON: Herald-Gazette Press, 1979.

____. *A Good Town Grew Here: The Story of Bracebridge.* 2nd ed. Bracebridge, ON: Oxbow Press, 2002.

____. *Celebrating a Ninetieth Birthday: Family History of Ethel Victoria Boyer.* Bracebridge, ON: Herald-Gazette Press, 1976.

____. *Power from Water: Bracebridge, Canada — First Municipality to Own and Operate Electrical Generation from Water Power.* Bracebridge, ON: Muskoka Publications Press, 1994.

Brown, Desmond H. *The Genesis of the Canadian Criminal Code of 1892.* Toronto: The Osgoode Society, 1989.

Clarke, John. *Land, Power, and Economics on the Frontier in Upper Canada.* Montreal: McGill-Queen's University Press, 2001.

Cotton, Larry D. *Whiskey and Wickedness. Vol. 3, Muskoka and Parry Sound Districts, 1850 to 1900.* Barrie, ON: Cotton Associates, 2004.

de la Fosse, Frederick. *English Bloods: In The Backwoods of Muskoka, 1878.* Edited by Scott D. Shipman. Toronto: Natural Heritage Books, 2004.

Demaine, Marjorie. *Chronicles of Stisted Township.* Bracebridge, ON: Herald-Gazette Press, 1976.

Denison, George T. *Recollections of a Police Magistrate.* Toronto: Mussen Book Company, 1920.

Denniss, Gary. *Macaulay Township in Days Gone By.* Bracebridge, ON: Herald-Gazette Press, 1970.

____. *A Brief History of the Schools in Muskoka.* Bracebridge, ON: Herald-Gazette Press, 1972.

____. *Going to School in Macaulay.* Bracebridge, ON: Garden Press, 2009.

Flaherty, David H., ed. *Essays in the History of Canadian Law. Vol. II.* Toronto: The Osgoode Society, 1983.

Foster, Hamar, Benjamin L. Berger, and A.R. Buck, eds. *The Grand Experiment: Law and Legal Culture in British Settler Societies.* Vancouver: UBC Press; Toronto: The Osgoode Society, 2008.

Francis, R. Douglas, and Donald B. Smith. *Readings in Canadian History, Post-Confederation.* Toronto: Harcourt Brace, 1994.

Glazebrook, G.P. de T. *Life in Ontario: A Social History.* Toronto: University of Toronto Press, 1968.

Guillet, Edwin C. *Pioneer Days in Upper Canada*. Toronto: University of Toronto Press, 1933.

Hamilton, W.E. *Guide Book and Atlas of Muskoka and Parry Sound Districts, 1879*. Toronto: H.R. Page & Co., 1879.

"James Boyer." In *Men of Canada, or Success by Example*. Edited by William Cochrane. Bradford, ON: Bradley, Garretson & Co., 1891.

Johnson, George H. *Port Sydney Past*. Cheltenham, ON: Boston Mills Press, 1980.

Long, Gary. *This River the Muskoka*. Erin, ON: Boston Mills Press, 1989.

Mackenzie, Norman, and William Bothwell. *The Lost One Found; or Adventures of British Subjects during the Civil War in the United States*. Compiled by F.J.B.A. Montreal: John Lovell Printing, 1868.

McKay, Ami. *The Virgin Cure*. New York: HarperCollins, 2012.

McMurray, Thomas. *The Free Grant Lands of Canada — from Practical Experience of Bush Farming in the Free Grant Districts of Muskoka and Parry Sound*. Bracebridge, ON: Northern Advocate Press, 1871.

Muldrew Lake Cottagers Club. *A History of Muldrew Lakes*. Orangeville, ON: Cline Printing, 1977.

Murray, Florence B. *Muskoka and Haliburton, 1615–1875: A Collection of Documents*. Toronto: The Champlain Society, 1963.

Oliver, Peter N. "The Place of the Judiciary in the Historiography of Upper Canada." In *Essays in the History of Canadian Law in Honour of R.C.B. Risk*. Edited by G. Blaine Baker and Jim Phillips. Toronto: The Osgoode Society, 1999.

Osborne, Bertram. *Justices of the Peace, 1361–1848: A History of the Justices of the Peace for the Counties of England*. Dorset: Sedgehill Press, 1960.

Penson, Emily Mary. *Muskoka: A Pioneer Memoir*. Coulee City, WA: Frolen, 1989.

Renwick, Riddell William. *The Legal Profession in Upper Canada in its Early Periods*. Toronto: Law Society of Upper Canada, 1916.

Rubbinaccio, Michael. *Abraham Oakey Hall: New York's Most Elegant and Controversial Mayor*. Seattle, WA: Pescara Books, 2011.

Splane, Richard B. *Social Welfare in Ontario, 1791–1893: A Study of Public Welfare Administration*. Toronto: University of Toronto Press, 1965.

Swaine, Robert T. *The Cravath Firm and Its Predecessors, 1819–1947*. New York: Ad Press Ltd., 1946.

Swainson, Donald, ed. *Oliver Mowat's Ontario. Papers Presented to the Oliver Mowat Colloquium, Queen's University, November 25-26, 1970*. Toronto: Macmillan Canada, 1972.

Thomas, Redmond. *Bracebridge, Muskoka: Reminiscences*. Bracebridge, ON: Herald-Gazette Press, 1969.

Waite, P.B. *Canada 1874–1896: Arduous Destiny*. Toronto: McClelland and Stewart, 1971.

Index

Numbers in italics refer to images and their captions.

Tookey, James, 150
Toronto, Ontario, 10, 12, 83, 85, 87, 88, 89, 91,
    95, 116, 119, 122, 123, 126, 139, 143, 144,
    149, 153, 196, 197, 205, 212, 219, 223, 240,
    245, 248, 249, 250, 254, 262, 263, 265, 266,
    275, 276, *277*, 278, 283, 290, 291
Tower, Florence, 290
Tower, Walter C., 290
Township of Cardwell's Local Board of Health,
    254
tradesmen, 151, 154, 156, 171, 234–35
Trading Lake (later Lake of Bays), 219
Traill, Mary, 226
trapping, animal, 219–20
Tweed, William "Boss," 66, 67, 258–59

Ukee, Chief Mesqua, 166–67
Umber & Snowden, 21
Union Army, 45, 46, 47, 50, 51, 52, 53, 75, 76,
    123
Union Jack, 83, 196, 197–98
United Kingdom, 42, 140
United States Army, 77
United States Patent Office, 58
Utterson, Ontario, 125
Uxbridge, Ontario, 269

vacationing, 223, 224
Vanderpoel, Aaron J., 65
Vanderpoel, Benjamin W., 46
Victoria, North, 87
Victoria County, 122

War of 1812, 166
Washago Mills, 86
Washington, D.C., 254
Watt Township, 226
Weis, Elizabeth, 276, 278
welfare, government, 171, 172, 254
Westchester Farm School for Boys, 54, 57, 81,
    110, 209, 240
White, Elizabeth, 32, 35
White, Mary, 33
White, Tom, 33
Whitten, James, 278
Wilkes Booth, John, 54
Williams, Francis, 166–67, 267, 268

Wilson, George, 285
Windermere House, 225–28, 233, 293–95
Winnipeg, 283
"Woodstone Lodge," 33
woollen mills, 151
Wright, Charles, 20

Young, Brigham, 121

About the Author

J. Patrick Boyer, Q.C., is a former Member of Parliament and author of many books, including *A Passion for Justice* and this book's companion volume, *Raw Life*, both available from Dundurn. He lives in Muskoka and Toronto

Also by the Author

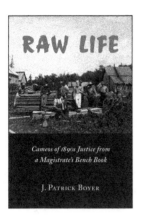

Raw Life
Cameos of 1890s Justice from a Magistrate's Bench Book
978-0978160043
$39.99

Rare views of human lives in turmoil are revealed in several hundred trials conducted in 1890s Muskoka by Magistrate James Boyer of Bracebridge. The charges and evidence show how raw life really was in Canada's frontier towns, with cases ranging from nostalgic and humorous to pitiable and deeply disturbing. While dispensing speedy justice, Boyer, who was also town clerk and editor of the *Northern Advocate*, the first newspaper in Ontario's northern districts, kept a careful record in his handwritten "bench book" of all these cases. That bench book, recently found by his great-grandson, lawyer J. Patrick Boyer, provides the raw material for *Raw Life*.

A Man & His Words
Robert J. Boyer Through Changing Times
978-1550024869
$19.95

Robert Boyer was a consummate Canadian, whose long career can be measured by words. An author, journalist, researcher, editor, printer, and public speaker, Boyer's professional life began at the age of nineteen when he became a newspaper editor, and continued through the publication of his twelfth book at the age of eighty-eight. He was also a church organist, a member of the Ontario Legislature for seventeen years, and the first vice-chairman of Ontario Hydro.

Of Related Interest

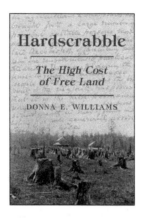

Hardscrabble
The High Cost of Free Land
by Donna E. Williams
978-1459708044
$22.99

When the Free Grants and Homestead Act was first introduced in 1868, fierce debates erupted in Ontario's Legislature over whether land in the Muskoka region should be opened to settlement or reserved for the Aboriginal population. From the beginning, many people vented serious doubts about the free-grant scheme, citing the district's poor agricultural prospects. In the end, such caution was ignored by overeager boosters. The story in *Hardscrabble* also takes readers to Britain, where emigration philanthropists urged their government to send the country's poor to Canada, then follows these emigrants as they left the familiar behind to make a new life in the Canadian wilderness. The initial romance of living off the land was soon dispelled as these hapless souls faced clearing the land, building shelters, and sowing crops in desolate, remote locations. Donna Williams's extensive research leads her to conclude that Muskoka's experience epitomizes the wrongheadedness of placing already-poor people on remote land unsuited for farming.

No Return

A novel of the Canadian election that vanished in Muskoka's backwoods

by Gordon Aiken

9781926577043

$24.95

Canadians took politics seriously in the years following Confederation and Gordon Aiken's novel about pioneer Muskoka and the fledgling nation's capital shows why. Unique events in the Dominion's second election, in 1872, inspired Aiken to write about Muskoka's returning officer, Richard Bell, who refused to declare Liberal candidate A.P. Cockburn elected, even though he got the most votes. Consequent groundbreaking events included Bell's summons to give an accounting of himself to the House of Commons, the first and only time an MP would be elected to Parliament by members of the Commons itself, and reforms in Canadian election law including introduction of the secret ballot. The political intrigues woven into Gordon Aiken's rich tale of local and national affairs from 140 years ago will resonate with readers today, if its essential plots and human ambitions were simply updated by new technology and a fresh cast of characters to re-enact timeless dramas. *No Return* tells of one man's struggle to support his chosen party, maintain his independence, confound his enemies, and hold his family together under duress.

VISIT US AT

Dundurn.com
Definingcanada.ca
@dundurnpress
Facebook.com/dundurnpress